The
German Regiment

of
Maryland and Pennsylvania

in the
Continental Army

1776-1781

—Revised Edition—

Henry J. Retzer

HERITAGE BOOKS
2006
Waldorf West Branch
10405 O'Donnell Place
Waldorf, MD 20603

HERITAGE BOOKS

AN IMPRINT OF HERITAGE BOOKS, INC.

Books, CDs, and more—Worldwide

For our listing of thousands of titles see our website
at
www.HeritageBooks.com

Published 2006 by
HERITAGE BOOKS, INC.
Publishing Division
65 East Main Street
Westminster, Maryland 21157-5026

International Standard Book Number: 978-1-58549-202-7

CONTENTS

FOREWORD

This history is an attempt to bring a little-known unit of General Washington's army some recognition. It is now known the German Regiment smelled powder smoke often. They tasted success at Trenton I and II, Princeton, and Newtown. They experienced the fear of losing at Brandywine and Germantown. They shivered at Valley Forge and hungered in Northumberland County. In short, they were seasoned veterans of the Revolution. The veteran could proudly say, "Ich war da."

The German Regiment qualifies for at least two firsts. They were one of the first units to be enlisted for three years after it was realized that the war was not going to be a short affair. The Regiment also represents the first of a long series of ethnic-American U.S. Army units. This tradition was continued by Negro-American units from the Civil War through World War II. The ethnic unit is epitomized by the Japanese-American 442nd Regimental Combat Team, the most decorated U.S. Army unit of World War II.

There are many gaps in the story of the German Regiment - some as long as four months. Government records, after 200 years, are far from complete. Original documents were lost in several fires, including the British raid on Washington, D.C. in 1814. State records are likewise incomplete. From a variety of federal and state records, plus personal journals and letters, a sometimes hazy, sometimes clearer story emerges.

Perhaps the reluctance of historians to treat the history of the German Regiment stems from the poor behavior of its leaders. The unit had to endure an alcoholic brigadier general, a colonel who defected, another colonel who was more interested in diplomacy than in tactics, a captain who was convicted of misbehavior before the enemy, and a large number of resignations. As so often happens, it was the junior officers who persevered, rose in rank, and completed their mission.

Neither the histories of Maryland or Pennsylvania gave the German Regiment much attention - perhaps because of its bi-state structure. Its companies were paid and supplied by their respective states. While General Washington once referred to the Germans as a large regiment [of nine companies of 400+ men]; to Maryland, for example, it was just a minor unit of four companies.

Although German was undoubtedly spoken in the ranks, the officers must have been bilingual. All correspondence found was written in comparatively good English, but with the poor spelling and haphazard capitalization of the period. Only a few sentences of Germanic structure, with the verb at the end, were noticed.

In regard to music, that important aspect of military maneuver and marching, there is nothing that can be attributed to the German Regiment. The only song text of the period found that might have been sung by ethnic Germans is:

England's Georgel, Kaiser, König,
Ist für Gott und uns zu wenig. [1]

England's Georgie, Emperor, King,
Is for God and us too small a thing.

Likewise, nothing can be found regarding distinctive uniforms. They put on whatever was available in Baltimore and Philadelphia in 1776. A 1777 deserter was described as wearing an "old green coat over his regimentals." Another 1778 deserter wore a white hunting shirt and breeches. [2] Subsequent clothing issues were probably in standard state colors - blue uniforms with red facings and white linings - for both Maryland and Pennsylvania. [3]

Military rank was found to be quite similar to the modern army. The full General [Washington] was commander-in-chief. Major generals commanded divisions, consisting of two or more brigades. Brigadier generals commanded brigades, consisting of two or more regiments. Colonels commanded regiments [also interchangeably known as battalions], consisting of four to nine companies. Lieutenant Colonels were colonel's deputies, but also commanded regiments when they could not be promoted to colonels. Captains commanded companies, consisting of up to 75 men. Lieutenants seem to be captain's assistants, rather than commanding a small unit of men. Ensigns were flag bearers of regimental and company colors.

This will acknowledge that there was another German Regiment from Virginia. This was raised in the Shenandoah Valley in 1776 and was also made up of ethnic Germans. When the numbering of units became prevalent they became the 8th Virginia Regiment. Theirs is another untold story.

REFERENCES

1 - Bittinger, L.F.: The Germans in Colonial Times, Phila., 1901, p242.
2 - Katcher, Philip: Uniforms of the Continental Army, York PA, 1981, p66.
3 - Richardson, E.W.: Standards and Colors of the American Revolution, Phila., 1982, p39.

SECTOR OF PENNSYLVANIA FRONTIER DEFENDED BY GERMAN REGIMENT

Oct 1779 to Sept 1780

[Modern cities are shown in ghost letters.]

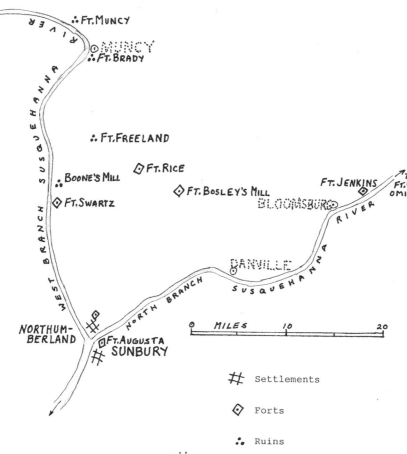

INTRODUCTION TO REVISED EDITION

Since the printing of the first edition the author has uncovered additional information which has been added at the end of the book, pp. 141 - 161. The index has been revised to include this new information.

Henry Retzer
1996

CHAPTER 1 - CONGRESS RESOLVES

Early in 1776 the Second Continental Congress seemed to realize that the war with Great Britain was not going to be a short affair. The Delegates in Philadelphia were faced with the need to mobilize many more men than they had in 1775. They found it necessary to involve the entire sympathetic population of the United Colonies.

It is no surprise then that the Congress turned to their second largest ethnic group. These were the Germans of Pennsylvania, Maryland, and Virginia. In 1776 they numbered about 130,000 in the three colonies; and most of them were staunch patriots.[1]

This reasoning was formalized on 25 May 1776 when the Congress resolved, "that one battalion of Germans be raised for the service of the United Colonies." The resolution was then turned over to an ad hoc committee to work out the details.[2]

At this time General George Washington was calling for a reorganization of the Army. In addition to more men, he needed them for a war that might last several years. He saw that with three and six month enlistments an army could literally melt away in the middle of a campaign. Congress heeded Washington's pleas and the proposed German Regiment and Stevenson's Maryland & Virginia Rifle Regiment became the first units in the Continental Army to be composed of three-year men.[3]

On 27 June 1776 the Congressional committee made its report:
"Resolved, That four companies of Germans be raised in Pennsylvania, and four companies in Maryland, to compose the German Battalion.
"That it be recommended to the Committee of Safety of Pennsylvania, immediately to appoint proper officers for, and direct the enlistment of the four Companies to be raised in that Colony.
"That it be recommended to the Convention, or in their recess, to the Committee or Council of Safety of Maryland, immediately to appoint proper officers for and direct the enlistment of the four Companies to be raised in that Colony.
"That the said Companies be enlisted to serve for three years unless sooned discharged, and receive bounty, pay, rations, and all other allowances, equal to any of the Continental Troops.
"That the said Companies be entitled to pay and subsistance from the time of enlistment.
"That the said Companies when raised, be formed into a Battalion, under the command of such Field Officers as the Congress shall direct.
"That the rank of Captains in the said Companies be regulated as the Congress shall hereafter direct.
"That $5,000 be sent to the Committee of Safety of

Pennsylvania, and $5,000 to the Convention, or in their recess, to the Committee of Safety of Maryland, to defray the expense of raising the German Companies."
The above resolution was voted on, passed, and forwarded by John Hancock to the Councils of Safety on 29 June 1776.[4]

The Pennsylvania Council of Safety took up the resolution on 01 July 1776 and made some additions:
"The Committee taking into consideration the Resolution of Congress for raising a Battalion of Germans, and being of the opinion that the Public Service requires that it be carried into execution without any delay, and the Recruiting Service be entered on as soon as possible,
"Resolved, that this Board will on Friday the 5th inst., appoint Captains, and on Friday the 12th inst., Lieutenants and Ensigns for the four Companies of Germans directed to be raised in this Province by order of Congress; and that it is the opinion of this Board, that consistant with the resolve of Congress, no persons but such as are Germans born, or the sons of Germans, should hold any office in the said Companies.
"All such gentlemen who fall under the above description, and are desirous to enter into the service, are requested to send in their applications as early as may be."[5]

The Maryland Convention of June 1776 passed the measure on 06 July 1776:
"Resolved, that this Province will raise four Companies..., two Companies of Germans to be raised in Baltimore County, and two in Frederick County, each to consist of 1 Captain, 2 Lieutenants, 1 Ensign, 4 Sergeants, 4 Corporals, 1 Drummer, 1 Fifer, and 76 Privates."[6]

As the search for officers of the German Regiment began, Congress voted to accept The Declaration of Independence on 04 July 1776. On the next day the German Community of Philadelphia was able to read about it in the German-language Pennsylvanischer Staatsbote, this was the first newspaper report about the Declaration published anywhere. The Pennsylvania Evening Post published the full text of the Declaration on 06 July. The Staatsbote followed with the full text on 09 July, as publisher Henrich Miller was unable to translate it in time for his earlier paper. The newly expressed idea of independence probably increased the rate of enlistment in the German Regiment in subsequent weeks.

Information on the selection of field officers is sparse. The Maryland Committee of Safety recommended George Stricker of Frederick County on 08 July 1776.[7] The process must have been completed by early September, for on the 11th B. H. Harrison of the Congressional Board of War wrote Major General Horatio Gates that they had appointed Major Nicholas Haussegger to the

2

command of the German Regiment and asked him to send Haussegger to Philadelphia.[8]

On 11 July the Baltimore County Committee of Observation recommended as officers for its two companies:
"Capt Graybill, 1st Lt Lorah, 2nd Lt Myers, Ens Shugart.
Capt Geo. Peter Keeport, 1st Lt Saml. Gerock, 2nd Lt Wm. Ritter, Ens Lindenberger."[9]

The Pennsylvania Committee of Safety, on 06 July 1776, recommended Daniel Burchardt, George Hubley, Jacob Bunner, and Benjamin Weiser to be captains in the German Regiment. [10] Several days later they received a letter of 08 July from General Washington at New York City recommending 1st Lieutenant John David Woelpper [a Virginia-German] to a captaincy in the Regiment.[11] Congress approved the addition of another company for Woelpper on 16 July 1776.[12] The Pennsylvania Committee of Safety concurred on 17 July.[13] On 22 July Washington ordered the 3rd Pennsylvania Regiment lieutenant, then in the New York City area, to join the German Regiment in Philadelphia.[14]

On 12 July 1776 the Pennsylvania Committee recommended the following Lieutenants and Ensigns to the Congress:
"1st Lts: F. Rowlwagen, P. Boyer, Wm. Rice, Jacob Bower;
2nd Lts: G. Hawbaker, J. Laudenberger, Geo. Schaffer, F. Yeiser;
Ensigns: J. Weidman, Chr. Helm, J. Cramer, C. G. Swartz."[15]

The last round of officer appointments began 09 August 1776 when the Pennsylvania Committee of Safety recommended 1st Lt Lewis van Linkensdorf and 2nd Lt Philip Shrawder for the fifth Company.[16] The same day van Linkensdorf was named Adjutant of the German Regiment. [17] The Committee then named Bernard Hubley, Jr for the first lieutenant vacancy on 14 August.[18]

Recruitment for the German Regiment began in mid-July in both states. In Maryland the recruiting territory was defined by the Assembly - two companies from Baltimore County and two companies from Frederick County.[19] In Pennsylvania there was also no need to recruit statewide; it could be limited to areas where there were German Lutheran and Reformed congregations. There was no need to go among the pacifist Amish, Brethren, Dunkards, and Mennonites.

Inspection of surviving muster rolls shows most Pennsylvania enlistees were from the city of Philadelphia or from Philadelphia County, especially Germantown and Kensington. Smaller numbers signed up from around Lancaster and Lebanon in Lancaster County and from the Reading area in Berks County. There was only a sprinkling of men from Chester and Northampton Counties.

From the remaining German area of Pennsylvania - York County, several men can be found in the Maryland companies. This is

3

not surprising as York County is contiguous to Maryland and had strong economic ties to Baltimore.

The only clue to recruitment procedures is found in the first muster roll of a Maryland company for which Captain Philip Graybill enlisted 56 men, one lieutenant enlisted 12, the other lieutenant 14, and the ensign enlisted eight men.[20] The officers must have gone out individually for volunteers.

Most of the enlistments in the Maryland companies occurred between 14 July and 31 August 1776. Captain Graybill's Account Book sheds some light on this period. He paid an enlistment bonus of three pounds, 15 shillings [=$10] and the monthly pay for a private was two pounds, 6 shillings [=$7]. The cost of clothing issued averaged 12 pounds, which was deducted from wages.[21] Note that it would take over five months wages to pay off the clothing.

In Pennsylvania the enlistment bonus was $10 and a private's pay was $7 per month.[22]

It was surprising to find it was possible in 1776 to allocate part of one's wages for the loved ones back home. Graybill's Account Book records deductions of 12, 20, and 25 shillings per month for wives and mothers.[23]

Some recruiting was still done as late as November 1776. Second Lieutenant Michael Bayer and another unidentified Maryland officer are known to have been in the Fort Lee, New Jersey area to enlist Maryland men from the main army. Presumably they were recruiting Maryland flying camp men with short enlistments. It was recorded that the two officers met General Washington on the road about 13 November 1776 and showed him their orders and instructions from Congress. Washington read their papers over at least twice before handing them back, saying he would not permit it.[24]

On 25 September 1776 the names of the officers of the German Regiment were announced by the Congressional Committee:

Rank	Name	Date of Rank	Hometown/County	State
Col	Nicholas Haussegger	17Jul76	Lebanon	Pa.
Lt Col	George Stricker	17Jul76	Frederick Co	Md.
Maj	Ludwick Weltner	17Jul76	Frederick	Md.
Capt	Daniel Burchardt	08Jul76	Phila	Pa.
Capt	Philip Graybill	08Jul76	Balto	Md.
Capt	George Hubley	08Jul76	Lancaster	Pa.
Capt	Henry Fister	12Jul76	Frederick Co	Md.
Capt	Jacob Bunner	08Jul76	Phila	Pa.
Capt	George Keeport	08Jul76	Balto Co	Md.
Capt	Benjamin Weiser	08Jul76	N'umberld Co	Pa.
Capt	William Heiser	12Jul76	Hagerstown	Md.
Capt	John D. Woelpper	12Jul76	?	Pa/Va.
1st Lt	Frederick Rawlwagen	12Jul76	?	Pa.
1st Lt	John Lohra	12Jul76	Balto Co	Md.
1st Lt	Peter Boyer	12Jul76	Phila	Pa.
1st Lt	Charles Baltzel	12Jul76	Frederick Co	Md.
1st Lt	F. Wm. Rice	12Jul76	Kensington	Pa.
1st Lt	Jacob Kortz	12Jul76	Frederick Co	Md.
1st Lt	Jacob Bower	18Jan76	Reading	Pa.
1st Lt	Samuel Gerock	12Jul76	Balto Co	Md.
1st Lt	Bernard Hubley, Jr	12/15Aug76	Lancaster	Pa.
2nd Lt	George Hawbaker	12Jul76	?	Pa.
2nd Lt	Christian Myers	12Jul76	Balto	Md.
2nd Lt	John Landenberger	12Jul76	?	Pa.
2nd Lt	Michael Bayer	12Jul76	?	Md.
2nd Lt	George Schaeffer	12Jul76	?	Pa.
2nd Lt	Adam Smith	12Jul76	Frederick Co	Md.
2nd Lt	William Ritter	12Jul76	Balto Co	Md.
2nd Lt	Frederick Weiser	12Jul76	?	Pa.
2nd Lt	Philip Schrawder	12Aug76	Phila	Pa.
Ensign	John Weidman	12Jul76	?	Pa.
Ensign	Martin Shugart	12Jul76	Balto Co	Md.
Ensign	Christian Helm	12Jul76	?	Pa.
Ensign	Jacob Grometh	12Jul76	?	Md.
Ensign	Jacob Cramer	12Jul76	Phila	Pa.
Ensign	Paul Christman	12Jul76	?	Md.
Ensign	C. Godfried Swartz	12Jul76	Phila	Pa.
Ensign	John Landenberger	12Jul76	Balto Co	Md.[25]

With all the officers of the Regiment named it is interesting to examine the field officers previous military experience.

Colonel Haussegger was previously a Major in the 4th Pennsylvania Battalion under Colonel Anthony Wayne and had participated in the Canadian campaign of 1775-76. During the French and Indian War he was a lieutenant in Captain Atlee's Company in 1760 and was promoted to captain in the 1st Pennsylvania Battalion on 11 November 1763. [26]

Lieutenant Colonel Stricker was the captain of a Light Infantry company in Colonel William Smallwood's Maryland Battalion formed in January 1776.[27] Major Weltner was 1st Major of the 1st Battalion of Frederick County Militia.[28] For experience of other officers, see chapter notes.

On 16 September 1776 Congress authorized an enlarged army of 88 regiments. To promote enlistments for this new army the bounty was increased from $10 to $20 plus 100 acres of land for those who would enlist for the duration of the war.[29] A significant number of men from four of the Pennsylvania companies took the extra $10 in October, but, probably because of the language barrier, did not understand that they had signed up for the duration of the war. One of the four companies can be indentified as Captain Hubley's, where at least 15 men who had been enlisted for three years are shown on the rolls as having enlisted 23 October 1776 for the duration of the war.[30] This situation caused serious problems for the German Regiment in 1779.

With the war going badly for Washington in the New York City area, the presence of the Germans must have been noticed around the Philadelphia Barracks, as on 23 September Congress resolved that they join the main Army. The men must not have been dressed too well as Congress also ordered the Pennsylvania Committee of Safety to supply them with such clothing as needed.[31]

On 16 October 1776 the Pennsylvania Committee of Safety proposed that the German Regiment, two Virginia regiments, and four companies of Marines be kept in Philadelphia or Trenton to protect the military stores and facilities in the Philadelphia area.[32]

As Washington retreated across New Jersey during November the German Regiment remained in Philadelphia.

CHAPTER 2 - BAPTISM UNDER FIRE AT TRENTON AND PRINCETON

At the end of November 1776 the German Regiment was still in Philadelphia awaiting equipment. On 01 December their presence again came to the attention of Congress. They directed their Board of War to order the Regiment to join General Washington, who was retreating across New Jersey.[1] Whether the Germans received their needed equipment is not known, but four days later Washington wrote John Hancock that part of the German Regiment had arrived at Trenton to join the main army.[2]

On 07 December Washington retreated across the Delaware River into Pennsylvania.[3] The next day he noted that the German Regiment had arrived and was assigned to guard Coryell's Ferry [now New Hope].[4]

The Germans were made part of Brigadier General Matthieu Fermoy's Brigade on 10 December.[5] Fermoy was a newly-arrived French mercenary who had been commissioned by Congress on 05 November.[6] His Brigade consisted of the German Regiment (Colonel Haussegger), with about 370 fit men, and the 1st Pennsylvania (Rifle) Regiment (Colonel Edward Hand), with about 260 fit men.[7] Fermoy's Brigade in turn was part of Major General Nathanael Greene's Division.

Regimental Adjutant Louis van Linkensdorf on 11 December for the second time requested the advance of six months pay from Congress. He had lost his horse and equipage and claimed he could not perform the duties of Adjutant without a horse and could not afford to replace it without an advance.[8] Since he is not mentioned again, he may have resigned.

On Christmas morning Colonel Haussegger received surprising orders. He called in his Captains and read:
"You are to see that your men have three days' provisions ready cooked before noon, everyone fit for duty, except a Sergeant and six men to be left with the baggage, will parade with arms, accroutements, and ammunition (40 cartridges) in best order and with provisions and blankets. No man is to quit his Division on pain of instant punishment. Each officer is to provide himself with a piece of white paper stuck in his hat for a field mark. You will order your men to assemble and parade them at 4 PM in the valley immediately over the hill from McKonkey's Ferry, to remain there for further orders."[9]
The Colonel then sent his officers off to prepare for the march.

While waiting for departure time Haussegger had a visitor. He was Captain John Lacey, whose home was nearby. They had served together in the Canadian campaign under Colonel Anthony Wayne. Hausegger seemed happy to see Lacey and they reminisced about their difficulties with "Mad Anthony" Wayne. Lacey was shocked to learn that Hausegger was disgusted with the patriot cause and planned to leave the Army soon.[10] This visit was probably cut short as the Regiment had to begin their march to McKonkey's Ferry [now Washington Crossing, Pa].

By late afternoon the entire Army was moving from the assembly area toward the ferry landing. While waiting there in the cold Washington had Thomas Paine's new tract," **Crisis**," read to the men.[11]

Fermoy's Brigade made the icy crossing at the rear of Greene's Division and just ahead of Sullivan's Division.[12] Since the crossing began at 7 PM and was not completed until after 3 AM, the Germans must have crossed about midnight, when it started sleeting.

It was almost 4 AM when the men were again formed up to resume the march. Fermoy's Brigade followed Greene's Division east on Upper Ferry Road, then south on Scotch Road. Before the junction of Pennington Road the brigade cut southeastward across the fields to the Trenton-Princeton Road. Their assignment was to secure this road to prevent any reinforcements from reaching the Hessians at Trenton.[13]
The brigade was in position when musket fire was faintly heard through the sleet at 8 AM. Then when artillery fire was heard they knew that the battle was on.

Before long new orders were received from Washington. They were to do an "about face" and advance toward Trenton to keep the Hessians from breaking out and escaping toward Princeton. The Hessian regiments Rall and Lossberg had been driven out of town and were milling in an apple orchard. Here Fermoy's and Stephen's Brigades closed in on them. As Fermoy's men were firing they closed to about 50 paces and called for the Hessians to surrender in both English and German. Lieutenant Colonel Franziscus Scheffer of the Hessians called out for quarter and the battle was over for about 600 men in the orchard.[14]

The Hessian Knyphausen Regiment surrendered shortly afterward at about 10 AM in another part of Trenton. Word was then received that the Americans would return immediately to their camp in Pennsylvania. Prisoners and booty were quickly rounded up and the return march was begun. It was the morning of 27 December before the last men arrived back in camp.[15]

On the morning of 30 December 1776 a second crossing of the Delaware was begun. Even in daylight this crossing was more hazardous than the last due to presence of larger blocks of floating ice. The Army moved through Trenton and across the Assunpink Creek Bridge and posted itself on the south side where they would be safe from surprise attack.[16]

On the last two days of the year Washington urged the men whose enlistments were about to expire to reenlist. When appeals to duty and patriotism failed, he offered $10 bounty for six week's additional service. This yielded about 1200 men, enough to continue the campaign.[17] The German Regiment and Hand's Riflemen did not have to be paraded to hear Washington's reenlistment talk. They were already enlisted for three years or longer.

With the enemy approaching from [New] Brunswick, Fermoy's Brigade was again assigned to cover the Princeton Road. This time they were supported by Stephen's Brigade, commanded by Colonel Charles Scott. This Brigade consisted of: Elliot's 4th Virginia Continental Regiment (Maj Josiah Parker), with about 229 men; Scott's 5th Virginia Continental Regiment (Lt Col Robert Lawson), about 129 men; and Buckner's 6th Virginia Continental Regiment (Maj Richard Parker), about 191 men.[18]

The two Brigades were ordered to acertain the strength of the enemy and delay them as long as possible. Their main defensive position was to be set up at the Five Mile Run [now Little Shabakunk Creek] Bridge.[19]

Apparently the German Regiment was in the lead as they marched north from Trenton on 31 December 1776. Meeting no enemy, they crossed Five Mile Run, passed by Maidenhead [now Lawrenceville], then crossed Eight Mile Run [now Shipetaukin Creek] and Stony Brook. When they were within $\frac{1}{2}$ mile of Princeton, Major Ludwick Weltner became worried.[20]

Weltner rode up to the head of the column to find out what was going on as it was known the enemy occupied Princeton. He argued about this with Colonel Haussegger and finally said he would not let the regiment go a step farther without reconnoitering the town. The colonel said this was mutiny and that he would personally lead Lieutenant Bernard Hubley and 10 men in a reconnaisance. Weltner ordered Hubley to stand fast and Haussegger went off with the 10 men.[21]

In Princeton Colonel Haussegger went directly to a housedoor and knocked. It was opened by what the men thought to be a Hessian general, but could only have been Colonel von Donop or one of his officers. The Hessian shook Haussegger's hand and asked where his regiment was. Haussegger blamed his Major for usurping command and refusing to let the men march on. At this point it became clear to the men that this was a prearranged defection. The Hessian then pulled out his purse and gave Haussegger some gold coins and called to the guard to take the men away. Haussegger asked for one man to be his servant and was told to pick one. Haussegger then followed the Hessian inside and closed the door on his Regiment.[22]

This shameful story was related by the man picked as the servant, Private Conrad Housman of York, Pa. After going to New York City with Haussegger for about a week, both were back in Philadelphia by 17 Jan 1777 and Housman returned to the regiment. [23] The identity and fate of the nine captured men is not known. If they were taken to the infamous New York City prisons, their chances of survival were very slim.

When his colonel's last patrol did not return from Princeton, Major Weltner took the regiment back to the main brigade defense line set up at Five Mile Run.

At daybreak of New Year's Day the 1st Battalion of British Light Infantry and two companies of Hessian Jaegers [Captains Wreden and Ewald] marched out of Princeton toward Maidenhead. About one and a half miles beyond Maidenhead they skirmished at the Five Mile Run position with Fermoy's Brigade. They then returned to Princeton claiming "the rebels lost four men killed." After the skirmish Fermoy withdrew most of his men to the Shabakunk Creek position.[24]

During the night British Lieutenant General Cornwallis arrived in Princeton and ordered an advance on Trenton in the morning. The British and Hessian vanguard started out about 8 AM on 02 January 1777. They passed through Maidenhead about noon and routed Fermoy's small force at Five Mile Run. Not long afterward, as the enemy was seen approaching the Shabakunk position, Fermoy suddenly left his brigade and rode rapidly back toward Trenton. Colonel Edward Hand, as senior officer, then took command of the brigade. He waited for the Five Mile Run defenders to get across the wooden bridge, then had it pulled down. He allowed the Jaegers to get within pointblank range before firing from concealment. The Jaegers fell back in confusion and waited for artillery support. The artilley was moved up and blasted the woods for a half-hour.[25]

During this cannonade Generals Washington, Greene, and Knox rode out to encourage the men. Washington urged Hand to hold the enemy until dark. By the time the enemy forced Hand back it was approaching 4 PM. In the retreat from the Shabakunk position Hand's Riflemen and the German Regiment took the main road while Colonel Scott's Virginians remained between the road and Assunpink Creek to aviod being outflanked.[26]

Colonel Hand's next holding position was where the road passed through a ravine known as Stockton Hollow, about a half-mile outside Trenton. Two fieldpieces, commanded by Captain Thomas Procter, were set up here and they duelled with the British for a half-hour, effectively stopping their advance at the road. The main enemy effort was then directed at Scott's Virginians. As they fell back toward the Assunpink Bridge, the sun set. During the artillery duel Washington sent Hitchcock's New England

Brigade over the bridge to cover Hand's retreat. Hitchcock's men opened ranks on Bridge Street to let Hand's and Weltner's men pass through. The New Englanders then collided with the Hessians.[27]

When Hitchcock's men in turn fell back from the Hessian attack, their retreat was to be covered by part of the German Regiment positioned at the north end of the Assunpink Bridge. When the British Light Infantry attacked the German Regiment in the flank, there was much confusion and intermingling of soldiers in the twilight. Finally those who didn't make it to the bridge had to take to the water to escape. Assunpink Creek was icy but fordable below the bridge.[28]

Private John Bottomer of Pennsylvania, in his pension application, stated that he was wounded in the side and fell near the bridge. He was then run over by about fifty men until he got Lieutenant Bernard Hubley's attention. Hubley had him carried to safety and he was treated by a surgeon. Even though he was considered mortally wounded, Bottomer recovered, returned to the regiment.[29]

The enemy made several attempts to storm the bridge, but were turned back by American artillery.[30] It was after dark when Lord Cornwallis rode into Trenton, the brigade - now Hand's - had completed its mission successfully. This day's action is now known as the Second Battle of Trenton.

The only misconduct reported to Washington after the battle was that of the German Regiment. They were accused of breaking ranks and fleeing too soon at the Assunpink Bridge.[31] This criticism seems to be overly harsh. Washington himself was at the south end of the bridge as his troops streamed across in the twilight; he saw what was happening.[32] No action was taken on the complaint.

Reports fail to show the whereabouts of the German Regiment after it fled over and around the Assunpink Bridge. It is assumed they remained in Colonel Hand's Brigade. Hand's Brigade slipped out of camp during the night and marched with the main army up a little-known back road to attack the British rear at Princeton on the morning of 03 January 1777.

Hand's Brigade was there to help repulse the attack of the British 17th Foot Regiment that was fatal to Brigadier General Hugh Mercer. Led in a rapid advance by Washington, Hand attempted to turn the 17th's left flank. They had nearly succeeded when the British fled in disorder toward Pennington and toward Trenton. Hand's units led the pursuit toward Pennington until after dark, joined for a time by General Washington.[33]

11

In the meantime other units of the main army recaptured the town of Princeton and made good use of the military stores there. About two hours after the shooting stopped the march was resumed on the road toward [New] Brunswick. They turned off the main road beyond Rocky Hill and reached Somerset Court House about dusk and bivoaced there. Washington ordered a day of rest on 04 January while they waited for Hand's Brigade to return.[34]

Hand's Brigade was cut off from making a direct return to the main army when the British reoccupied Princeton. They had to take a roundabout route and had been "obliged to encamp on the bleak mountains, whose tops were covered with snow, without even blankets to cover them."[35]

On 05 and 06 January the army marched north to Morristown where they went into winter quarters.

CHAPTER 3 - THE DEFENSE OF NEW JERSEY IN 1777

After their double defeat at Trenton and Princeton the British-Hessian forces withdrew from all of New Jersey except [New] Brunswick, [Perth] Amboy, and Paulus Hook [Jersey City]. To keep the enemy in New York City and on Staten Island, Washington positioned his Army in the hills around Middle Brook, with the left flank on the Hudson River and the right flank at Princeton.[1] The German Regiment seems to have been with the main army in the Middle Brook-Rahway area.

By mid-January the army had time for garrison details. On 17 January 1777 a general court-martial sat at Morristown for Captain Henry Fister of Maryland and 1st Lieutenant Frederick Rawlwagen of Pennsylvania. The details are not recorded, but Fister was found guilty of "quitting his Company and Regiment, being absent a fortnight without leave from his commanding officer." Rawlwagen's charges are not known, but he was also found guilty. Washington reviewed and approved the sentences on 31 March. Fister was dismissed or resigned 07 April, Rawlwagen was cashiered on 15 April 1777.[2]

On 15 February 1777 1st Lieutenant Jacob Bower of the 1st Vacant [ex-Weiser] Company was promoted to captain and transferred to the 6th Pennsylvania Regiment.[3] This was not the first transfer out of the regiment, 2nd Lieutenant John Lindenberger of Pennsylvania was promoted to 1st lieutenant and transferred to the 4th Continental Artillery on 01 January 1777.[4]

A large enemy foraging party of about 4000 men came out from Amboy on 23 February 1777. They were attacked about 11 AM near Spanktown [now Rahway] by Maxwell's New Jersey Brigade, plus Hand's 1st Pennsylvania Regiment, the German Regiment, and part of McKay's 8th Pennsylvania Regiment. Lieutenant Colonel George Stricker of the Germans reported to Major General Greene that the Americans killed or wounded three wagon loads of men and that 11 of the enemy were seen dead in one place. The Americans followed the enemy toward Amboy and continued their attacks until dark.[5]

In March the German Regiment was stationed at Spanktown with 125 rank and file fit for duty.[6] On 28 March 1st Lieutenant John Lorah of Maryland was promoted to captain.[7] He was the replacement captain for the Second Vacant [ex-Fister's] Company.

At the beginning of April the Regiment received word that they were getting a new colonel and losing their general. Brigadier General Fermoy was transferred to the northern army.[8] The new colonel was Henry Leonard Philip, Baron de Arendt, a German mercenary. The Congress had commissioned him on 19 March to replace Hausegger.[9] Arendt was described as a military engineer having 22 years experience in the Prussian Army.[10]

13

Two additional majors for the Regiment were created in April - Captain Daniel Burchardt of Pennsylvania was promoted 07 April and Captain George Hubley of Pennsylvania on 09 April 1777.[11,12]

In April Lieutenant Colonel George Stricker aroused General Washington by asking to resign. On 09 April Washington replied to Maryland Governor Thomas Johnson, "Heard you appointed George Stricker to command of a regiment, he doesn't deserve such an appointment. He received my permission yesterday to resign, if I had a replacement for him I would have accepted his resignation on the spot." Stricker resigned on 29 April.[13] On the same day Major Ludowick Weltner of Maryland was promoted to lieutenant colonel.[14]

On 19 April Congress resolved "that the Rev. Mr. Henry Miller be and he is hereby appointed Chaplain to the German Regiment."[15] Pastor Miller [also Moeller/Mueller], a Lutheran, had a very short tenure with the Germans as on 24 April he was appointed Chaplain of the Pennsylvania Regiment of Foot.[16]

Congress accepted a bill on 26 April 1777 "due to [Maryland Private] Thomas Polehouse, to be paid to Mr Weltner, for bleeding 95 Privates of Col Hausegger's Rgt, the sum of 12 and 60/90 dollars."[17] This is an indication of the medical state-of-the-art during the Revolution.

There were more personnel changes in the Regiment in May. Captain George Keeport of Maryland resigned on 04 May. He was replaced by 1st Lieutenant Charles Baltzel of Maryland who was promoted to captain on 10 May.[18] Also, 1st Lieutenant Peter Boyer of Pennsylvania was promoted to captain on 09 May.[19]

During May the Regiment was active in New Jersey. A muster roll of Captain William Heiser's Company listed a man missing at Bonumstown [now Edison] on 10 May. This roll was dated 22May 1777 at Quibbletown [now New Market].[20]

A major organizational shakeup occurred for the Germans on 24 May 1777 when Major Generals Greene and Sullivan agreed to trade regiments. Sullivan, for unstated "good reasons," desired to keep Hazen's Canadian Regiment. Greene had no objection to accepting the German Regiment in exchange.[21]

The Regiment was assigned by Greene to the brigade of John Peter Muehlenberg, also a German-American.[22] Pastor Muehlenberg was the patriot who, from the pulpit, is said to have stated there was a time for worship and a time to fight, as he revealed himself in uniform.[23] He raised the 8th Virginia Continental Regiment, also originally known as a German Regiment, and served as their colonel in the southern army. Upon his promotion to brigadier general on 21 February 1777 Muehlenberg was transferred

14

to the main army.[24]

Muehlenberg took command of his brigade on 26 May 1777 at Middlebrook, NJ.[25] It was organized as follows:
German Regiment (Col Baron Arendt) with about 285 fit men,
1st Virginia Coninental Regiment (Col Isaac Read) with about 137 fit men,
5th Virginia Continental Regiment (Col Josiah Parker) with about 133 fit men,
9th Virginia Continental Regiment (Col George Matthews) with about 308 fit men,
and [they seem to have joined later]
13th Virginia Continental Regiment (Col Wm. Russel).[26,27]

On 24 May 1777 the Regiment received orders to move to Princeton. It was hoped they would get tents at Boundbrook. At this time Colonel Arendt requested ten days leave upon arrival at Princeton to go to Philadelphia on important business.[28] The nature of this business became clear a month later.

Washington joined the main Army at Middlebrook on 28 May to begin the years campaigning.[29]

During June the Regiment continued to support pickets and scout enemy movements. On 09 June 1777, for example, they received orders for a detachment of three captains, six lieutenants, six sergeants, and 150 men to parade that afternoon at the Artillery Park with three days' provisions. They were to be commanded by Major [sic] Weltner, who would receive his orders from Brigadier General Maxwell.[30] Where they went is not known.

General Howe began the enemy offensive in New Jersey by marching 18,000 troops from Amboy to Bruswick on 13 June.[31] Brunswick was only seven miles from Washington's forces at Middlebrook. The main Army at this time consisted of only 8,000 men, but the strength of their positions in the hills more than made up for their lack of numbers.

On 25 June 1777 Washington responded to Colonel Arendt: "Regarding your request to go to Philadelphia, at this season heads of regiments can be ill-spared, but it is impossible for me to refuse your request. I have considered your project for a treaty between this country and the King of Prussia, but I must refer you to Congress."[32] From this it is obvious that Arendt went to Philadelphia in May to promote a pact with Prussia.

During the second half of June there was much marching and countermarching as Howe and Washington played cat and mouse. Washington avoided serious confrontations and frustrated Howe. By the end of June, Howe marched his Army through Metuchen and back to Amboy. The enemy then went into camp on Staten Island. For the first time in eight months New Jersey was free of the enemy.[33]

There is no record of the marches made by the German Regiment. It is known that during this time Colonel Arendt suffered a rupture when his horse fell during a skirmish at Quibbletown and Raritan Bridge.[34]

Back at the regiment, 1st Lieutenant Samuel Gerock of Maryland was promoted to captain on 01 July 1777.[35]

In response to a feint made by Howe the brigades of Maxwell and Muehlenberg were ordered on 19 July to march north to the Hudson River.[36] When it became clear to Washington that Howe's troopships went out to sea on 23 July, the two brigades were recalled on 24 July.[37] Muehlenberg's Brigade was back at Morristown on 27 July when word was received that the enemy fleet was off Cape May, NJ and might come up the Delaware. Washington reacted by starting the army south toward Philadelphia.[38]

The defense of New Jersey ended on 09 August 1777 when the army crossed into Pennsylvania. On 11 August the army stopped on the banks of the Neshaminy River (20 miles north of Philadelphia and 20 miles west of Trenton) to await Howe's next move. They camped here until 22 August when word was received that the enemy fleet had entered Chesapeake Bay.[39] It was now clear that Philadelphia was to be attacked from the southwest. It was time to march to meet the threat.

CHAPTER FOUR - BRANDYWINE AND GERMANTOWN

Knowing the British fleet was in the Chesapeake Bay, Washington started his army south from its camp on the Neshaminy on 23 August 1777. In the lead was Muehlenberg's Brigade, which included the German Regiment.[1] They stopped early that day to prepare for a parade through Philadelphia the next day.

On Sunday morning the 24th it was necessary to start marching at 3 AM in order to reach the city by 7 AM. It took three hours for all the brigades to pass.[2] Hopefully some of the Philadelphia men of the German Regiment were able to see their families.

On 25 August 1777 Howe's British and Hessian troops began landing at Head of Elk [now Elkton], Md. On this day Muehlenberg's Brigade was camped along White Clay Creek in Maryland to observe Howe's progress. Behind them the main body of the American army was positioned on the left bank of Red Clay Creek.[3]

After taking a week to collect horses and wagons, Howe began to move slowly toward Philadelphia. When it became apparent that his right flank was in danger, Washington began a withdrawal. By 01 September Muehlenberg's Brigade had retreated to Red Clay Creek.

As the enemy approached Red Clay Creek on 08 September, Washington decided to move to a new position. Muehlenberg's Brigade began their retreat about 2 AM on the 9th. By nightfall they were encamped on the east side of Chadd's Ford on Brandywine Creek in Pennsylvania. Here they were placed in the second line as a reserve unit.

On 11 September the Battle of Brandywine began. Greene's Division, consisting of Muehlenberg's and Weedon's Brigades, remained in its reserve position until about 5 PM. At this time the division was ordered to support the troops of Major General Sullivan, whose lines were crumbling.[4]

Greene's Brigades literally ran to their new positions. Greene later wrote that he moved Weedon's Brigade three to four miles in 45 minutes.[5] They began arriving at the new position at a ravine between two woods at about 6 PM.[6] Muehlenberg's Brigade passed to the right of Weedon and positioned itself on a road.[7]

The British attack came right at Weedon's Brigade. First with artillery fire, then with musket and bayonet, the brigade held off the enemy until dark. This allowed the entire army to retreat toward Chester. After dark Greene made a fighting withdrawal from the battlefield. The British were content to occupy the

17

battlefield.

Muehlenberg's Brigade appears not to have been attacked that evening. The only known German Regiment loss at Brandywine was the capture of 1st Lieutenant John Weidman [#1] of Pennsylvania.[8]

From Chester the bruised Americans moved to Germantown. On 15 September Washington broke camp there and moved to the White Horse Tavern area. Howe moved toward them on the 16th and a major battle was in the making when a severe rain storm struck. All guns and paper cartridges were soaked so the next day the Americans were hurriedly marched to a supply depot at Warwick where there was fresh powder. Washington then moved to deny the British the use of Parker's Ford on the Schuykill River.

On 21 September Howe feinted toward Warwick and drew Washington away from the river fords. The next day the enemy crossed the Schuykill at Sweede's Ford. The defense of Philadelphia had failed. On 26 September the British entered a half-deserted city.

After being deceived by Howe's feint, Washington's Army camped at Pennypacker's Mill. Here, on 23 September, Colonel Arendt of the German Regiment received new orders from Washington: "To prevent a junction of the British fleet with the Army we must hold Fort Island [Fort Mifflin] below Philadelphia. I therefore appoint you to command of it, move there immediately."[9] With these orders Arendt left the German Regiment in command of Lieutenant Colonel Ludwick Weltner.

On 29 September Washington moved the army five miles south to the Skippack Road. He was going on the offensive again. The army had been reinforced by additional troops and now numbered about 8,000 continentals and 3,000 militia. Washington planned to attack the British-Hessian Camp at Germantown by approaching in four columns during the night and simultaneously attacking at daylight. In the afternoon of 03 October 1777 the plan was put into motion. Greene's column started off at 7 PM, after dark.[10]

The Brigades of Muehlenberg and Weedon were again under the command of Greene. Their mission was to advance into Germantown on Limekiln Road and attack the British camped around Luken's Mill.

Muehlenberg's Brigade was in the lead coming down Limekiln Road. At dawn, visibility stayed poor because of a heavy ground fog. They struck the outposts of Osborn's British 1st Light Infantry Battalion and drove them back toward Luken's Mill.

Around Luken's Mill the Brigade struck two more British battalions in the fog and broke through them with a bayonet charge. When the brigade reached the neighborhood of the Market

House they came under attack from two sides. Cornwallis had arrived from Philadelphia with three fresh battalions and on the other side of them was Grant who had just repulsed Generals Sullivan and Wayne on the Germantown Pike.[11]

The brigade began to fight its way back to Greene's main body of troops. Here the Germans' sister unit, the 9th Virginia Regiment, the most advanced, was surrounded and forced to surrender. Most of the men, including Colonel George Mathews, were taken prisoner and about 100 British prisoners were freed.[12] With his division reunited, Greene ordered a retreat about 10 AM.

During the retreat 1st Lieutenant Bernard Hubley of the Germans had some of his men break down a high fence so Muehlenberg's horse could jump it. While waiting Muehlenberg reportedly fell asleep in the saddle.[13] He had been without sleep for 48 hours. Greene's Brigade was followed up Limekiln Road for about five miles by Cornwallis' three battalions.[14]

What happened to the German Regiment that day must be inferred. They were in action beside or near the 9th Virginia ·Regiment. Their known casualties are probably only a fraction of the actual number. This was the Germans' worst day.

KNOWN CASUALTIES FROM PENNSYLVANIA

Private Philip Flowers, probably Burchardt's Co., died of wounds.
Private Philip Gillman, Rice's Co., wounded in left breast, recovered and returned to duty.[15]
Private Henry Hammrick, Bunner's Co., wounded in left shoulder recovered and returned to duty.[16]
Private Philip Klein, Rice's Co., wounded through left shoulder, recovered and returned to duty.
Private John Richcreek, Hubley's Co., wounded, recovered, but transferred to Invalid Corps.[17]
Private John Rysbecker, Hubley's Co., wounded through hand and shoulder by musket ball, recovered and returned to duty.[18]
Private John Snyder, Hubley's Co., wounded in the head [19] or breast and right side by splinters from fence rail struck by cannon ball, recovered and returned to duty.[20]

KNOWN CASUALTIES FROM MARYLAND

Captain Charles Baltzell, wounded, recovered and returned to duty.[21]
Private Henry Wagner, Heiser's Co., badly wounded in the leg.[22]
Private Henry Tomm, Heiser's Co., wounded, in hospital at Court House, Reading, Pa on 17Nov77.

After the Battle of Germantown, the German Regiment marched 20 miles back to their former campground at Pennypacker's Mill. Here they received word of Gates' victory at Saratoga on 14

October. News of Burgoyne's surrender arrived on 17 October and was celebrated by a 13-gun salute, a _feu de joie_ by the army drawn up in two lines, and short talks by the chaplains.

On 18 October Howe withdrew from Germantown and moved all his troops into Philadelphia. He then concentrated his efforts on capturing the American forts in the Delaware River. These were the forts to which Colonel Arendt, the former commanding officer of the German Regiment, had been reassigned.

On 22 October 1777 the German Regiment and the 5th Virginia Regiment were ordered to be ready to march at 6 PM without blankets or any encumbrances and with 40 rounds of ammunition.[23] Later orders restored the blankets and added a gill of rum for Greene's entire division.[24] The army was moving to Whitpin, to be closer to the Delaware River. Washington then moved the army to Whitemarsh, 12 miles from Philadelphia, on 02 November.

On 19 November Greene was placed in command of all troops in New Jersey to deal with Cornwallis and 4000 troops who had landed in Gloucester, NJ that day.

At 10 AM on 21 November Muehlenberg's and Weedon's Brigades arrived on the riverbank across from Burlington, NJ. They were expected to take most or all night to get the wagons and artillery over.[25] On 22 November Greene made his headquarters at Mount Holly and attempted to concentrate his forces there to meet Cornwallis. By the 25th Cornwallis had turned back and was returning to Philadelphia, so Washington directed Greene to return to Whitemarsh.[26] The Greene incursion into New Jersey ended 27 November 1777 when the division recrossed the Delaware into Pennsylvania.[27]

CHAPTER FIVE - VALLEY FORGE, MONMOUTH AND NEW YORK

On 12 December 1777 the German Regiment and the rest of the army completed their march from White Marsh to the new location which was to be their winter quarters. This place was unlike the Morristown area where they spent the previous winter - here there was only a barren, wooded hill known as "the Gulph." Nearby were several houses and a blacksmith shop known as "Valley Forge."

General Washington had chosen this desolate place as it was easy to defend and it was only 20 miles from Philadelphia. The main army's presence here would limit the foraging area of the British-Hessian Army in the city.

The first order of business in the new camp was the construction of quarters for the men. Trees were about the only thing not in short supply here. A prize of $12 was offered for the first log hut completed in each regiment. The 12-man cabins were to be 14 feet wide, 16 feet long, and 6½ feet high with a door in one end and fireplace and chimney at the other end. Construction began on 20 December, by 03 January 1778 most of the cabins were up and were occupied. [1]

When the work on the huts was completed the men of Muehlenberg's Brigade began fortifying their area of the perimeter, the southeastern corner of the camp. During the winter they built a redoubt called Fort Muehlenberg and two redans. [2]

On 17 December Washington issued a general order thanking the troops for their honorable service in 1777. He wished he had better winter quarters for them and pointed out that those who fled Philadelphia were also suffering. He concluded by stating he would spend the winter with the army. [3]

Tempers flared in those small log cabins. Lieutenant Martin Shugart of Pennsylvania, who had been tried by brigade court-martial for challenging Lieutenant Laudermilk of Maryland, was found guilty of violating section seven of the articles of war and was sentenced to be cashiered. On 26 January 1778 Washington approved the sentence and, on the recommendation of the court, restored Shugart's rank. [4] Laudermilk must have felt disgraced by the court-martial decision, he resigned on 08 April. [5]

First Lieutenant Philip Shrawder of Pennsylvania was promoted to Captain-Lieutenant on 08 February 1778. [6] This rank was then just below that of Captain, and he was the actual commander of the "Lieutenant Colonel's Company" in the regiment. [7] He had been a 1st Lieutenant since 13 May 1777. [8]

Other personnel changes took place in February. Captain John Lorah of Maryland resigned on 23 February 1778. [9] The next day 1st Lieutenant Bernard Hubley of Pennsylvania was promoted to captain and commanded Lorah's [ex-Fister's] Maryland company until June 1779. [10] This was the first, but not the last, 'interstate' transfer of officers within the German Regiment.

At the end of February 1778 the German Regiment was in very poor condition with only 73 fit men out of 308. Of the 308 men, 52 were without enough clothes to go outside, 48 were sick, 106 were detailed elsewhere, and 29 were on furlough. During February alone there were five deaths, one desertion, and two discharges in the regiment. [11] See Appendix 1.

On 23 February 1778 a Prussian mercenary - "Baron" Friedrich Wilhelm von Steuben - reported to Washington's Headquarters at Valley Forge. After several interviews, even though he spoke only German and French, he was named Acting Inspector General and placed in charge of troop training. Steuben threw himself into the task. Within days he had formed a "Commander-in-Chief's Bodyguard," a model company of 100 to 120 men (two from each regiment) which he drilled himself from 6 AM to 6 PM. Later he also selected an officer from each Brigade to be the "Brigade Inspector," whom he also drilled. These Brigade Inspectors also received evening classes in leadership, responsibility, and record keeping. [12] By 24 March the entire army was drilling by the Steuben system. There is no evidence the bilingual German Regiment's personnel assisted with Steuben's early training efforts.

Captain Philip Graybill, an original captain of the Regiment, resigned on 12 March. On the same day 1st Lieutenant Christian Myers was promoted to captain and took over Graybill's Company. [13] Graybill must not have been with his company prior to resigning as his men were listed for a time as the 3rd Vacant Company. First Lieutenant Jacob Kotz or Kortz of Heiser's Company resigned on 08 April. [14]

As the regimental clothing situation had not improved by April, the officers complained directly to Washington. Alexander Hamilton, Washington's aide, fired off this letter on 26 April to Clothier General James Meese: "By command of his Excellency, I inclose a letter to him of officers of the German Battalion. There appears to be something particular in the circumstances of that Batallion re clothing which deserves attention. Do whatever to put them upon equal footing with other regiments." [15] The clothing situation had been critical since March, as the end of March strength report lists 52 men as being unfit for duty for lack of clothes. [See Appendix 1.]

On 05 May 1778 Washington announced the alliance with France at Camp. Two treaties - one of amity and commerce, the other a defensive alliance - had been signed 06 February in Paris. The next day was set aside for celebration at Valley Forge. First there was a solemn thanksgiving by the brigade chaplains, then a grand parade, a 13-gun salute, a _feu de joie_, followed by much cheering and jubilation. [16]

Captain William Heiser, another original captain of the Regiment, resigned 21 May and his men became the 4th Vacant Company. [17] Four days later 1st Lieutenant Michael Bayer of Maryland was promoted to captain, but he was placed in command of George Hubley's Pennsylvania Company until June 1779. [18, 19] This was another case of 'interstate' assignment of officers within the German Regiment.

Second Lieutenant Martin Shugart was promoted to 1st lieutenant on 25 May 1778, he had been a 2nd lieutenant since 15 Nov 1777. [20] Ensign John Machenheimer resigned on 31 May, followed by Ensign George Cole on 02 June. [21]

Second Lieutenant Thomas Edison of Pennsylvania was tried by general court-martial on 16 May for abusing the family of Colonel John Nixon [3rd Pennsylvania Regiment]. He was found guilty of behavior unbecoming of an officer and a gentleman and was sentenced to be discharged. Washington approved the sentence on 22 May. [22]

To replentish the depleted ranks of the army at Valley Forge, Congress established quotas for the individual states. At the March session of the Maryland Assembly an act was passed to raise its quota of 2,902 men. This levy was apportioned among the counties according to the number of militia in each. Frederick County's quota was 309 men. County quotas unfilled by 20 May 1778, according to the act, were to be filled by draftees chosen from the county militia. [23]

Provision was also included in the act for the hiring of substitutes to reach the quotas. [24] This was done on a large scale as can be seen from two Frederick County lists of that period which survive. One shows 153 substitutes enlisted up to 20 May 1778, including 72 for the German Regiment. [25] The second list gives 69 substitutes furnished by the militia between 29 May and 09 June 1778, with 16 men for the Germans. [26]

On 09 June General Washington wrote a note to Colonel Louis Nicola of the Invalid Corps at Philadelphia asking him to accept Captain John D. Woelpper of the German Regiment into the Invalid Corps. [27] Two days later Woelpper was transferred to the Invalids. [28] He had been with the German Regiment since 22 July 1776.

Muehlenberg's Brigade strength at the beginning of June was:
    German Regiment   313 fit officers and men,

```
1st, 5th, & 9th Virginia Rgts    281          "
1st Virginia State Rgt           203          "
2nd Virginia State Rgt           229          " . [29]
```

By mid-June it was evident that the British were preparing to
evacuate Philadelphia and Washington's Army was ready to fight.
The British withdrawal began in the early morning of 18 June for
a march across New Jersey. Muehlenberg's Brigade was the last
brigade of the second line to leave Valley Forge. On 19 June
they marched northeastward toward Coryell's Ferry and crossed
into New Jersey on 21 June where they formed the rear guard of
the army.

When the leading two brigades of Americans caught up with the
British-Hessian Army near Monmouth Court House [now Freehold,
NJ] on 27 June, the rear guard was still 20 miles away. As the
battle developed the next day Muehlenberg's brigade spent most of
that humid, 100° day marching. They reached their reserve
position late in the afternoon. Here they briefly came
under British artillery fire. [30] If there were casualties in
the German Regiment that hot day, they most likely were from
heatstroke.

In the days following Monmouth the German Regiment moved with
the main army to keep the British confined to the New York City
area. Captain Christian Myers' extant orderly book begins here
and covers the rest of the summer. [31]

On 04 July 1778 the Germans were camped along the Raritan River
at Brunswick Landing. General Washington ordered "a feu de joie
of the whole line" and "a double allowance of rum will be served
out" on this second anniversary of the Declaration of
Independence.

The march was continued as shown by Myers' entries:
          07 July 1778 - Scotch Plains
          08 July 1778 - Springfield
          09 & 10 July 1778 - Second River
          12 July 1778 - 2nd line camp near Paramus
          14 July 1778 - Keaikeae [?]
          17 July 1778 - near King's Ferry
          20 July 1778 - Croton Bridge. [32]

While at Croton Bridge, Sgt John Johnson of the Regiment was
courtmartialled "for insolent behavior to Lt Hudson." He was
found guilty and sentenced to be reprimanded by Colonel Weltner
in front of his regiment that evening. The next day they marched
to North Castle. [33]

On 22 July Washington transferred the German Regiment from
Muehlenberg's Brigade to the 2nd Maryland Brigade. [34] He
carried out a Congressional Resolution of 26 February which

24

transferred the German Regiment to the quota of Maryland as of 04 May 1778. [35] Somehow this did not come to the attention of Pennsylvania officials for another 12 months.

Word of the transfer reached the Regiment on 22 July while they camped at North Castle. The next day they marched to Wright's Mill and on 25 July 1778 they were at White Plains, New York which would be their camp until December. [36]

The new 2nd Maryland Brigade at White Plains was organized as follows:

2nd Md Rgt [Col Thomas Price]	382 fit officers and men	
4th Md Rgt [Col J.C. Hall]	380	"
6th Md Rgt [Col O.H. Williams]	315	"
German Rgt [Lt Col L. Weltner]	310	" .[37]

Personnel changes within the German Regiment during July indicate a junior officer shortage. Sergeant-Major Jacob Smith, the regimental adjudant, resigned 15 July. Four sergeants of the Regiment were among five new ensigns commissioned between 23 July and 25 July. These were Sergeants David Diffenderfer and Christian Clackner of Pennsylvania and Jacob Reybold and Sergeants Henry Hain and William Trux of Maryland. [38, 39] Surgeon's Mate Charles Ritter resigned 01 August and Private Alexander Smith was named his replacement the same day. [40]

Two brigade courtsmartial were held on 06 Aug 1778. Private John Smith, recaptured near Hackensack, NJ, was charged with deserting at Paramus, NJ and attempting to go to the enemy. He was sentenced to receive 100 lashes on his bare back well laid on. In the other case, Sergeant George Wentz of Fister's Company complained of being detained in the service contrary to his enlistment. The court was of the opinion that he was unjustly detained and instructed Colonel Weltner to give Sergeant Wentz his discharge. [41]

During the first week of September, Peter Peris of Philadelphia was named regimental surgeon [42], and an older ensign, David Morgan, was promoted to 2nd lieutenant. [43] There was also time for paperwork, several Maryland muster rolls survive from this period at White Plains. [44]

On 29 September 1778 a belated court-martial was held for Captain-Lieutenant Philip Shrawder and Ensign Henry Maag. Both were charged with behaving in a cowardly manner at the Battle of Germantown [04 August 1777] by leaving their regiment in time of action and not rejoining it until the action was over. Lieutenant Shrawder was found not guilty, having acted in his capacity as quartermaster in carrying off the wounded. Ensign Maag was found guilty and ordered cashiered. His sentence was reviewed and approved by General Washington on 26 March 1779. [45]

25

Monthly strength reports show the Germans located at Fishkill, New York with the 2nd Maryland Brigade at the end of September and October. [46]

In November there are indications that Colonel Weltner was ill for some time. Washington wrote Weltner on 16 November asking him to take a furlough instead of resigning for health reasons. [47] Weltner seems to have been too ill to return home as he was still at Newburgh, New York on 01 December.

The German Regiment's duty with the 2nd Maryland Brigade turned out to be short. On 23 November 1778 General Washington mentions his intention to move the Regiment to Easton, Pennsylvania [48] to help protect the frontier against further Indian attacks. Enroute to their new post they were to help escort the prisoners taken at Saratoga (2200 British and 1800 Hessians) across New Jersey. [49]

By the end of November the Germans were stationed at Newburgh, New York, presumably waiting for the prisoners to arrive from Cambridge, Massachusetts.

With the prisoner escort march behind them the German Regiment moved to Easton to take their position on the frontier. On New Year's Day 1779 Washington wrote to Brigadier General Edward Hand at Minisink, New Jersey that, "should any pressing circumstances arise you may call [the German Regiment] from Easton." [50] It is known that the Germans celebrated New Year's with a _feu de joie_.

On 27 January Washington appointed Ensign Henry Shrupp regimental adjutant, as of 01 October 1778. [51]

In March the acting commander of the Germans, Major Daniel Burchardt, was called on the carpet. General Washington wrote him on 25 February 1779 to make him account for a large deficiency of ammunition. Burchardt responded on 20 March that the 10,000 paper cartridges were lost through damage on foraging expeditions in bad weather, a quantity were damaged by a careless wagoner while escorting the prisoners, and some were fired celebrating New Year's at Easton. [52]

While back in Philadelphia on furlough, Captain-Lieutenant Philip Shrawder was called before a committee of the Pennsylvania General Assembly on 04 March. He confirmed their suspicions, the German Regiment had been transferred to the State of Maryland as part of the quota of that state. This had been done by Congress on 26 Feb 1778. The committee was upset, their report stated this action was unfair since over half of regiment's men were from Pennsylvania, and perhaps Pennsylvania ought not give the German Regiment any supplies. These comments were read in

Congress on 30 March 1779 and referred to the Board of War. [53] It apparently resulted in each state taking care of its own companies.

With their enlistments expiring in four months there must have been a lot of talk in Easton about going home. Some men's hopes were dashed when they were told that they had enlisted for the duration of the war. They had enlisted in 1776 for three years and received $10 bounty. After three months, in October 1776, they had received an additional $10 bounty but it was not made clear to them that the acceptance of the second $10 enlisted them for the duration of the war. On 02 April the men of four Pennsylvania companies sent a grievance petition to Congress asking to be discharged after three years' service. The petition was read in Congress on 11 April 1779, but seems not to have been acted on. [54] This inaction caused more difficulties in July.

CHAPTER 6 - WITH THE SULLIVAN EXPEDITION IN 1779

The Western Indian Expedition, as it was originally called, was planned to prevent a recurrence of the disastrous 1778 raids on the New York and Pennsylvania frontier. The expedition planned to strike into the heartland of the Six Nations Indians, in what is now upstate New York, to destroy their villages and crops, and make it impossible for them to wage war.

Participation in this expedition must have been considered adventurous at the time as it resulted in at least 28 known journals and diaries, kept by both officers and men. Seventeen of these were collected and published by New York State after the Centennial observance in 1879; these diaries contain many details of the German Regiment's participation in this campaign. [1]

On 24 March 1779 General Washington ordered Brigadier General Edward Hand to move the German Regiment plus Armand's and Schott's Corps to Fort Wyoming [now Wilkes-Barre, Pa]. [2] Armand's Corps, at this time commanded by Major Lomaign, also contained many Germans, both ethnic Americans and ex-Hessian volunteers. Armand's Corps' duty in the western army was short, it was recalled by Washington to the main army on 30 June 1779. [3]

The German Regiment arrived at Minisink, NJ, 30 miles up the Delaware from Easton, Pa, before 04 April. Here Major Burchardt received further orders from General Hand for the march to Fort Wyoming. [4] They must have met up with Armand's And Schott's Corps at Fort Penn [now Stroudsburg, Pa.] about 07 April. On 08 April they were scheduled to camp at Learned's Tavern [now Tannersville, Pa.]. On 09 April their stopping point was in the Great Swamp. Another overnight camp at Bullock's farm brought them to Fort Wyoming on the morning of 11 April. That day Lieutenant John Jenkins, a scout, noted in his diary, "Arrived at Wyoming with Maj Birchard [sic] who commanded 400 men." [5]

At the time of the German's arrival, Fort Wyoming was an island in an Indian-controlled Wyoming Valley. Two weeks later, Major Powell, arriving from Easton with 200 men of the 11th Pennsylvania Regiment was ambushed about three miles from Fort Wyoming. Two officers and two men were killed. The Germans were called out to escort them in. During the next few weeks the fort commander, Colonel Zebulon Butler, made good use of the German Regiment to clear the open areas of the valley of Indians. [6]

On 08 May 1779 General Hand arrived at Fort Wyoming to assume command. During May it also became known that Major General John Sullivan would assume overall command of the Western Army.

After Congress approved the expedition on 25 February, Washington had tactfully offered the command to the senior Major General, Horatio Gates. Gates refused for health reasons and suggested Sullivan, Washington's real choice. Sullivan arrived at Easton on 07 May to set up his headquarters. [7]

At the end of May Major Burchardt had a roll prepared of the "Five Companies belonging to the State of Pennsylvania," one of the few extant lists of the Pennsylvania portion of the German Regiment. [8]

The organization of the western army was announced on 24 May by General Sullivan:
1st Brigade - Gen William Maxwell [four New Jersey regiments]
2nd Brigade - Gen Enoch Poor [three New Hampshire + one Massachusetts regiments]
3rd Brigade [the Light Corps] - Gen Edward Hand [three Pennsylvania regiments + artillery & misc units]
4th Brigade - Gen James Clinton [four New York regiments + artillery]. [9]

The 3rd Brigade was organized as follows:
4th Pa Rgt - Lt Col William Butler & ca 217 fit men,
11th Pa Rgt - Lt Col Adam Hubley, Jr & ca 340 fit men,
German Rgt - Maj Daniel Burchardt & ca 305 fit men,
Armand's Corps - Maj Lomaign & ca 73 fit men [recalled to Main Army 30 June 1779],
Morgan's Riflemen - Maj James Parr & ca 107 fit men,
Schott's Corps - Capt Anthony Selin & ca 37 fit men,
Procter's (Pa) Artillery - Col Thomas Procter,
plus any volunteers that may join the Army. [10]

By mid-June road building had progressed to the point that Sullivan, with the 1st and 2nd Brigades and the remaining troops, departed Easton on 18 June and arrived at Fort Wyoming on 23 June. [11]

When Sullivan arrived at Fort Wyoming he found that the expected supplies for the Army had not arrived, the salted meat there was not fit to eat, and the cattle were thin. He turned the supply problem over to General Hand, who detailed a number of companies, including Capt Rice's, to go down river and assist with bringing the supplies up to Fort Wyoming. The supply operation must have overtaxed the boat capacity of the lower Susquehanna as extra boats had been built at Middletown, Pa, to haul Sullivan's supplies. These boats came to be known on the river as "Continental boats." [12]

Sometime in June Major Burchardt left Captain Jacob Bunner in charge of the German Regiment and departed with Ensign Henry Shrupp, regimental adjutant, for Philadelphia. On 29 June, in Philadelphia, Burchardt petitioned the Congress for permission to resign, citing hardships to his family and estates during the recent British occupation of the city. [13] The Board of War voted not to accept his resignation. [14] On 02 July he again appealed to Congress, who resolved that his resignation be accepted. [15] On 03 July they also accepted the resignation of Henry Shrupp. Shrupp's stained and creased commission, a printed form signed by John Hancock and Charles Thomson, survives in the papers of the Continental Congress. [16]

Back at the Fort some regimental personnel changes were made. Captains Bernard Hubley and Michael Bayer were ordered to trade Companies on 19 June. This gave Hubley the command of the Pennsylvania Company of his late uncle, George Hubley, and gave Bayer the command of a Maryland Company. [17] On the next day 1st Lieutenant John Weidman [#2] was appointed regimental adjutant and Captain Peter Boyer became regimental paymaster. [18] Also on that day Ensign Henry Hain resigned, he had been with the Germans since 23 July 1778. [19] On 01 July Ensign William Trux resigned, he had enlisted in the Regiment as a private on 21 July 1776 and came up through the ranks. [20]

Army Orders were issued in July to permit bathing in the river either before reveille or after retreat on Tuesdays, Thursdays, and Saturdays. This change was made as some units were not able to bathe on schedule because of "unwholesome fogs." [21]

At morning roll call on 14 July 1779, 33 men of the German Regiment were found missing. Quizzing those remaining, it was quickly determined that the missing men felt their 3-year enlistments had expired and they were going home, discharge or no discharge. [22]

A friendly Indian was sent out to determine the direction in which the missing men had headed. When their route was determined, 50 mounted men were sent in pursuit. The deserters were captured "at the gap in the mountain," presumably then on the road to Easton. The mounted men returned to Fort Wyoming with 29 prisoners on 19 July; four men had escaped successfully. [23]

On 24 July 1779 a general courtmartial was held with General Poor presiding. There are no details available for this trial. All 29 men were found guilty. The five ringleaders: Fifer Joseph Alexander and Privates Jacob Bottomer, Philip Cook, Frederick Kerls, and George Ottenberger were sentenced to be shot. Corporals Henry Moser and Frederick Sipperel were reduced to the ranks and were to run the gauntlet through two brigades and the artillery. The remaining 22 privates were also to run the gauntlet. Sentences were to be carried out at 4 PM on 26 July. [24]

Unsettled weather on 26 July caused a 25-hour postponement. A petition from the prisoners was accepted and General Sullivan ordered a Board of General Officers to meet. This time cooler heads prevailed and when orders for 27 July were read they included:

"The Commander-in-Chief having received a petition from the prisoners of the German battalion now under sentence, manifesting their consciousness of the crimes for which they have been condemned, and promising in case of pardon to distinguish themselves in future as brave and obedient soldiers, which petition being laid before a board of general officers in hopes that an act of lenity may have a proper effect on their future conduct as well as that of others, they have unanimously advised a pardon of all the offenders without discrimination. The General, wishing to extend mercy where it can be done without injury to the public service, has accordingly consented to pardon each and every one of the offenders tried and sentenced by a general court martial, whereof Brigadier General Poor president, and directs that they be immediately released and restored to their duty. Lest this unparalleled act of lenity should be abused, and any soldier take the same unjustifiable measures hereafter, the Commander-in-Chief absolutely declares he will not in future pardon a deserter, or one who, though his time be expired, shall quit his corps without a proper discharge from his commanding officer." [25]

The prisoners rejoined their companies. Six of the seven named deserters appear on a later muster roll as reenlisted for the duration of the war, so reenlistment was apparently also a condition of the pardon, probably for all 29 men.

There is little doubt that all of the 33 deserters were Pennsylvanians. This mass desertion came about as there was no action on their April petition to Congress. Captain Bunner's advice on the Pennsylvania men must have been not to discharge them. His instructions from Maryland were different as he began discharging Maryland men while the deserters were still missing. This is shown by data from the muster rolls of two Maryland Companies:

Capt-Lt Shrawder's [Md] Co
==========================
16Jul: 4 men discharged
17Jul: 6 "   "
20Jul: 1 "   "
26Jul: 24 "   "
29Jul: 1 "   "
09Aug: 3 "   "
12Oct: 9 "   "
=========================. [26]

Capt M. Bayer's [Md] Co
==========================
20Jul: 10 men discharged
24Jul: 12 "   "
26Jul: 3 "   "
09Aug: 1 "   "
12Oct: 5 "   "
==========================

31

About 115 supply boats arrived at Fort Wyoming on 24 July. Thanks were given in General Orders to General Hand, Major Conway, Captain Rice [of the Germans], Captain Porter, and others involved in the supply operation. [27]

The Army broke camp at Fort Wyoming on 31 July and began a slow march up the North Branch of the Susquehanna River. Their initial destination was Tioga [now Athens, Pa], where the Chemung River joins the North Branch. Here the Army was to link up with the New York Brigade.

Several abandoned Indian villages were burned by the time the Army reached Tioga on 11 August. There they began erecting Fort Sullivan on the portage trail between the two rivers.

Six German Regiment Privates were searching for some missing pack horses on the afternoon of 17 August. They were 200 to 300 yards beyond the advance sentries when they were attacked by about a dozen hidden savages. They returned fire and four of the men returned safely to camp. A party of 50 men was sent out by Col Hubley [11th Pa Rgt] and met the fifth man returning with a shattered arm. The sixth man, Philip Hilter [Helter], was found killed and scalped. [28]

On 22 August General Clinton arrived at Tioga with his 4th Brigade. They had marched and floated down from the headwaters of the North Branch in New York.

The following day Sullivan reorganized his army for the Indian campaign. Lacking a field officer, the German Regiment was one of the targets. They were reorganized into four companies of 25 men each. This shows that there were only about 100 men left after discharging those whose enlistments had expired. Two German companies plus 200 other hand-picked men were formed into the right flanking division commanded by Colonel Lewis Dubois [5th NY Rgt] under General Poor. The other two companies were similarly merged with 200 men and formed into the left flanking division commanded by Colonel Mathias Ogden [1st NJ Rgt] under General Maxwell. [29]

The officers and men of the German Regiment were then so scattered that it is impossible to detail their activities until they were again reformed after the campaign.

Two hundred fifty men were left behind at Fort Sullivan on 26 August as Sullivan began his march up the Chemung River valley. It was known that the Indians were concentrating there to fight. When the chiefs of the Six Nations heard Sullivan was moving against them they insisted on making a stand in the valley. British support consisted of Major John Butler, 15 regulars of the 8th Rgt, plus tories. Butler advised the Indians against a stand there, but they began to prepare an ambush at

Newtown [just east of Elmira, NY], 15 miles from Fort Sullivan. [30]

At mid-morning on 29 August Sullivan's scouts discovered the concealed foe behind the wilting leaves of their cover. Artillery was brought up to fire on their line, while Poor's Brigade worked their way over a hill to flank the Indians. Demoralized by the artillery fire and a frontal charge, the Indians broke and fled. Combined Indian and British losses were around 30 killed. Sullivan's losses were four killed and about 30 wounded. [31] Among the dead was Private Cornelius Quinlan of the Germans. [32] Private Bartel Engle was either wounded or died on 29 August, or died on 06 August 1779. [33,34] The records give both dates.

Sullivan reported his success at Newtown to Washington by express messenger. Washington responded from West Point on 15 September with guidance:
"Two points which I wish to repeat. The one is the necessity of pushing the Indians to the greatest practicable distance from their own settlements and our frontiers; to the throwing them wholly on the British enemy. The other is making the destruction of their settlements so final and complete as to put it out of their power to derive the smallest succor from them in case they should attempt to return this season." [35]

This scorched earth policy was duly carried out as the army marched north into the Finger Lakes country and west as far as the Genesee River. During the month of September they burned 18 Indian villages and destroyed an estimated 150,000 bushels of corn. There were several more clashes with the Indians which increased casualties to 41 men killed. On 30 September the army returned to Fort Sullivan at Tioga. [36]

The only German Regiment member whose record of this period was found is Captain Christian Myers. His Orderly Book indicates he was assigned to the garrison of Fort Sullivan. This strong point in the rear of the Army was commanded by Colonel Israel Shreeve [2nd NJ Rgt]. Twohundred-fifty men, including sick and unfit, were stationed at Fort Sullivan to guard the boats, wagons, and heavy baggage. The fort also contained the forward hospital to treat casualties before they were sent downriver to Wyoming and the General Hospital set up at Sunbury. [37]

Captain Myers' book covers the period from 25 August to 02 October 1779. During that period the officers at the fort had to deal with shortages of flour and beef, rations were cut several times. Orders were issued to prevent cookfires from being built too close to the stored baggage and wagons. He also mentions "the women employed as nurses" and problems with the boatmen. [38]

The German Regiment was reformed at Tioga on 03 October and rejoined Hand's Brigade. The next day they started the return march toward Fort Wyoming. [39] Men without shoes were permitted to go by boat. On 07 October the Army began arriving at Wyoming, they were instructed to camp in the same positions as in July. [40]

On 08 October the Germans, along with Schott's Corps and Spaulding's Co were ordered to remain at Fort Wyoming with the garrison under the command of Colonel Zebulon Butler. Two days later, Sullivan and the rest of his army departed for Easton en route to rejoining the main army in the Hudson Valley. [41]

This was the first time in over two months that the German Regiment could stop and examine itself. Since discharging the original three-year men in July and August the Regiment's character had changed markedly. They were no longer an ethnic German unit; with every replacement they had become more and more American. Their numbers were also dwindling. Of the 350 men who camped at Fort Wyoming in the Spring, there were only about 120 remaining. They were now experienced Indian fighters and this probably determined their next assignment.

Word was received that Washington had congratulated the western army on 17 October in General Orders: "The whole of the soldiery engaged in the expedition, merit and have the Commander-in-Chief's warmest acknowledgements, for their important services." [42]

During this period at Fort Wyoming, Lieutenant Colonel Ludowick Weltner appears to have returned from sick leave to resume command of the Regiment. Perhaps Weltner had the German Regiment's marching orders in his pocket when he arrived at Fort Wyoming.

CHAPTER 7 - ON THE FRONTIER IN NORTHUMBERLAND COUNTY,
PENNSYLVANIA

Orders were received by the German Regiment to move to Sunbury, Pennsylvania to protect the settlers around the forks of the Susquehanna River from Indian attacks. The farmers in the area had been attacked repeatedly in the past six months and most had fled their farms.

Considerable correspondence to, from, and about the German Regiment survives in Pennsylvania's and Maryland's Archives from this period.

The 120 men of the German Regiment departed from Fort Wyoming on 29 October 1779. [1] It is not known if they floated down the North Branch of the Susquehanna on the Continental boats or if they had to march the 65 miles. They almost certainly overnighted at Fort Jenkins, about 30 miles above Sunbury. Fort Jenkins was described earlier that year as "a stockaded area of 1/8 acre containing a very good dwelling house located on a height above the river." [2]

The Regiment reached Sunbury and Fort Augusta before 05 November. [3] There they saw "about 150 houses, mostly of log construction; the population Irish and German." [4]

Upon arrival, Lieutenant Colonel Weltner met at Fort Augusta with Colonel Samuel Hunter, Lieutenant of Northumberland County, who filled him in on recent happenings. [5] The 11th Pennsylvania Regiment, commanded by Colonel Adam Hubley, had been recalled from the area at the end of June 1779 to join the Sullivan Expedition. This left Hunter's feeble force of Northumberland County militia and volunteers trying to protect the entire area from what is now Lock Haven to Berwick against an increasing number of raids. Hunter's pleas for help to General Sullivan were turned down as these raids were recognized as diversions. They were to keep Sullivan from marching into the heartland of the Six Nations Indians.

Local attacks culminated on 28 July 1779 with the fall of Fort Freeland with about 20 dead and 30 captured. Most of the local farmers then fled south to Sunbury and beyond. Forts Muncy, Brady, and Boone's Mill were then abandoned and burned. Only Forts Jenkins and Bosley's Mill were still intact in November. [6]

Colonels Hunter and Weltner developed a defense strategy as ordered. They agreed that the McClung farm, about 15 miles due north, should be defended and a detachment of 40 men was sent there on 05 November 1779. Twenty men were sent back to Fort Jenkins to reinforce that post. [7]

35

From his correspondence, there is no doubt that Colonel Hunter was upset by the small size of the German Regiment. He had been led to believe, probably by President Joseph Reed of the Pennsylvania Supreme Executive Council , that the Regiment had about 200 men. [8] When only 120 arrived, he must have felt deceived. This may account for Hunter's critical attitude toward the German Regiment.

The German Regiment men sent out to the burned-out McClung farm found it "devoid of shelter and barren of timber," and moved to the abandoned John Montgomery farm nearby. [9] This place was equally well situated and according to Colonel Weltner, "the troops have erected barracks and other necessary defenses." [10] This fort was built by Captain F. William Rice's Company and became known as Fort Rice. The barrack here was a one and a half story limestone house (23'x26') with the basement built over a spring in the Montgomery farm yard. The building had gunports in the second story and typically small windows and was surrounded by a stockaded yard. [11] Colonel Weltner always referred to it as Fort Montgomery in his reports, it was also referred to as Fort Bunner in a June 1780 citizen's petition for aid. [12] Fort Rice will be mentioned again.

Colonel Weltner originally planned to keep half his force, 60 men, in Sunbury to relieve the others monthly. [13] Colonel Hunter must have prevailed on him to post more men in the field as Weltner wrote on 13 December 1779 he "had only enough men at Sunbury to mount a couple of sentries." [14]

During the winter Colonel Weltner moved across the river to Northumberland. Here he was at once an hour closer to his forts and away from Colonel Hunter. Weltner's new headquarters were at or near a fortification Hunter had ordered built in September 1778 for the local people. It consisted of a fort [a strong building] and two redoubts with cannons. [15] Weltner mentions in a 09 April 1780 letter, "I have scarcely as many men in Town as will man two pieces of artillery." [16]

In December 1779 President Reed and the Congressional Board of War proposed merging Schott's [formerly Ottendorf's] Corps and Captain Selin's Company into the German Regiment. A 28 December 1779 letter from the Board of War to Colonel Weltner stated that 42 men from these units whose enlistments were about up could be reenlisted for the duration of the war. The officers were to agree among themselves on who was to continue in the service. [17]

In March 1780 Weltner asked the Board to choose between Captain Schott and Captain Selin for command of the proposed new company. In response, the Board suggested that a board of officers make the choice. [18] On 27 April 1780 General Washington commented to the Board of War that he was withholding comment on the incorporation for the time being. [19]

The extra men were never merged into the German Regiment. Muster rolls of both Schott's Corps and Selin's Company show them still at Fort Wyoming at the end of March 1780. [20] Inspection of these muster rolls shows none of the men on later rolls of the German Regiment.

THE SOLDIERS' FINANCIAL SITUATION

The financial situation of all Continental soldiers deteriorated seriously during 1779 due to inflation. For example, the widely circulating Spanish eight reales or dollar coin could be exchanged for $8 in Continental paper money in January, $16 in April, $19 in July, and $30 in October. On 17 June 1779 most of officers of the Maryland Line signed a petition to the Governor and the Assembly requesting relief from the inflation. [21]

The Maryland Assembly passed an Act on 22 July 1779 to allow officers to buy at a fixed price "four good shirts and a complete uniform, suitable to his station." They were also to be allowed a ration of tea, coffee, chocolate, sugar, soap, and tobacco. For 1779, in lieu of these commodities, they were to receive $2000. [22] There is a record of the $2000 being authorized for Colonel Weltner on 18 September. [23] On 11 November Captains Baltzel, Myers, and Bayer, Lieutenants Shugart, Grometh, and Morgan, Ensign Raybold, and Surgeon's Mate Smith in a joint letter to the Governor pleaded that they had not yet received any of the money allowed by the State. [24]

For non-commissioned officers and privates the Maryland Assembly also made an allowance of rum and tobacco which was calculated at 20 Pounds for 1779. [25] The Maryland Treasurer was authorized to pay this money for the German Regiment on 07 February 1780. [26] Another provision of the Maryland Act provided that three-year and duration-of-the-war enlistees should receive a hat, stockings, and overalls in addition to State and Continental bounties. [27]

At the end of January 1780 the German Regiment counted its Maryland men and sent a report to Annapolis:

	NCOs & Pvts
Lt Col Weltner's Co:	13
Capt Myers' Co:	18
Capt Baltzel's Co:	25

```
          Capt Bayer's Co:                24,  80 in all. [28]
```

Based on the above return, 1600 Pounds, or 20 Pounds per man, was ordered paid on 07 February to Captain Michael Bayer, to be delivered to Captain Peter Boyer, paymaster of the German Regiment, for the soldiers of the Maryland portion of the Regiment. [29] Hopefully the Pennsylvanians also received some money at this time.

The above document also orders Captain George P. Keeport [one of the original captains of the German Regiment], now Commissary of Stores at Baltimore, to deliver to Captain Bayer three and one-fourth yards of cloth and three yards of shalloon, as part of the articles allowed by the Maryland Assembly. [30] If Captain Bayer went in person to pick up the goods, he probably enjoyed a cup of Maryland rye whiskey with his former fellow officer.

On 25 February 1780 the Congress gave up the charade of trying to purchase supplies for the Army with paper money. At the same time they called on the States to deposit goods at designated depots. By this return to the barter system the Congress acknowledged the failure of the nation's first fiscal policy.

The Continental Treasury was saved by the availability of new funds from loans placed in France. With these credits the Congress issued new paper money in mid-March 1780. This printing was known as the "new emanation" or "new emission." Old "not worth a Continental" paper money was to be accepted at $40 for each of the new dollars.

This infusion of new money did not help the State treasuries, however. An appeal for supplies from Colonel Weltner in Northumberland brought this response from Annapolis: "The exhausted state of our Treasury renders it impracticable [to send you supplies], but you may rely on it, Sir, that the German Regiment has not been forgot by us...." [31]

Pennsylvania had a similar reply: "You are acquainted...with the state of our Treasury, which is not altered for the better; tho' we hope in a short time the collection of taxes will relieve us from the present difficulty...." [32]

In March 1780 it came to Colonel Weltner's attention that Captain William Rice and his 1st Lieutenant C. Godfried Swartz had sold some of their state-issued clothing. This is not surprising, knowing how short of money the men were. Weltner wrote to the Board of War on 18 March for advice on how to deal with this situation. [33] The Board was shocked, but noted that there was no regulation against it for officers. [34] President Reed was notified and he felt they should be prosecuted as an example to others. [35] The officials in Philadelphia finally agreed on 06 April to send copies of the correspondence to General Washington for his advice. [36] There is no evidence Washington acted on this minor infraction.

By September money seemed to be available again. On 19 September the Maryland Treasurer was ordered to pay each officer 1,149/15 Pounds in lieu of the items promised by the Assembly for the period 01 January to 01 October 1780. [37] The next day the Treasurer was ordered to pay Captain Michael Boyer 4/18/8 Pounds in **coin**, in lieu of 343/5 Pounds due him on an expense account. [38] This indicates that one pound in silver was worth 70 paper Maryland pounds.

THE SUPPLY SITUATION

Just as the states had difficulty paying the troops, they also had difficulty buying supplies with their inflated paper money. The new emanation money did not improve the situation in the short run. The lack of supplies was a continuous problem for the German Regiment while in Northumberland County. Here are some comments regarding supplies from Colonel Weltner's correspondence:

"Posts, even Sunbury, likely soon destitute of provisions, was asked to to use my influence to have provisions brought up [the river], especially salt from Estherton [now Rockville, Pa.].... The salt is only now arrived and the cattle are miserably fallen away.... Flour and liquors we are now informed are not to be had. Local purchases will not support us. I blame the Quartermaster." [To Board of War, 13 December 1779]. [39]

"...Sufficient quantities of provisions...must be sent...or I will be obligated to evacuate the post myself." [To Board of War, 09 April 1780]. [40]

"Am exceedingly sorry to inform you that if I do not get a speedy supply of provisions, there being but 6 days on hand, am afraid I shall be obligated to quit my post...." [To President Reed, 06 May 1780]. [41]

"We are ill-supplied, we seldom have over 6 days supply on hand and lately some of our outposts have been on $\frac{1}{2}$ allowance which should the enemy block, they must surrender. [To President Reed, 08 May 1780]. [42]

"...This place has not afforded a drop of good liquor since the beginning of March last." [To President Reed, 20 June 1780]. [43]

These blunt regimental situation reports received equally blunt replies.

The Maryland Council responded on 24 June with, "It gives us much concern that we have it not in our power to furnish you [the supplies] your regiment is entitled to." [44]

Pennsylvania President Reed commented, "We really have the greatest difficulties in supplying [the German Regiment]." [45]

In September Colonel Weltner received word that was a little more optimistic. He received supplies sufficient to last until January and was promised necessary clothing. More rum than needed for the officers was shipped - the surplus was to be issued to the soldiers "in the proportion ordered by the Assembly." [46]

THE MILITARY SITUATION IN 1780

During the winter months Indian raids ceased and the German Regiment settled down to manning and improving their line of forts. Numerous men were kept busy felling trees and skidding logs. They also had to contend with what is known as the "Winter of the Deep Snow" and "the Hard Winter of 1779-80." Beginning about 02 January 1780 the Northern States were gripped by a period of heavy snow and extreme cold that lasted at least a month. In New York City it was the only winter on record when it was possible to cross on the ice from Manhattan to Staten Island. [47]

In March Colonel Weltner recommended a full captaincy for Captain-Lieutenant Philip Shrawder in a letter to the Pennsylvania Supreme Executive Council. [48] This bid must have been unsuccessful as ten months later Shrawder still signed his name as "Capt-Lt." [49]

During March Capt Christian Myers and his Company of 18 men were stationed at Fort Montgomery. Myers copied into his Company Orderly Book four orders he issued there. These orders show that the area was not completely devoid of people, and there was some form of fellowship outside the stockade. They also show that the defences were still being improved in March. [50]

On 09 April 1780 Colonel Weltner mentioned that the German Regiment was manning three outposts. [51] When they took over Bosley's Mill [now Washingtonville], is not known. The mill was supposed to have been stockaded in 1777 when the Indians became troublesome. It is believed to have been a small, but strong post manned by 10 to 30 men. There is no mention of an attack on this fort. [52]

Just a month later Weltner reported the Regiment was occupying four forts! He describes the new location as being "on the West

Branch near Boone's Mill." [53] This fort consisted of a log building surrounded by a stockade; it overlooked the West Branch about one mile north of downtown Milton. The fort became known as Fort Swartz for its builder, 1st Lieutenant C. Godfried Swartz. It appears also not to have been attacked. [54]

At the end of March, while snow was still on the ground, Indian raids began anew. This alarmed the farmers, they had to get their crops in if they were to continue living there. It was claimed the German Regiment garrisons at the forts did not go out to pursue the raiders. This caused a campaign to have the German Regiment, or at least its commanding officer, replaced. Colonel Weltner was projected as an out-of-stater with no sensitivity for the local farmers.

Colonel Hunter and others complained to President Reed. Hunter claimed, "the German Regiment thats stationed here is in no ways adiquit to Grant us the Necessary Reliefe Required." [55] A local politician complained, "The German Regiment is posted at four different places, but I do not find they ever stir a foot out of their posts without some other support." [56] Reed responded to Hunter, saying, "You must spirit them to turn out and not lay in their posts, when their exertions might be honorable to themselves and useful to you." [57]

Colonel Weltner must have been aware of the complaints against him as he also wrote to President Reed defending his handling of the situation. He also included some endorsements from important citizens of the county who agreed with him. The situation escalated as both Reed and Weltner sent appeals to General Washington in May. Washington was noncommittal in his reply to the Board of War, and he solved the problem about two months later. [58]

Proof that the Regiment was not derelict is given in a 27 June 1780 report by Hunter to Reed: "Scouting parties on the frontier [are] sometimes joined by some of Col Weltner's Regiment." [59] A citizens' petition for aid, dated 16 August 1780, stated: "Our [wheat] harvest being generally cut and saved, in which important service the German Battalion rendered us great assistance." [60] Their help was appreciated after all.

General Washington on 01 August 1780 at West Point, NY, signed orders for the German Regiment to rejoin the main army, which was then on the east side of the Hudson River. [61] It would have taken Army message riders about three days to get these orders to Weltner at Northumberland. So the German Regiment garrisons probably left their forts on 04Aug and the Sunbury area the next day.

Word evidently leaked out to the Tories and Indians that the German Regiment had departed. On 06 August a combined force of about 300 Indians and Tories attacked Fort Rice. Fortunately Colonel Hunter had reinforced the fort with 20 militiamen after the Germans had departed.

Hunter later reported, "The enemy attacked the fort about sundown and fired very smartly, the garrison returned the fire with spirit, which made them withdraw a little, and in the night they began to set fire to a number of houses and stacks of grain." [62] The arrival of reinforcements the next day forced the enemy to depart. Some of these reinforcements came from Fort Jenkins, which was left vacant. While unoccupied the enemy raiders burned Fort Jenkins.

Fort Rice survived the siege and became the Montgomery family's home when they returned after the war. The fort was in use as a springhouse in 1897 when the Commonwealth of Pennsylvania surveyed its old fort sites. [63] Fort Rice was found standing in 1987 with water still flowing from its spring. This landmark is located about two miles out Paradise Road from Turbotville.

The only known man of the Germans to return to this area after the war was Captain Bernard Hubley, who settled in Sunbury. In 1807 he published the first volume of his "History of the Revolution," illness prevented further writing; he died in 1808. [64]

CHAPTER 8 - RECALLED BY WASHINGTON

From the day the German Regiment marched away from their
frontier forts until they reappeared in northeastern New Jersey
there is a six-week gap in their story. It can be assumed the
men gathered at the fort in Northumberland, Pa. about 04 August
1780 and that they were quickly ferried across to Sunbury. From
Sunbury there was easier marching on the road to Reading which
was opened 10 years before as the King's Highway. From Reading
they probably marched via Bethlehem and Easton into New Jersey.

For the period from mid-September to mid-December á German
Regiment Orderly Book is available. [1] Ensign John Weidman
(#2) was adjutant at this time and some of his entries are very
useful.

In mid-September the Germans were located in northeastern New
Jersey. They had linked up with the main army, which was keeping
the British bottled up in the New York City area. They were
again attached to the Division of General Nathanael Greene, and
were in the New Jersey Brigade with the 1st, 2nd, and 3rd New
Jersey Regiments. [2] These were men with whom they had served
on the Sullivan Expedition in 1779.

On 01 October 1780 the Regiment was camped near Tappan, NY.
The Adjutant mentioned that the spy trial of the captured British
Major Andree was held that day, that he was to be hanged the next
day, and that the Regiment was to send a detachment to the
execution. [3]

The Regiment was camped at Haverstraw, NY on 07 October, and
two days later they were located at West Point, NY, where
they apparently went into garrison duty. [4]

Captain Rice was tried on 23 October by general court-martial,
charged with insulting and abusing Colonel Weltner in his
quarters when on business of importance in a manner unbecoming of
an officer and a gentleman. He was found not guilty, the
sentence was approved and he was released. [5]

On 03 November 1780 the German Regiment received word of
General Washington's Order of 01 November for the reorganization
of the army. They were shocked to learn that the Regiment would
be disbanded on 01 January 1781, that the men would be
incorporated with troops of their respective states, and that
they would join their new units before 01 January. [6] Adjutant
Weidman did not comment about his feelings on receiving this
news.

This second major reorganization of the Continental Army had
been planned by Washington for some time, and had been approved

by Congress at the beginning of October. The primary reason for the reorganization was to achieve uniformity in unit size throughout the army, as recommended by Inspector General von Steuben. Up to now companies had varied in size from 20 to 80 men and regiments contained six to eleven companies. A new infantry regiment was to consist of nine companies, one of which was light infantry, with 53 privates and three corporals each. [7]

At the end of November the German Regiment was listed on monthly strength reports as moving to winter quarters with the New Jersey Brigade. [8]

On the home front, the Maryland Assembly passed a bill to compensate soldiers who had served three years in the Continental Army for the depreciation of the Continental paper money with which they had been paid. [9]

On 17 December 1780 Colonel Weltner received his last order from General Washington. He was told to send the Pennsylvania men to Brigadier General Anthony Wayne at Morristown, NJ. He was then to march the Maryland men back to Frederick or Baltimore, depending on where Brigadier General Mordecai Gist, at Baltimore, wanted them. [10]

By the end of December the reassignment of men must have been near completion. On Christmas Day Washington wrote General Heath: "The few men belonging to Maryland may be delivered to Lt Col Weltner commanding the German Regiment to be found at Sufferans [NY] or with the New Jersey Line near Pomton [NJ]." [11]

An officer was also returned to the roster in those last days. Prisoner of war 1st Lieutenant John Weidman (#1) arrived at Elizabeth[town], NJ on 30 December 1780 in a prisoner exchange. He had spent the last 39 months in captivity following his capture at the Battle of Brandywine. [12]

On 01 January 1781 the reorganization of the Army went into effect. Since the rank and file had been moving to their new units since the middle of December, this must have been the day the officers learned of their new assignments.

Maryland's apportionment in the new army was five regiments, down from seven. Officers not needed in the new structure were declared supernumerary and were given the opportunity to retire and receive a half-pay pension for seven years. All Maryland officers of the German Regiment were declared supernumerary:

Lt Col Ludowick Weltner
Capt Charles Baltzel
Capt Christian Myers
Capt Michael Bayer

1st Lt Jacob Grometh
2nd Lt David Morgan
Ensign Jacob Raybold
Surg Mate Alexander Smith.

1st Lt Martin Shugart

Pennsylvania's apportionment was six regiments, down from eleven. Unneeded officers here also were declared supernumerary and offered the half-pay for seven years retirement. All of the Pennsylvania officers of the German Regiment were also declared supernumerary, they were:

Capt Jacob Bunner
Capt Peter Boyer
Capt William Rice
Capt Bernard Hubley, Jr.
Capt-Lt Philip Shrawder
1st Lt John Weidman [#1]

1st Lt Godfried Swartz
1st Lt Marcus Young
1st Lt Jacob Cramer
Ensign Christian Clackner
Surgeon Peter Peris.

On New Year's Day 1781 the five Pennsylvania Companies of the German Regiment arrived from Sufferan, NY to join Wayne's Pennsylvania Brigade at Mount Kemble, west of Morristown, NJ. There they were assigned to temporary quarters. [13] The following day their officers were invited to join the 10th Pennsylvania Regiment at a regimental farewell dinner. The 10th was also being reorganized and became the new 2nd Pennsylvania Regiment. [14]

Following their dinner the officers heard gunfire. [15] This was the beginning of the mutiny of the Pennsylvania Line which began in Wayne's Brigade. The problem was that old one that kept reccurring in the Continental Army. The men demanded eleven months back pay due them, adequate clothing, and supplies. These men decided to take their gripes to Congress and began a march to Philadelphia. Negotiations finally ended the mutiny at Trenton on 25 January 1781. [16]

By the end of February Wayne's Brigade was under orders to march to Virginia to assist General Lafayette. They halted at York, Pa to refit until 20 May 1781 and reached Lafayette on 07 June. [17] This campaign ended with the siege of Yorktown and surrender of Cornwallis on 19 October 1781.

On 13 January 1781 the Continental Treasury Board reported that the Deputy Paymaster General was requested by General Washington to pay the German Regiment $65,319 in old emissions and $10,534 in new emissions. The Paymaster also mentioned that the [Pennsylvania] officers were then in Philadelphia and were destitute. [18] When they had not received their money by 26 January, they petitioned Congress directly for the 14 months back pay and sustenance due them. [19]

The unpaid Pennsylvania men were less subtle, they marched to the office of the Board of War on 24 January and demanded pay. "Twenty or thirty Men of the German Reg't invested the doors in rather an hostile manner, and could not be satisfied, till they were assured that their Officers were in no better situation with

45

respect to pay than themselves." So wrote Ben Stoddart, secretary of the Board to the President of Congress. [20]

Colonel Weltner arrived back in Frederick, Md on 01 February. He must have ridden on ahead as the men were expected the next day. When the Maryland House of Delegates heard of their arrival, they resolved to make them part of the guard of the British prisoners being held at Frederick. [21]

Brigadier General Gist forcefully pointed out to Maryland Governor Lee on 08 February that these were Continental troops who did not take orders from the State government. The ex-German Regiment men were turned over to Captain Thomas Lansdale of the 3rd Maryland Regiment who marched them to Baltimore to equip and forward them to the southern army. [22] As members of the 3rd Maryland Regiment under Lieutenant Colonel Peter Adams [Gist's Brigade], they participated in the siege of Yorktown. [23] A detachment of the 3rd Maryland, commanded by Major Thomas Lansdale, reappeared near Newburgh, NY with the main army in November 1782. [24]

General Washington, in a 19 February 1781 letter to the Board of War, requested they honor Colonel Weltner:
"The board will also be pleased to pay attention to a Memorial of Lieut. Colo. Weltners [sic] of the German Battalion. He is a very deserving Officer, and always conducted himself and the Affairs of the Regt, the charge of which was in fact always upon him, with singular propriety. His Health is much impaired by the service, and if the Baron D'Arent was considered as having quitted the command of the Regiment, when he returned to Europe, I think Colo. Weltner is justly intitled to the emoluments of a Lt. Colo. Commandant from that time." [25]

CHAPTER 9 - EPILOGUE

It would not be fair to the reader to end the story of the German Regiment with the reorganization of the Army. The war was not over and the men continued to serve. This is compilation of what happened to some of the individuals.

The Maryland officers seem to have gone home content with their half-pay for seven years pensions. None appear to have joined other units.

Lieutenant Colonel Weltner settled into retirement with his wife Mary at his house in Frederick, Maryland. In the following months various military men gravitated to his house for talk and a sip of rye. He entertained the diarist John Adlum, who, as a paroled prisoner-of-war had to sit out the rest of the war working for his uncle in Frederick. [1] Another known visitor was Major Friedrich Heinrich Scheerer of the Hessian von Bosse Regiment who was quartered in Frederick after becoming a prisoner at Yorktown. [2]

References to Ludowick Weltner's poor health were not without foundation. He died less than a year after returning home. His date of death is not known, but his will was proved 17 January 1782 at Frederick. Part of his estate consisted of a state certificate for depreciation pay for 914/1/0 Pounds, $11,000 Continental, and $25 Maryland. [3]

Several Pennsylvania officers served in other units later in the war. Captain Philip Shrawder commanded his own [Frontier] Ranger Company beginning 10 February 1781. Lieutenant Jacob Cramer joined Shrawder's Company on the same day. [4] Shrawder's Company was sent back to the Wyoming Valley in 1783 to prevent violence in the Pennsylvania-Connecticut land dispute. In May 1784 Shrawder was a company commander of The Corps of Pennsylvania Infantry commanded by Major James Moore. [5]

Captain Bernard Hubley became Brigade Inspector of Northumberland County,and settled down in Sunbury, Pennsylvania. [6] Lieutenant Godfried Swartz joined Armand's Legion as a Lieutenant and was Adjutant of the Legion by November 1783. [7]

On 23 November 1783 the Maryland Branch of the Society of the Cincinnati was formed at Annapolis. Among the original members were Captains Charles Baltzel, Martin Shugart, William Heiser, and Paul Bentalou. Michael Bayer joined later. [8]

The Pennsylvania Branch of the Society was organized in December 1783. Original members included Captains William Rice, Bernard Hubley, Philip Shrawder, Jacob Bower, Lieutenant John

Bernard Hubley, Philip Shrawder, Jacob Bower, Lieutenant John Weidman, and Surgeon Peter Peris. [9]

Colonel Nicholas Haussegger, when he stepped into that house on 01 January 1777 in Princeton, ceased to be a part of the German Regiment. But the Regiment had to live it down. Rumors and stories began to spread about what happened.

Haussegger and his new orderly, Private Conrad Housman, soon arrived in New York City. Here they visited the house where Colonels Magaw, Miles, Atlee, and other Pennsylvania prisoners lived. The orderly, Corporal John Adlum, answered the door and let them in. He related in his memiors that the arrival of Haussegger really shocked the other officers. They asked Haussegger if another battle had occurred. He replied, "No, I went to reconoiter at Princeton and I was with ten men taken by the Hessians. [10]

During the course of the evening Corporal Adlum was asked to pump Private Housman for information. This was easy as they knew each other from York, Pennsylvania - Housman's brother was the Adlum family's butcher. By the end of the evening all the details of the Colonel's sudden appearance were known. [11] Captain Alexander Graydon, in his memiors, relates that Colonel Haussegger even undertook to persuade the other officers to make terms with the British. [12]

Paroled by the British within a week, Haussegger returned to Philadelphia, where he was questioned by a Congressional Committee on 17 January 1777. Their suspicions were quieted by his version of how he came to be captured. [13] He then returned to his home at the corner of Market and Cumberland Streets in Lebanon, Pennsylvania.

Word of Haussegger's action also spread quickly in the Army. He was ordered to be taken to army headquarters by General Gates. Six troopers from the Pennsylvania Light Horse Cavalry and an officer escorted Haussegger to Morristown, New Jersey, arriving there 12 February 1777. General Washington would not see him and sent him home again under the same escort. In a note to Gates, Washington requested that Haussegger be watched by reliable people. [14]

Haussegger was either recalled or willingly returned to captivity before 17 February 1779, as on that day he co-signed a petition to Congress requesting exchange. [15] There must have been some progress on this exchange, as the lists crossed General Washington's desk. On 19 August 1779 Washington wrote, "You are not to exchange Col Haussegger..., [he] was taken in a manner which will not suffer us to consider him in the light of a common prisoner."[16] From this it is clear that Washington had made up his mind regarding Haussegger's disloyalty.

On 30 June 1780, Haussegger and five other prisoners on Long Island addressed a letter to Washington requesting exchange. [17] When nothing came of this Hausegger must have realized his situation, on 01 February 1781 he submitted his resignation and returned his commission to Washington. [18]

Haussegger's house, stable, hatter's shop, and lot in Lebanon which had been siezed due to his treason, were sold at public auction on 11 January 1782 for 2,200 Pounds. His 5-acre lot on the edge of town was likewise sold for 775 Pounds. [19]

Nicholas Haussegger's postwar situation is confusing. One author has him joining the British. [20] Another has him returning to live with relatives in the Lebanon area and dying there in July 1786, with the relatives receiving post-war soldier lands. [21]

By the end of March 1785 a total of 260 German Regiment veterans of Maryland had applied for and received depreciation certificates. This payment, which amounted to about 57 Pounds for Privates, was additional wages for three-year men to make up for their underpayment during the inflation of 1779 and 1780. [22]

When 44 applicants could not be found on 1779 muster rolls, the Maryland Auditor General's office became suspicious of fraud. Muster rolls were exchanged with their counterparts in Pennsylvania. Ten of the 44 problem men were found to have served in Pennsylvania companies. Discharge certificates were then obtained from the remaining 34 men. Most of the discharges were found to have been signed by Captain Bunner in July 1779 at Fort Wyoming. The Maryland officials on 01 April 1785 asked Pennsylvania for help in verifying Bunner's signature. Bunner was located in or around Philadelphia and verified his signature. [23] This ruled out forged discharges.

Suspicion then fell on the identity of the applicants. It was thought that the discharges were purchased by imposters, who then applied for the benefits. No arrests seem to have been made. The Maryland Auditor General solved his problem on 25 May 1785 by stopping payment on the fraudulently obtained depreciation certificates. [24] It is not known how those applicants whose names were wildly misspelled or moved from one state to the other fared.

The muster roll exchange mentioned above is one reason there are so many German Regiment rolls extant today. Pennsylvania saved the Maryland rolls and later inadvertantly included six of them among their own when they were published in Pennsylvania Archives.

1 -   This was conservatively estimated at 110,000 in
      Pennsylvania, 20,000 in Maryland, and 25,000 in Virginia
      by A.B. Faust: The German Element in the United States, v1,
      Boston & NYC, 1909. Cited by Wandel, Jos.: The German
      Dimension of American History, Chicago, 1979, pp1-2.
2 - Ford, W.C., ed: Journals of the Continental Congress
      [hereafter JCC], 1774-89, 34 vols, Washington DC, 1904-37,
      v4p392.
3 - JCC, v5pp487-88.
4 - JCC, v5p486.
5 - Minutes of the Provincial Council of Penna [hereafter MPCP],
      Harrisburg Pa, 1852(1968), v10p622.
6 - Archives of Maryland [hereafter AMd], Balto., 1900, v18p181.
7 - Force, Peter: American Archives [hereafter Force], s5v1p114.
8 - Force, s5v3p293.
9   Force, s5v1p182.
10 - MPCP, v10p634.
11 - Fitzpatrick, J.C., ed: Writings of Washington [hereafter
      WW], 39 vols, Washington DC, 1931-44, v5pp237ff-38.
12 - WW, v5pp324-25.
13 - MPCP, v10p643.
14 - MPCP, v10p679.
15 - Pennsylvania Archives, 9 series, Phila, 1874-1914, s5v3p789.
16 - MPCP, v10p685.
17 - AMd, v18p181.
18 - AMd, v18pp265-6.
19 - Original in Maryland Historical Society Library, Balto.
20 - AMd, v18pp265-266.
21 - Capt Graybill's Account Book, Md Hist Soc Libr, Balto.
22 - Adlum, John: Memiors of the Life of John Adlum, Chicago,1968.
23 - Names are from JCC, v5p571 and v5pp825-26; date of rank
      and hometown from various muster rolls.
24 - Richards, H.M.M.: Valley Forge and the Penna-Germans,
      Penna-Ger Soc, v26pp27-28, 1918.
25 - Scharf, J.T.: History of Md, 1879, v2p192.

Previous military service of captains and below is as follows:
Captain George Keeport was 3rd Lt in the 1st Co of Matrosses
at Annapolis on 14 January 1776 [AMd, v18p563].
Captain Daniel Burchardt was transferred to the German Regiment
from the 4th Penna Battalion [Col Anthony Wayne] where he was
a company commander [MPCP, v10p649]. Captain Woelpper was
commissioned a 1st Lt in the 3rd Penna Battalion [Col John Shea]
on 06 January 1776. He had served in the Virginia Provincial
forces under Col Washington during the entire French & Indian
War [WW, v5pp237ff-38].
First Lt Lohra may have been a 2nd Lt in the 3rd Battalion
[Anne Arundel County] of the Maryland Flying Camp in July 1776
[AMd, v18p38]. Adjutant van Linkensdorf had been a lieutenant

in a Swiss regiment of Sardinia [P.A., s5v3p789].

Captain Benjamin Weiser was the colonel of a Northumberland County, Penna Militia Battalion in July 1776 [P.A., s5v5p24]. He was in the New York City area in September 1776, probably with the Pennsylvania brigade of BGen Thomas Mifflin in the division of MGen William Heath.

Washington authorized Heath to attempt a surprise recapture of Montresor's [now Riker's] Island. A dawn attack on 23 Septmber 1776 by 240 men in three boats was led by Lt Col Michael Jackson of the 16th Massachusetts Continental Regiment. When the first boat, with the commanding officers, hit the shore it came under heavy musket fire and the other two boats turned away and fled. By the time the first boat extricated itself, Major Thomas Henley, Heath's aide, was killed and Jackson was wounded. In all 14 Americans killed, wounded, or captured [Roberts, R.B.: New York's Forts in the Revolution, Cranbury, NJ, 1980, p295].

Weiser, who must have been on the second or third boat, was charged "with misbehavior before the enemy in the attack on Montresor's Island." The date of his court-martial is not known, but he was found guilty and ordered "cashiered with infamy." Washington approved the sentence on 31 October 1776 and ordered Weiser's dismissal [WW, v6p234].

If Capt Weiser ever served with the German Regiment it could only have been during the month of October 1776 while his sentence was under appeal. This possibility is strengthened by the existence of a muster roll entitled "Capt Weiser's Co," dated 23 October 1776 at the Barracks in Philadelphia [P.A., s5v3pp791-93]. A later muster roll of the same company was designated "First Vacant Company" [P.A., s5v3p799].

This reverse did not break Weiser's patriotic spirit, he returned to the Northumberland County Militia. He was the captain of a militia company stationed in Philadelphia on 30 January 1777, according to a muster roll [P.A., s5v8p668].

Several regimental personnel changes were made about the same time the list of officers was issued. Jacob Laudermilk of Maryland was commissioned an Ensign on 19 September [Steuart, R.: The Maryland Line, 1969, Md Soc of Cincinnati, p40], apparently to fill the position of Christian Helm. Paul Bentalou of Baltimore was commissioned a 2nd lieutenant on 25 September 1776 [Steuart, p40], in William Ritter's place. Both Helm and Ritter seem not to have accepted their commissions.

27 - JCC, v5pp762-63.
28 - P.A., s5v3pp790-91pp813-14.
29 - Force, s5v3p293.
30 - P.A., s1v10p757.

Ensign Paul Christian of Maryland became the first man to resign from the regiment on 08 November 1776.

REFERENCES - CHAPTER 2

1 - Force, Peter: American Archives [hereafter Force], s5v3p1595.
2 - Fitzpatrick, J.C. ed: Writings of George Washington [hereafter WW], 39 vols, Washington DC, 1931-44, v6p333.
3 - Dwyer, W.M.: The Day is Ours! [hereafter Dwyer], NYC, 1983, p102.
4 - WW, v6p343.
5 - Ibid.
6 - WW, v6p326.
7 - Lesser, C.H. ed: The Sinews of Independence [hereafter Lesser], Chicago, 1976, p43.
8 - Force, s5v3p1164.
9 - Adapted from Dwyer, p228.
10 - Penna Magazine of History & Biography, v5p513.
11 - Ketchum, R.M.: The Winter Soldiers, Garden City NY, 1973, p295
12 - Smith, S.S.: The Battle of Trenton [hereafter T-Smith], Monmouth Beach NJ, 1965, p19.
13 - T-Smith, p20.
14 - Ketchum, p312.
15 - Ketchum, p315.
16 - Ketchum, p329.
17 - Ketchum, p332.
18 - Lesser, p43.
19 - Ketchum, p341.
20 - Adlum, John: Memoirs of the Life of John Adlum, Chicago, 1968, pp119-121
21 - Ibid.
22 - Ibid.
23 - Ibid.
24 - T-Smith, p17.
25 - Ibid.
26 - Ibid.
27 - Ibid.
28 - Ibid.
29 - Pennsylvania Archives, s5v4p586.
30 - T-Smith, p17.
31 - Freeman, D.S.: George Washington, 6 vols, NYC, 1954, v4p343.
23 - Smith, S.S.: The Battle of Princeton, Monmouth Beach NJ, 1967, p17.
33 - Ketchum, p361.
34 - Ketchum, p373.
35 - Ketchum, pp378-79.
36 - Ibid.

REFERENCES AND NOTES - CHAPTER 3

1 - Boatner, M.M.: Encylopedia of the American Revolution, New York City, 1958, p746.
2 - Fitzpatrick, J.C., ed: Writings of Washington [hereafter WW], 39 vols, Washington, DC, 1931-34, v7p19,338.
3 - Richards, H.M.M.: Valley Forge and the Penna-Germans [hereafter Richards], Penna-German Society, 1918, v26p25.
4 - Steuart, R.: A History of the Maryland Line in the Revolutionary War [hereafter Steuart], [Towson, Md.], 1969, p39.
5 - Showman, R.K., ed: Papers of Gen Nathanael Greene [hereafter Greene], Chapel Hill, 1980, v2pp26-27.
6 - Papers of the Continental Congress, Microfilm at National Archives, Washington DC, M247, r167, i152, v4, p15.
7 - Steuart, p39.
8 - Ford, W.C., ed: Journals of the Continental Congress [hereafter JCC], 1774-89, 34 vols, Washington, DC, 1904-37, v7p211.
9 - JCC, v7p185.
10 - Syrett, H.C., ed: The Papers of Alexander Hamilton, NYC, 1961, v1pp238-39.
11 - Richards, v26p28.
12 - Heitman, F.B.: Historical Register of Officers of the Continental Army, (1893,1914)1973, Baltimore, pp133,306.
13 - WW, v8p382.
14 - Steuart, p39.
15 - JCC, v8p284.
16 - Pennsylvania Archives [hereafter P.A.], s5v2p516.
17 - JCC, v8p302.
18 - Steuart, p39.
19 - Richards, p28.
20 - P.A., s5v3p795.
21 - Greene, v2pp90-91.
22 - Greene, v2p90.
23 - Wallace, P.A.W.: The Muhlenbergs of Pennsylvania, Phila., 1950, pp116-117.
24 - Greene, v2p90.
25 - Muhlenberg, H.A.: Life of J.Peter Muhlenberg, Philadelphia, 1849, p76.
26 - Greene, v2p90.
27 - Muhlenberg, H.A.: Life of J.Peter Muhlenberg, Philadelphia, 1849, p76.
28 - Greene, v2pp91-92.

On 31 May a court-martial was held for Pvt William Hardy, [company unknown] of the German Regiment for deserting and enlisting in two different regiments. He was sentenced to be reprimanded by his commanding officer. Cited in Orderly Book of BGen Muhlenberg, reprinted in Penna Magazine of History & Biography [hereafter JPM], v33p267.

29 - Dupuy & Dupuy: The Compact History of the Revolutionary
     War [hereafter D&D], New York City, 1963, p194.
30 - JPM, v33p460.
31 - D&D, p220.
32 - WW, v8pp301-02.
33 - D&D, p220.
34 - JCC, v11pp808-09.
35 - Steuart, p39.

On 07 July 1777 Pvt Herman Wynch [unknown company] of the German
Regiment was court-martialled at Morristown, NJ. He was charged
with mutiny, neglect of duty, absence, and refusal to take up
arms and accoutrements. For this he was sentenced to receive
39 lashes on his bare back. Two days later Pvt John Rysbecker,
of Hubley's Co was charged with desertion and enlisting in another
regiment, his sentence was postponed for further evidence. Cited
in WW, v8p361,209 resp.

36 - Greene, v2p128n.
37 - JPM, v33p459.
38 - D&D, p222.
39 - D&D, p223.

In time for this march guidelines were issued for the regimental
utilization of wagons:
    one for field officers,
    one for staff officers,
    one per 100 men, plus five spare wagons to follow the brigade
to pick up the sick or to take on packs should the men need to
be disencoumbered. For Muehlenberg's Brigade the wagons were
distributed on 21 August 1777 as follows:
    1st Va Rgt: 3 wagons + 1 for staff,
    5th Va Rgt: 4 wagons + 1 for staff,
    9th Va Rgt: 6 wagons,
    German Rgt: 5 wagons. Cited in JPM, v34p439.

Several weeks later, on 13 September 1777, instructions were
also distributed on tent usage:
    one soldier's tent for field officers,
    one soldier's tent for 4 common officers,
    one soldier's tent for 8 sgts, drummers, and fifers,
    one soldier's tent for 8 privates; and
no more than 50 tents to be loaded on each wagon. Cited in JPM,
v34p466.

1 - Muehlenberg's Orderly Book [hereafter JPM], reprinted in Penna Magazine of History and Biography, v34(1910)p444.
2 - Scheer & Rankin: Rebels and Redcoats, Cleveland, 1957, p233.
3 - JPM, v34(1910)p449.

On 03 September 1777 General Washington had time to pardon Private Henry Hargood of a Pennsylvania company of the German Regiment. Hargood had been found guilty of desertion and had been under death sentence, but with a recommendation of clemency. Cited in Fitzpatrick, J.C., ed: Writings of George Washington [hereafter WW], 39 vols, 1931-44, Washington, DC, v9p170.

4 - Boatner, M.M.: Encyclopedia of the American Revolution [hereafter Boatner], New York, 1966, p108.
5 - Showman, Richard K. ed: The Papers of Gen Nathanael Greene [hereafter Greene Papers], 3vols, Chapel Hill, 1976-83, v2p471.
6 - Muhlenberg, H.A.: The Life of MGen Peter Muhlenberg [hereafter Muhlenberg], Phila, 1849, p95.
7 - Ibid.
8 - Trussell, J.B.B.: The Pennsylvania Line 1776-83, Harrisburg, 1977, p226.
9 - WW, v9pp256-57.
10 - Greene Papers, v2p174.
11 - Boatner, p428.
12 - Boatner, p429.
13 - Muhlenberg, p113.
14 - Boatner, p428.
15 - Boatner, p429.
16 - P.A., s5v4p561.
17 - P.A., s5v4p562.
18 - P.A., s5v3p830.
19 - P.A., s5v3p831.
20 - P.A., s5v4p574.
21 - Steuart, R.: A History of the Maryland Line in the Revolutionary War, Towson, Md., 1969, p158.
22 - P.A., s5v4p576.
23 - JPM, v35p89.
24 - Greene Papers, v2p181.
25 - Ibid., v2p202.
26 - Ibid., v2p217.
27 - Ibid., v2p222.

REFERENCES AND NOTES - CHAPTER 5

1 - Busch, Noel F.: Winter Quarters [hereafter Busch], NYC, 1974, pp49-51.
2 - Muhlenberg, Henry A.: The Life of Major-General Peter Muhlenberg [hereafter Muhlenberg], Philadelphia, 1849, p124.
3 - Fitzpatrick, J.C., ed: Writings of Washington [hereafter WW], 39 vols, Washington, DC, 1931-34, v10pp167-68.
4 - Ibid., v10p351.
5 - Steuart, R.: A History of the Maryland Line in the Revolutionary War [hereafter Steuart], Towson, Md., 1969, p40.
6 - Penna Archives [hereafter P.A.], s5v3p821.
7 - Trussell, J.: The Pennsylvania Line - 1776-83, 1977, p224.
8 - P.A., s5v3p811.
9 - Heitman, F.B.: Historical Register of Officers of the Continental Army, Baltimore, (1893,1914)1973, p357.
10 - P.A., s5v3p821.
11 - Lesser, C.H., ed: The Sinews of Independence [hereafter Lesser], Chicago, 1976, p60.
12 - Doyle, Joseph B.: Frederick William von Steuben and the American Revolution, NYC, (1913) 1970, pp89-91.
13 - Steuart, p39.
14 - Ibid.
15 - Syrett, H.C., ed: The Papers of Alexander Hamilton, NYC, 1961, v1pp479-80.
16 - Busch, pp148-149.
17 - Steuart, p39.
18 - Ibid.
19 - P.A., s6v14p23.
20 - Steuart, p40.
21 - Ibid.
22 - WW, v11p432.
23 - Scharf, J.T.: History of Maryland, 1879(1967), v2p344.
24 - Ibid.
25 - Maryland Historical Magazine, 1911, v6pp256-61.
26 - ASSIGNMENT OF FREDERICK COUNTY, MD. SUBSTITUTES WITHIN THE GERMAN REGIMENT IN 1778.

	Enlisted Subs	Militia Subs
4th Vacant Co [ex-Heiser's]	4	2
Bayer's Co [ex-Fister's]	12	4
Baltzell's Co [ex-Keeports']	19	3
3rd Vacant Co [ex-Graybill's]	16	3
Company undeterminable	16	4
Musicians	5	0
TOTAL	72	16

    Adapted from AMd, v18pp324-26.
27 - WW, v12p38.
28 - Heitman, p602.
29 - Lesser, p72.
30 - Muhlenberg, p156.

31 - Orderly Book of Capt Christian Myers [hereafter
     CMOB], Manuscript Div No. MMC1259, Library of Congress,
     Washington, DC.
32 - Ibid.
33 - Ibid.
34 - WW, v12pp215-217.
35 - Ford, W.C., ed: Journals of the Continental Congress - 1774-
     89 [hereafter JCC], 34 vols, Washington, DC, 1904-37,
     v10p200.
36 - CMOB, see date.
37 - Lesser, p76.
38 - Steuart, p39.
39 - P.A., s5v3p788.
40 - Steuart, p39.
41 - CMOB, see date.
42 - P.A., s5v3p789.
43 - Steuart, p40.
44 - AMd, v18pp262,264-5,266-7.
45 - WW, v14p293.
46 - Lesser, pp88,92.
47 - WW, v13p270n.
48 - WW, v13pp373-374.
49 - WW, v13p381.
50 - WW, v13p475.
51 - WW, v14p50.
52 - WW, v14pp154, 156-157, 157n.
53 - JCC, v13p392.
54 - Papers of the Continental Congress, Microfilm at National
     Archives, Washington, DC, M247, r47, i41, v3, p376.

NOTES

One day in early July Private Christian Castner had a little too much to drink, so Jacob Kaufman went out to take his place on guard duty. When Lieutenant Jacob Grometh discovered this he immediately sent Kaufman off to fetch Castner, who then received a few strokes and was sent back to the guard house. Later Castner claimed that Lieutenant Grometh had taken a $60 bill [Continental paper money, worth about $3 in silver in 1779] from him after his punishment. Castner told this story to Lieutenant Shugart and Captain Myers. The story spread and Castner was arrested for speaking disrespectfully of Grometh's character.

A regimental court-martial was held 09 July by order of Captain Bunner, acting commanding officer. Captain Peter Boyer was court president, with Lieutenants Shugart and Swartz and Ensigns Diffenderfer and Clackner as members.

Captain Myers testified that Castner came to him with the story and he told Castner that without proof he better keep quiet. Lieutenant Shugart stated he heard the same story from Castner. Sergeant Jacob Lowe said he also heard the accusation, but didn't see any money in Castner's hand. Corporal Burk stated he saw the bill in Castner's hand a half-hour after the punishment. Private David Robinson also saw a bill in Castner's hand at the guard house.

The prisoner had nothing to say in his own defense, so the court deliberated and found Castner guilty of injuring Lieutenant Grometh's character and sentenced him to run the gauntlet "once up and once down the regiment." The sentence was approved to be carried out at that evening's roll call.

Cited in P.A., s6v14pp39-40.

The wording of the discharges issued at this time was:

"Wyoming, July ___st, 1779

This is to certify that the bearer, _____,
a Private in the German Regiment in Capt _____'s Company,
Served three years as a good Soldier from the time of his
Inlistment he is hereby Discharged from the same. Given under
my hand the Day and Date above written.

/s/ Jacob Bunner, Capt.
Commanding the German Regt."

Adapted from AMd, v18p271.

Corporal Philip Snyder [Shrider] of Captain Bunner's Company was court-martialled on 28 July 1779. He was charged with insolence and mutiny, found guilty, and sentenced to be reduced to the ranks and receive 100 lashes. General Sullivan approved the sentence and ordered it carried out that evening at roll call before his unit. Cited in P.A., s6v14p61.

On 10 August 1779 a court-martial was held for Captain John
Van Anglen, 3rd Brigade Commissary, for "brutally assulting"
Sergeant Lewis Reiskly of the German Regiment. Van Alglen was
found guilty and sentenced to be severely reprimanded in general
orders.   Cited in P.A., s6v14p77.

On 12 August "a board of field officers appointed to settle
the rank of Lieutenants Swartz and Cramer reported that Lt Cramer
ought to retain his rank. General Sullivan therefore directed
he hold his rank as heretofore."   Cited in P.A., s6v14p77.

The court-martial of Private John Ammersley of Captain
Baltzell's Company was held on 01 Sepember 1779 at Fort Sullivan.
Ammersley was charged with stealing and selling clothing belonging
to Catharina Castner. Found guilty, he was sentenced to receive
100 lashes bare back well laid on at the head of the garrison
troops. In addition, one-half of his pay was stopped until
Catharina Castner was paid $45, the sum she paid for the clothing,
and Catty Castner received $15 for stockings and sleeve buttons
not yet found. The sentence was to be carried out that evening
at roll call.   Cited in Capt Myers' Orderly Book.
The Castner women were probably the wife and daughter of Private
Christian Castner of Maryland, the subject of a court-martial
in July at Fort Wyoming.

REFERENCES - CHAPTER 6

1 - New York (State) Secretary of State: Journals of the Military
    Expedition of Major General John Sullivan Against the Six
    Nations of Indians in 1779 [hereafter Journals], Auburn,
    NY, (1887) 1972.
2 - Fitzpatrick, J.C., ed: Writings of George Washington
    [hereafter WW], 39 vols, Washington DC, 1931-44, v14p286.
3 - WW, v15p338.
4 - Pennsylvania Archives [hereafter P.A.], s2v11pp73-74; also
    s5v3pp785-86.
5 - Journals, p169.
6 - Miner, Charles: History of Wyoming, Phila., 1845, p263.
7 - Journals, pp342-43.
8 - P.A., s5v3pp807-815.
9 - Journals, pp315-329.
10 - Ibid.
11 - Journals, pp344-45.
12 - Ibid.
13 - Papers of the Continental Congress [hereafter PCC], Microfilm
     @ Natl. Archives, M247, r91, i78, p327
14 - Ford, W.C., ed: Journals of the Continental Congress,
     34 vols, Washington DC, 1904-37, v14p788.
15 - PCC, M247, r48, i41, v1, p184.
16 - PCC, M247, r102, i78, v20, p427.
17 - Orderly Book, P.A., s6v14p23.

18 - P.A., s6v14p23.
19 - Steuart, R.: The Maryland Line, Md Soc of Cincinnati, 1969, p40.
20 - Ibid.
21 - P.A., s6v14pp39-40.
22 - Journals, pp252-54.
23 - Ibid.
24 - Ibid.
25 - Ibid.
26 - Archives of Maryland [hereafter AMd], v18pp262,264-5.
27 - Journals, p253.
28 - Journals, p263.
29 - Journals, p356.
30 - Journals, pp356-61.
31 - Ibid.
32 - AMd, v18p212.
33 - Wright, A.H.: Sullivan's Expedition of 1779 - The Losses, Ithaca, NY, 1943, pp14,25.
34 - AMd, v18p262.
35 - WW, v16p293.
36 - Journals, p378.
37 - Orderly Book of Capt Christian Myers, Manuscript Division No. MMC1259, Library of Congress, Washington, DC.
38 - Ibid.
39 - Journals, p166.
40 - Journals, p379.
41 - Ibid.
42 - Ibid.

NOTES & REFERENCES - CHAPTER 7

1 - New York [State] Secretary of State: Journals of the Military
    Expedition of Major General John Sullivan Against the Six
    Nations of Indians in 1779 [hereafter Journals], Auburn,
    NY, 1887, p177.
2 - Journals, p4.
3 - Pennsylvania Archives [hereafter P.A.], Phila.,
    1852-1935, s1v8pp40-41.
4 - Journals, p4.

Two wounded Maryland men, Thomas Proctor of Myers' Company
and Adam Mussler of Baltzell's Company were patients at the
General Hospital at Sunbury. They were admitted before 04
September; one was discharged between 18 October and 07 December
1779, the other between 07 and 14 February 1780. See Jordan,
J.W.: Continental Hospital Returns 1777-80, Phila, 1899,
reprinted in Pa. Mag. Hist. & Bio., April 1899.

5 - P.A., s1v8pp29-30.
6 - P.A., s1v8p41.
7 - Ibid.
8 - P.A., s1v8pp29-30.
9 - P.A., s1v8p41.
10 - Ibid.
11 - Buckalew, John M.: Report of the Commission to Locate the
     Sites of the Frontier Forts of Penna [hereafter Frontier
     Forts], Harrisburg, Pa, 1896, v2pp375-381.
12 - Snyder, C.F., ed.: Northumberland County in the American
     Revolution [hereafter Snyder], Northumberland Pa, 1976,
     p517.
13 - P.A., s1v8pp29-30.
14 - P.A., s1v8pp40-41.
15 - Snyder, p242[ff61].
16 - P.A., s1v8p171.
17 - P.A., s1v8p62.
18 - P.A., s1v8pp153-154.
19 - Fitzpatrick, J.C., ed: Writings of George Washington
     [hereafter WW], 39 vols, Washington DC, 1931-44, v18p302.
20 - P.A., s5v3p909.

THE SOLDIERS' FINANCIAL SITUATION

21 - Nead, D.W.: The Penna-German in the Settlement of Maryland
     [hereafter Nead], Lancaster Pa, 1914, pp255-258.
22 - Nead, p259.
23 - Archives of Maryland [hereafter AMd], 71 vols, Baltimore,
     1883-1970, v21p531.
24 - AMd, v43p364.
25 - Nead, p259.
26 - AMd, v43p81.

27 - Nead, p259.
28 - AMd, v43p81.
29 - Ibid.
30 - Ibid.
31 - AMd, v43p204.
32 - P.A., s1v8pp205-06.
33 - Minutes of the [Pa] Supreme Executive Council, v12pp296-97.
34 - P.A., s1v8pp153-54.
35 - P.A., s1v8p161.
36 - P.A., s1v8pp165-66.
37 - AMd, v43p295.
38 - AMd, v43p297.

THE SUPPLY SITUATION

39 - P.A., s1v8p40.
40 - P.A., s1v8p171.
41 - P.A., s1v8p270.
42 - P.A., s1v8p233.
43 - P.A., s1v8p341.
44 - AMd, v43p204.
45 - P.A., s1v8p166.
46 - AMd, v43p297.

THE MILITARY SITUATION IN 1780

47 - Roberts, R.B.: New York's Forts in the Revolution, Cranbury
     NJ, 1980.
48 - Minutes of [Pa] Supreme Executive Council, v12pp296-97.
49 - Papers of the Continental Congress, M247, r100, i78, v1,
     p119, Microfilm at National Archives, Washington DC.

50- Garrison Orders   Fort Montgomery   March 5th 1780
                   Countersign: Hubley
     The wood in future is to be Left out side of the Garrison
and cut small before it is brought in[. T]he men are Desired
to Keep their Quarters Clean, as filth at this Time in the year
will Breed Distembers ---- A Fateage to be Turned out Tomorrow
to raise a Scaffell [scaffold] for the Sentinels to be placed
on[. T]he Guard to continue as Usual Till further Orders.

     Garrison Orders   Fort Montgomery   March 7th .80
                   C: Sign - [blank]
     A Fateague to Turn out Tomorrow Morning at Troop Beating in
order to Clean the Fort of the Quantity of filth it Contains[.]
     The Commdt. observed that many of the Troops Ease themselves
close by the Fort. As there is a Necessary and Vaults Handy[,]
Anyone that will be Aprehented in Easing himself at any other
place Near the Fort, May Depend on Being Punished Without the
Benefit of a Court Martial.----

Garrison Orders   Fort Montgomery   March 10th 1780
                   C: Sign - [blank]
No Soldier in future to go one Quarter of a Mile from the
Fort, without a written Pass from an Officer. There has been
Complaint mad[e] Lately that some of the Soldiers of this
Garrison, was Straggling in the Night amongst the Neighboughrs
in a sort of an Indian Habbit, in which there Could be no Good
Design ---- The Corpl. of the Guard will Give Strict orders
to the Sentinels, that Every Such Offender May be Aprehended.
The gates are to be Locked at Eight OClok in the Evening,
and Not a Man to Go out, Without one of the guard to Go with
him to the Gate, and see it well Fastened when he comes in -
any one found Guilty of a Breach of this order May Depent on
being Punished ---- this to be a Standing Order.----

Garrison Orders   Fort Montgomery   March 29th .80-
The Commdt. is sor[r]y that so Little respect is Paid to the
former Orders, Especially to the Order of the Tenth Instand,
Concerning the Soldiers Leaving the Garrison after Night without
Leave, but is resolved[. A]ny found Guilty of a breach of that
kind for the future, shall not Com[e] of[f] with a Reprimant,
one Hundred Lashes shall be Inflicted on Every such Offender
without the Benefit of a Court Martial. The Non Commisd. Officr.
of the Guard, is once more Called upon to Take Perticular Care
to Apprehend all such Delinquents ---- Last Night some of the
Soldiers absented themselfs After Tatoo Beating, the Non Commisd.
Officr. Commanding the Guard Shall for the future be answerable
for all Such Offences ---- As there is Three Sergts. at this
Post the troops are Divided in two Divisions, & Each to be
Commanded by a Sergt., the Eldest Sergt. to do the Duty of Sergt:
Major.   - Copied from MS MMC1259, Manuscript Div., Library
of Congress, Washington, DC.

51 - P.A., s1v8p171.
52 - Frontier Forts, v2pp374-75.
53 - P.A., s1v8p233.
54 - Frontier Forts, v2pp386-87.
55 - P.A., s1v8p157.
56 - P.A., s1v8p172.
57 - P.A., s1v8pp205-06.
58 - WW, v18p480.
59 - P.A., s1v8p369.
60 - Snyder, p517.
61 - WW, v19p296.
62 - P.A., s1v8p567.
63 - Frontier Forts, v2pp375-381.
64 - Northumberland County [Pa] Historical Society Proceedings,
     v25pp1-10.

On 01 October 1780 Privates Jacob Shepard, Jacob Myers, and Frederick Hersh of Captain Bunner's Company were tried for desertion. They were found not guilty and released. Cited in 1 below.

1 - Pennsylvania Archives [hereafter P.A.], s6v14pp125-207.
2 - Lesser, C.H., ed: The Sinews of Independence - Monthly Strength Reports of the Continental Army [hereafter Lesser], Chicago, 1976, see date.
3 - P.A., s6v14pp125-207.
4 - Ibid.
5 - Ibid.
6 - Ibid.
7 - Lesser, ppxxv-xxvi
8 - Lesser, see date.
9 - Archives of Maryland [hereafter AMd], v18pp513-514.
10 - Fitzpatrick, J.C., ed: Writings of George Washington [hereafter WW], 39 vols, Washington DC, 1931-44, v20p487.
11 - WW, v21pp12-13.
12 - Saffel, W.T.H., ed: Records of the Revolutionary War, New York City, 1858, pp320-21.
13 - Van Doren, C.C.: Mutiny in January, New York City, 1943, p42.
14 - Reeves, Enos: Extracts from the Letterbooks of Lt Enos Reeves of the Penna Line, reprinted in Penna Magazine of History & Biography, v21pp72-83, 1897.
15 - Ibid.
16 - Tucker, Glenn: Mad Anthony Wayne and the New Nation, Harrisburg, Pa, 1973, p192.
17 - Ibid.
18 - Ford, W.C., ed: Journals of the Continental Congress [hereafter JCC], 1774-89, 34 vols, Washington DC, 1904-37, v19p55.
19 - Papers of the Continental Congress, Microfilm at National Archives, Washington DC, M247, r100, i78, v17, p119.
20 - Burnett, E.C., ed: Letters of Members of the Continental Congress, 8 vols, Washington DC, 1921-36, v5p544.
21 - AMd, v47pp44-45.
22 - AMd, v47p58
23 - Lesser, see date.
24 - Ibid.
25 - WW, v21pp250-51.

REFERENCES - CHAPTER 9

1 - Adlum, John: Memoirs of the Life of John Adlum [hereafter Adlum], Chicago, 1968, pp77-78.
2 - Adlum, p77.
3 - Frederick County [Md] Will Book GM-1-122, 218.
4 - Pennsylvania Archives [hereafter P.A.], s2v15pp668-69.
5 - P.A., s5v4pp832-33.
6 - P.A., s5v3p787.
7 - P.A., s5v3p864,876.
8 - Saffel, W.T.R., ed: Records of the Revolutionary War [hereafter Saffel], New York City, 1858, pp488-490.
9 - Saffel, pp483-88.
10 - Adlum, p118.
11 - Adlum, pp119-122.
12 - Graydon, Alexander: Memoirs of His Own Time, Philadephia, 1846, p237.
13 - Papers of the Continental Congress [hereafter PCC], M247, r150, i137, v4, p93. Microfilm at National Archives, Washington,DC.
14 - Fitzpatrick, J.C., ed: Writings of George Washington [hereafter WW], 39 vols, Washington, DC, 1931-44, v7pp141-42.
15 - PCC, M247, r52, i41, v10, p59.
16 - WW, v16p131.
17 - PCC, M247, r170, i152, v9, p113.
18 - WW, v16p131ff.
19 - P.A., s6v12p260.
20 - Van Doren, C.C.: Secret History of the Revolutionary War, New York City, 1941, pp231-32.
21 - Richards, H.M.M.: Valley Forge and the Penna-Germans, Penna-German Society Proc., v26[1918]p28.
22 - Archives of Maryland, v18, pp268-272.
23 - Ibid.
24 - Ibid.

GERMAN REGIMENT STRENGTH TABLE*

Date	Present and Fit					Unavailable					GRAND TOTAL	Remarks
	Officers	NCO	Staff	Rank and File	TOTAL	Sick, present	Sick, absent	On Command	On Furlough	Without Clothes		
22 Dec 1776	35	40	5	294	374	36	18	10	11		449	
21 May 1777	22	22	5	236	285	29	56	37	7		414	
31 Dec 1777	18	30	5	176	229	11	39	54	7		340	
End of Mar 1778	10	17	5	41	73	24	24	106	29	52	308	1 deserted
" Apr 1778	18	14	3	168	203	27	20	46	14		310	5 deaths, 1 deserted, 2 discharged
" May 1778	18	18	3	160	199	16	36	57	7		315	
" Jun 1778	16	25	3	269	313	4	40	57	5		397	1 death, 3 discharged, 3 joined.
" Jul 1778	17	30	4	249	300	4	48	44	3		399	2 deserted
" Aug 1778	15	31	3	261	310	14	26	42	3		395	9 deaths, 8 deserted, 5 discharged, 12 joined.
" Sep 1778	12	39	4	254	309	7	34	45	2		397	2 deaths, 2 deserted, 1 joined.
" Oct 1778	11	31	5	185	232	12	25	113	3		385	
" Nov 1778	4	23	5	182	214	6	20	133	4		377	1 deserted, 8 joined.
" Mar 1779	13	32	5	236	286	2	19	27	49		383	
" May 1779	14	36	5	250	305	22	16	20	18		381	
" Jul 1779	17	42	2	280	341	5	9	15	2		372	6 deserted, 1 discharged.
" Sep 1780	12	20	6	132	170	10	1	12	2		195	4 joined.
" Oct 1780	8	22	5	96	131	8	1	54	2		194	2 deserted.
" Nov 1780	13	25	5	121	164	4	1	15	0		184	14 deserted, 3 discharged.
" Dec 1780	13	22	5	95	135	5	1	36	1		178	3 deserted.

* Data from Lesser's Sinews of Independence.

66

FACSIMILE SIGNATURES OF THE FINAL GERMAN REGIMENT OFFICERS AND
STAFF

Traced from letters of 1780 and 1781 pleading for their pay.

MARYLAND MEN   PENNSYLVANIA MEN

APPENDIX 3 - PERSONNEL LISTS

These lists were compiled while working on the history of the German Regiment. It is my hope that the lists will make the reader feel that these German-Americans were real people - our ancestors - and not faceless masses.

This was not the only unit in the Continental Army to contain German-Americans. They enlisted from 1775 onward in various units from Maryland, Pennsylvania, Virginia and other states.

I have tried to give each man's entry a sentence for 1) his names, trade, and hometown, 2) his military service from enlistment to discharge, and 3) pension and other personal data. Unfortunately, many entries are less than complete.

Where there was conflicting data on dates and places, all data is shown separated by a /. Sources of the data are shown to the right of the surname. Abbreviations of common military and geographical terms are also listed with the references.

In conclusion, some negatives. These lists are not complete. These lists contain errors. In some cases I may have merged two people into one. In other cases I may have the same person listed twice with slightly different name spellings. Anyone with additional or corrective data on German Regiment personnel is urged to contact the author in care of the publisher.

Henry J. Retzer

PERSONNEL LIST ABBREVIATIONS

Adlum - MEMOIRS OF THE LIFE OF JOHN ADLUM, Chicago, 1968.
AMd   - ARCHIVES OF MARYLAND, vol 18 [1900], Baltimore, 1972.
appld - applied.
beg   - beginning.
BGen   - Brigadier General.
Brum   - G.M.Brumbaugh: MARYLAND RECORDS..., vol.2, Balto,
           (1928)1967.
BWCo   - Capt Weiser's [Pa.] Co, 03Oct76 muster roll, in P.A.
ca   - circa, about.
Capt   - Captain.
Capt-Lt - Captain-Lieutenant.
CBCo   - Capt Baltzel's [Md.] Co., 09Sep78 muster roll, in AMd..
CHG   - C.H.Glatfelter: PASTORS & PEOPLE, 2 vols, Breinigsville,
           Pa., 1979,81.
CMOB   - Capt Myers' Orderly Book, orig in MS Div, LC.
CO   - Commanding officer.
Co   - Company, County.
Col   - Colonel.
comm   - commissioned.
Cpl   - Corporal.
deprec - depreciation.
des   - deserted.
DB79   - Muster roll of five Pa. Companies of GR of ca. Mar 1779,
           signed by Maj. Daniel Burchardt, in P.A.
disch - discharged.
Eelking - M.v.Eelking: THE GERMAN ALLIED TROOPS..., Albany, 1893.
enl   - enlisted.
FBH   - F.B.Heitman: HISTORICAL REGISTER OF OFFICERS OF THE
           CONTINENTAL ARMY, Baltimore, 1982 (1914)
FCDAR - FRANKLIN COUNTY (PA.) PATRIOTS, DAR publication.
FCM   - Substitutes from the Frederick County Militia, 13 Jun
           1778, in AMd, vol 18, pp324-26.
FC78   - List of Frederick County, Md. substitutes, dated 20May79,
           in MHM, vol.6 [1911], pp 256-61.
Force - AMERICAN ARCHIVES, ed Peter Force, 5th Series.
for war - for the duration of the war.
Fredk - Frederick County, Md.
GAB   - Capt P. Graybill's [Md] Co Account Book, 1776-77, in
           MHS Library.
GHCo   - Capt Hubley's Co., undated roll, in P.A.
GKCo   - Capt Keyports'[Md] Co 19Sep76 Muster Roll, in AMd.
GR   - The German Regiment of the Continental Line.
HCP   - H.C.Peden: REV PATRIOTS OF BALTO TOWN & CO, Sil.Spg,
           Md., 1988
HFCo   - Capt Fister's Co 1776 Muster Roll, in AMd.
HMMR   - H.M.M.Richards: THE PENNA-GERMAN IN THE REV WAR, Penna
           German Society, vol 26, pp22-32, 1915 [1918].
HWN   - H.W.Newman: MARYLAND REVOLUTIONAY RECORDS, Balto, 1938,67,
HYCO   - Prowell, G.R.: HISTORY OF YORK CO., PA., Chicago, 1907.

JBCo - Capt Bunner's Co, undated roll, in P.A.
JCC   - JOURNALS OF THE CONTINENTAL CONGRESS, Washington, 1904-37.
LC   - Library of Congress, Washington, DC.
Lt   - Lieutenant.
Lt Col - Lieutenant Colonel.
LW80 - Muster roll of five Pa. Companies of GR, ca. May 1780,
        signed by Col Ludwig Weltner, in P.A.
Maj   - Major.
MB79 - Capt Bayer's Co Oct 1779 pay roll, in AMd.
Md   - Maryland.
MdDAR - DIRECTORY OF MD DAR & ANCESTORS, n.p., 1966.
MdHR - Md. Hall of Records, Annapolis.
MGen - Major General.
MHM   - MARYLAND HISTORICAL MAGAZINE.
MHS   - Maryland Historical Society, Baltimore.
ML   - R.Steuart: THE MARYLAND LINE IN THE REV WAR, Towson,
        Md, 1969.
mo, mos - month, months.
Pa   - Pennsylvania.
P.A. - PENNA. ARCHIVES, Series 5, vol 3, et al, Harrisburg,.
PBCo - Capt Boyer's [Pa] Co undated muster roll, in P.A.
PCC   - PAPERS OF THE CONTINENTAL CONGRESS, National Archives
        Microfilm Publication M247, Washington, D.C.
Penna - Pennsylvania.
pens - pension
PGCo - Capt Graybill's [Md.] Co, 1776 muster roll, in AMd.
Phila - Philadelphia.
PL   - J.B.B.Trussell: THE PENNA LINE, Harrisburg, 1977.
P.M. - PENNA MAGAZINE OF HISTORY & BIOGRAPHY.
prom - promoted.
PVR   - PENNA VITAL RECORDS, 3 vols, Baltimore, 1983.
Pvt   - Private
rec   - received.
red   - reduced, demoted.
reenl - reenlisted.
res   - resided.
Rgt   - regiment.
Saffel- W.T.H.Saffel: RECORDS OF THE REV WAR, New York, 1858.
Sgt   - Sergeant
sub   - substitute
S&H   - Strassburger & Hinke: PENNSYLVANIA GERMAN PIONEERS, 3
        vols, Norristown, 1934.
transf - transferred.
WDA   - Capt Woelpper's deserter advertisement, in PENNA GAZETTE,
        19 Mar and 02 Apr 1777.
WHCo - Capt Heiser's [Md.] Co, 23Oct76 muster roll, in AMd.
WP78 - List of GR recruits at White Plains, NY, 05 Sep 1778,
        in AMd.
WW   - WRITINGS OF WASHINGTON, ed J.C.Fitzpatrick, Washington,
        D.C., 1931-44.
yr,yrs - year, years.
1Vac - 1st Vacant Co, undated roll, in P.A.

```
2Vac   - 2nd Vacant Co, undated muster roll, in P.A.
3Vac   - 3rd Vacant Co, undated muster roll, in P.A.
3-78   - 3rd Vacant Co, 31 Mar 1778 muster roll, in P.A.
4Vac   - 4th Vacant Co, undated muster roll, in P.A.
5Vac   - 5th Vacant Co, undated muster roll, in P.A.
5-77   - Capt Heiser's Co, 22May77 muster roll, in P.A.
79PR   - Col Weltner's Co pay roll Oct 1779, in AMd.
/      - Separates conflicting information.
?=     - Entry above and below this sign may be the same person.
```

Maryland Soldier Land data is from J.T. Scharff: HISTORY OF WESTERN MARYLAND, vol 1, Baltimore, 1882(1968).

ARENDT, Baron d'/de   P.A., JCC, WW, PCC.
   Henry Leonard Philip; German Mercenary, military engineer,
formerly in the Prussian service. Commissioned Colonel of the
German Rgt on 19 Mar 1777, transferred by General Washington to
command of Ft Mifflin in Delaware River 18 Oct 1777, received
leave of absence for one year for health reasons 18 Aug 1778,
returned to Europe. He visited Franklin in Paris to request
return to Contl Army, he was given an advance of 25 Louis 22
May 1780; he was in Phila by 05 Jan 1781 till at least 25 Feb
1782.

BALTZEL, BALTZELL, BULSEL   ML.
   Charles, of Frederick County, Md. Commissioned 1st Lt in GR as
of 12 Jul 1776, prom to Capt 10 May 1777, wounded @ Battle of
Germantown 04 Oct 1777, in GR when disbanded 01 Jan 1781, took
supernumerary's ½-pay retirement. Born 15 Oct 1737 in what is now
Alsace, France; was original Md member Society of the Cincinnati;
died 31 Dec 1813 in Woodstock, Md.

BALTZEL   HFCo, AMd, ML.
   John, of Md. Enlisted 1776 in GR as Pvt, prom to Sgt
01 Dec 1776, commissioned Ensign in GR 10 Aug 1777, separation
date not known.

BAYER, BOYER, BOWYER   ML, Brum.
   Michael, of Md. Commissioned 2nd Lt in GR as of 12 Jul 1776,
prom to 1st Lt 15 Nov 1777, prom to Capt 25 May 1778, in GR when
disbanded 01 Jan 1781, took supernumerary's ½-pay retirement.
Original Md member Society of the Cincinnati, 1788 Md Soldier Land
assignee 200A.

BENTALOU   ML, Saffel, FBH.
   Paul, of Baltimore, Md. Commissioned 2nd Lt in GR 25 Sep 1776,
prom to 1st Lt 21 Jun 1777, resigned 10 Dec 1777; transf to
Pulaski's Legion (Cavalry), prom to Capt of 1st Troop 12 Apr 1778,
wounded @ Battle of Savannah 09 Oct 1779, retired 01 Jan/Jun
1781. He was born 1735, was original Md member Society of the
Cincinnati, was active in committee welcoming Lafayette and
published **Pulaski Vindicated** in 1824, died in Baltimore 26 Sep
1826 from a fall in a warehouse, buried in Westminster Cemetery,
Balto.

BOWER, BAUER, BOYER   P.A., HMMR, PVR.
   Jacob, of Reading, Pa. Enlisted in Jun 1775 as Sgt in Capt
George Nagel's (Reading) Co; prom to 1st Lt 18 Jan 1776;
transferred to GR as 1st Lt about Sep 1776; prom to Capt &
transferred to 6th Pa Rgt 15 Feb 1777; transferred to 2nd Pa Rgt
01 Jan 1783. Born 1757, died @ Womelsdorf, Pa as a General

03 Aug 1818.

BOYER, BOWYER   DB79, LW80, P.A.
   Peter, of Philadelphia, Pa. Commissioned 1st Lt in GR as of
12 Jul 1776; prom to Capt 09 May 1777; appointed GR Paymaster
20 Jun 1779; in GR when disbanded 01 Jan 1781, took
supernumerary's ½-pay retirement.

BUCHER   CHG.
   John Conrad, Reformed pastor, of Lancaster [now Lebanon] County,
Pa. Appointed Chaplain of the GR 08 Jul 1776 as it was being
formed, probably never served actively except very briefly;
resigned 01 Aug 1777 because of ill-health. Born 13 Jun 1730 at
Schaffhausen, Switz; arrived in Penna before 1758; died at
Annville, Pa 15 Aug 1780.

BUNNER   DB79, LW80, P.A., AMd.
   Jacob, of Philadelphia, Pa. Commissioned Capt in GR as of
08 Jul 1776; acting CO of GR Jul 1779 to Oct 1779; in GR when
disbanded 01 Jan 1781, took supernumerary's ½-pay retirement.
Resided in Philadelphia in 1785.

BURCHARDT, BURKHARD   DB79, P.A., HMMR, PCC.
   Daniel, of Philadelphia, Pa. Commissioned Capt in GR as of
08 Jul 1776; prom to Major 07/09 Apr 1777; acting CO of GR Nov
1778 to Jul 1779; resigned 02 Jul 1779 at Philadelphia. Resided
in Philadelphia in 1786.

CHRISTMAN, CHRISTIAN   ML.
   Paul, of Md. Commissioned Ensign in GR as of 12 Jul 1776;
resigned 08 Nov 1776.

CLACKNER, GLECKNER   BWCo, PBCo, DB79, LW80, P.A.
   Christian, of Philadelphia, Pa. Enlisted 10 Jul 1776 in GR as
Sgt; appointed Ensign 23 Jul 1778; in GR when disbanded 01 Jan
1781, took supernumerary's ½-pay retirement.

COLE   GKCo, CBCo, AMd, ML, HCP.
   George, of Baltimore, Md. In Balto Mechanical Co of Militia
04 Nov 1775, enl 15 Jul 1776 in GR as Cpl, commissioned Ensign in
GR 17 Aug 1777; resigned 02 Jan/Jun 1778. Died 21 Aug 1828.

CRAMER, CRAEMER   DB79, LW80, P.A.
   Jacob, of Philadelphia, Pa. Commissioned Ensign in GR as of
8/12 Jul 1776; prom to 2nd Lt 13/15 May 1777; prom to 1st Lt
08 Jan/Feb 1778; in GR when disbanded 01 Jan 1781, declared
supernumerary. A Lt Jacob Cramer joined ex-GR Capt Shrawder's
[Pa. Frontier] Ranger Co on 10 Feb 1781. See also Pvt Jacob
Kremer of Capt Burchardt's Co.

DIEFFENDERFER   5Vac, DB79, P.A., FBH.
   David, of Lancaster, Pa. Enlisted 25Aug76 in GR as Pvt; prom to

Cpl 01 Dec 1776; taken prisoner 10 May 11777 near Monmouth, NJ, rejoined GR 24 Apr 1778; Sgt on 5th Vac Co muster roll; appointed Ensign 23 Jul 1778; resigned 23 Jun 1780. Resided in Lancaster County in 1832, aged 80.

EDISON, EDDISON   WW., JCC.
    Thomas, of Philadelphia, Pa. Commissioned 2nd Lt in GR 07 Jun 1777; court-martialed for behavior unbecoming of an officer and a gentleman, found guilty, discharged 22 May 1778. Later clerk in office of Secretary to Congress.

FISTER, FEASTER   ML, JCC.
    Henry, of Jefferson, Frederick County, Md. Commissioned a Capt in GR as of 08/12 Jul 1776; court-martialed 17 Jan 1777 for quitting his company & regiment, absent a fortnight without leave, found guilty, dismissed or resigned 07 Apr 1777. Death date unknown, but will is dated 13 Jul 1822.

GEROCK, GERROCK, GERRECK   ML, AMd, MdHR, CHG, HCP.
    Samuel L., of Baltimore County, Md. Commissioned 1st Lt in GR as of 12 Jul 1776; transferred to Md Artillery in Balto 05 Jun 1777, prom to Capt 01 Jul 1777, on duty with Capt Furnival's Co of Md Artillery 04 Jun 1778, resigned as Lt 19 Sep 1778. Born 1754, son of German-born Lutheran Pastor John Siegfried Gerock of Balto city.

GRAYBILL, GRAYBELL   GAB, ML, MdHR, HCP.
    Philip, of Baltimore, Md. Commissioned a Capt in GR as of 08 Jul 1776, resigned 12 Mar 1778. He served on Balto Salt Committee 14 Oct 1779, and seems to have been Capt of a Co of Balto Town Militia Batl. Elected Sheriff of Baltimore for 1785, died in Balto 25 Oct 1819.

GROMETH, CRUMMET, GOMATH   ML, FBH.
    Jacob, of Baltimore County, Md. Commissioned Ensign in GR as of 12 Jul 1776; prom to 2nd Lt 12 May 1777; prom to 1st Lt 04 Jan 1778; in GR when disbanded 01 Jan 1781, took supernumerary's ½-pay retirement. He was a 1788 Md Soldier Land assignee 200A.

HAIN, HEAN, HAYNE   HFCo, 2Vac, ML, HWN, AMd, FBH.
    Henry, of Md. Enlisted 18/25/26 Jul 1776 as Pvt in GR, prom to Cpl 01 Mar 1777, prom to Sgt 12 Jun 1778; commissioned Ensign 23 Jul 1778, resigned 20 Jun 1779. Applied for pension.

HAUSSEGGER,
HOUSACKER, HONSSECKER   P.A., PCC, Adlum, HMMR.
    Nicholas, hatter, of Lebanon, [then] Lancaster County, Pa. Was Lt & Capt during French & Indian War; commissioned Major in 4th Pa Batl 04 Jan 1776; comm Colonel of GR as of 17 Jul 1776; surrendered himself & 10 men to enemy @ Princeton, NJ 01 Jan 1777; returned to Penna on parole by 17 Jan 1777; returned to captivity on Long Island before 17 Feb 1779; resigned while a prisoner at

NYC 01 Feb 1781. His Lebanon property was seized as loyalist and sold at auction 11 Jan 1782. He died on his farm near Lebanon in Jul 1786.

HAWBACKER, HAUBECKER   P.A., FBH.
George, of Pa. Commissioned 2nd Lt in GR as of 12 Jul 1776; prom to 1st Lt 10 Aug 1777; resigned Jan 1778.

HEISER, HEYSER, KEISER   ML, MdHR, CHG, MdDAR.
William, of Hagerstown, Md. Commissioned Capt in GR as of 12 Jul 1776, resigned 21 May 1778. He was born 1737 in Germany or ca 1745 in Amsterdam, Holland, arrived in Colonies before Sep 1765, naturalized by Provincial Court @ Annapolis 10 Sep 1772, was original Md member Society of the Cincinnati, was active in Reformed church in 1784, died 1828/ca 1790 @ Hagerstown.

HELM   P.A., FBH.
Christian, of Pa. Commissioned Ensign in GR as of 12 Jul 1776, prom to 2nd Lt 13 May 1777, superceeded 12 Sep 1777.

HUBLEY   DB79, LW80, P.A., P.M.
Bernard, Jr., of Lancaster, Pa. Commissioned 1st Lt in GR as of 12/15 Aug 1776; prom to Capt 24 Feb 1778; in GR when disbanded 01 Jan 1781, took supernumerary's ½-pay retirement. Later Brigade Inspector of Northumberland County, was original Pa member Society of the Cincinnati, resided in Sunbury, published 1st volume of **History of the Revolution** in 1805/07. Born 1758, died 1808.

HUBLEY   P.A.
George, of Lancaster, Pa. Commissioned Capt in GR as of 08 Jul 1776, prom to Major 09 Apr 1777, on sick leave, died 07 Feb 1779. His Company was commanded by his nephew, Capt Bernard Hubley, Jr, after 19 Jun 1779.

KEEPORT, KEYPORTS,
KEPHART, KUHBORD   ML, AMd, MdHR, HCP.
George Peter, of Baltimore, Md. Was 3rd Lt in 1st Co of Matrosses @ Balto 14 Jan 1776, commissioned Capt in GR as of 08 Jul 1776, resigned 04 May 1777. Was Commisary of Stores @ Balto Feb 1780. Postwar in insurance business, appointed Notary Public in Jan 1787. Born 1718; died 1814, buried in Westminster Cemetery, Balto.

KORTZ, KOTZ   ML, FBH.
Jacob, of Frederick [now Washington] County, Md. Commissioned 2nd Lt in GR as of 12 Jul 1776, prom to 1st Lt 25 Sep 1776, resigned 08 Apr 1778.

LANDENBERGER, LINDENBERGER   ML, Eelking, FBH.
John, cabinetmaker of Md. Commissioned 2nd Lt in GR as of 12 Jul 1776, promoted to 1st Lt 01 Jan 1777 & transferred to 4th Continental Artillery Regt; escorted Hessian officer-prisoners

to Dumfries, Va 18-24 Jan 1777; prom to Capt-Lt 27 Apr 1777, resigned 03 Feb 1779.

LANDENBERGER, LINDENBERGER   HMMR, HCP, FBH.
   John, of Baltimore County, Md/Pa. Commissioned Ensign in GR as of 12 Jul 1776; 1st Lt in 4th Continental Artillery 20 Apr 1777, resigned 17 Mar 1778.

LAUDERMILK, LOWDERMILK   ML.
   Jacob, of Md. Commissioned Ensign in GR 19 Sep/Nov 1776, prom to 2nd Lt 13 May 1777, resigned 08 Apr 1778.

LINKENSDORF, de/van   P.A., Force, FBH.
   Louis/Lewis, of Pa. Was Lt of a Swiss Rgt of Sardinia; recommended for 1st Lt in GR on 09 Aug 1776, appointed Adjutant of GR 09 Aug 1776, requested six months advance pay from Congress on 11 Dec 1776 to replace his stolen horse, retired Jun 1779.

LORAH, LOHRA   ML, HCP, FBH.
   John, of Baltimore County, Md. Was 2nd Lt of 3rd Batln, Md Flying Camp, Anne Arundel County Jun/Jul 1776; commissioned 1st Lt in GR as of 12 Jul 1776, prom to Capt 28 Mar 1777, resigned 23 Feb 1778. Born 1747, married to Maria E. Zellers, died after 1809.

MAAG   P.A., P.M., FBH.
   Henry, of Philadelphia, Pa., stepson of Major Burchardt. Enlisted in GR as Sgt 10 Jul 1776; commissioned Ensign in GR 15 Aug 1777; court-martialed 29 Sep 1778 for cowardice @ Battle of Germantown, found guilty & cashiered 26 Mar 1779. He became a wheelwright's apprentice Mar 1773.

MACHENHEIMER,
MACKENHEIMER, McINHEIMER   GAB, PGCo, ML, HCP.
   John, of Baltimore, Md. Enlisted 29Jul76 in GR as Sgt, commissioned Ensign 17 Aug 1777, resigned 31 May 1778. Was 2nd Lt in Balto Town Militia 25 Sep 1780. Died before 27 Oct 1823.

MICHAEL   P.A., JCC.
   Eberhard, of Lancaster Co, Pa. Appointed GR Paymaster 1776-77; died 16 Jul 1778, buried in Lutheran Cemetery, Lancaster, Pa.

MUELLER, MOELLER, MILLER   JCC, P.A., CHG.
   Henry, Lutheran pastor @ Reading, Pa. Appointed Chaplain of the GR by Congress 19 Apr 1777 but apparently did not accept, appointed Chaplain of Pa [State] Rgt of Foot 24 Apr 1777, appointed Chaplain "to the Germans in the main army" by Congress 18 May 1778, resigned 07 Aug 1779. Born ca 1750 prob @ Hamburg, Ger, arrived in Colonies ca 1764; died 16 Sep 1829 at Sharon, NY.

MORGAN, McCORGAN   WHCo, 5-77, ML.
   David, of Md. Enlisted 05Nov76 in GR as Sgt; commissioned

Ensign 13 Aug 1777; prom to 2nd Lt 08 Apr 1778; in GR when disbanded 01 Jan 1781, declared supernumerary. Was 1788 Md Soldier Land assignee 200A.

MYERS, MEYERS, MYER   ML, CMOB, HCP.
   Christian, sadler of Baltimore city, Md. In Balto Mechanical Co of Militia 04 Nov 1775. Commissioned 2nd Lt in GR as of 12 Jul 1776; prom to 1st Lt 12 May 1777; prom to Capt 12 Mar 1778; in GR when disbanded 01 Jan 1781, took supernumerary's ½-pay retirement. Was 1788 Md Soldier Land assignee 200A.

MYLE, MEIL   P.A., FBH.
   Jacob, of Pa. Quartermaster of GR 24 Oct 1776 to Jul 1778.

PERIS, PERES   DB79, LW80, P.A., PVR.
   Peter, physician, of Philadelphia, Pa. Warrented GR Surgeon 01 Sep 1778; in GR when disbanded 01 Jan 1781, took supernumerary surgeon's ½-pay for life retirement ($32.50/mo). Died 17 Aug 1825 in Phila, aged 79 yrs & 11 mos.

RAWLWAGEN, ROWLWAGEN,
ROHLWAGEN   P.A., WW, FBH.
   Frederick, of Pa. Commissioned 1st Lt in GR as of 12/19 Jul 1776; courtmartialled 17 Jan 1777 for quitting his Company & Regiment, found guilty & cashiered 31 Mar 1777.

RAYBOLD, REYBOLDT   ML, HMMR.
   Jacob, of Md. Quartermaster Sgt in GR 13 Nov 1777; commissioned Ensign 24 Jul 1778; appointed GR Quartermaster 24/30 Jul 1778; in GR when disbanded 01Jan81, took supernumerary's ½-pay retirement. Was 1788 Md Soldier Land assignee 200A.

RICE   DB79, LW80, P.A., PL.
   Frederick William, of Kensington, Phila County, Pa. Commissioned 1st Lt in GR as of 12 Jul 1776; prom to Capt 04 Jan 1777/78; court-martialed for insulting and abusing Col Weltner, found not guilty 23 Oct 1780; in GR when disbanded 01 Jan 1781, took supernumerary's ½-pay retirement. Died Jan/Jun 1805.

RITTER   ML, FBH.
   Charles, of Md/Pa. Named Surgeon's Mate 20 Dec 1777, resigned 01 Aug 1778.

RITTER   HMMR, FBH.
   William, of Baltimore County, Md. Commissioned 2nd Lt in GR as of 12 Jul 1776; he apparently rejected this commission as his replacement was named 25 Sep 1776; he was 1st Lt in 4th Continental Artillery 01 Apr 1777, resigned 11 May 1779 .

SCHAEFFER, SHAFFNER   HMMR, FBH.
   George, of Pa. Commissioned 2nd Lt in GR as of 12 Jul 1776; Lt

in Ottendorf's/Schott's Corps 04 Feb 1777, prom to Capt of 3rd Cavalry in Pulaski's Legion 08 Feb 1778, prom to Major.

SHRAWDER, SCHRAWDER, SCHRADER   DB79, LW80, P.A., P.M., FBH.
   Philip, of Lancaster/Philadelphia, Pa. Commissioned 2nd Lt in GR as of 12 Jul or Aug 1776; prom to 1st Lt 13 May 1777; prom to Capt-Lt 08 Feb 1778; court-martialed for cowardice 29 Sep 1778, found not guilty; in GR when disbanded 01 Jan 1781, declared supernumerary; Capt of Pa Militia [Frontier] Ranger Co 10 Feb 1781, he arrived with this Co at Ft Wyoming on 21 Mar 1783 to prevent violence in Pa-Conn land dispute. Resident of Smithfield, died 1822.

SHRUPP, STRUPP   PCC, Brum, PVR, FBH.
   Henry, of Pa. Enl in GR as Pvt/Sgt 20 Jul 1776; commissioned Ensign in GR 20 Aug 1777, appointed GR Adjutant by GW 27 Jan 1779 as of 01 Oct 1778, resigned 20 Jun or after 29 Jun 1779. His original commission certificate is extant in PCC. Received Lts pension Jan 1820, died as a Col in Apr 1821 in Phila in his 66th year.

SHUGART, SHUGARTH, SUGART, SUGARS   AMd, ML, WW, HCP.
   Martin, of Baltimore County, Md. Commissioned as Ensign in GR as of 12 Jul 1776; prom to 2nd Lt 15 Nov 1777; court-martialed for challanging Lt Laudermilk, found guilty, cashiered, but rank & position restored 26 Jan 1778; prom to 1st Lt 25 May 1778; in GR when disbanded 01 Jan 1781, took supernumerary's ½-pay retirement. Was original Md member of Society of the Cincinnati, 1788 Md Soldier Land assignee 200A.

SMITH   ML, HWN.
   Adam, of Frederick [now Washington] County, Md. Commissioned 2nd Lt in GR as of 12 Jul 1776, resigned 04 May 1777. Was born 1753, applied for pension.

SMITH   FC78, ML, P.A.
   Alexander, of Md. Enlisted in GR as Frederick County substitute 20 May 1778; appointed Surgeon's Mate 01 Aug 1778; in GR when disbanded 01 Jan 1781, declared Md supernumerary; served to at least 01 Jan 1783, but not later than 15 Nov 1783.

SMITH   GKCo, ML, HCP, FBH.
   Jacob, of Baltimore Co, Md. Enl 15Jul76 in GR as Sgt, promoted to Sgt-Major 01 Oct 1776, appointed GR Adjutant 15 Dec 1777, resigned 15 Jul 1778.

STRICKER   ML, P.A., MHM, WW.
   George, of Frederick County, Md. Commissioned Capt in Col Smallwood's Md Batl 03/14 Jan 1776; comm Lt Col in GR as of 17 Jul 1776, resigned 29 Apr 1777. Was Frederick County Delegate

to Md Genl Assembly 1779-80. He was born 1732 in Winchester, Va, and died in Wheeling, now W.Va. in 1810.

STRICKER   GKCo, HCP.
  John, son of George, above. Was enlisted as Cadet in Keeports' Co in 1776, became Sgt in 4th Contl Artillery Jan 1777. Later BGen in War of 1812. Born 15 Feb 1759 in Fredk Co, died 23 Jun 1825 in Balto.

SWARTZ, SCHWARTZ   DB79, LW80, P.A., FBH.
  Christopher/Christian   Godfried,   of   Philadelphia,   Pa.
Commissioned Ensign in GR as of 12/19 Jul 1776; prom to 2nd Lt 14 May 1777; prom to 1st Lt 12/24 Feb 1778; in GR when disbanded 01 Jan 1781, declared Pa supernumerary; later Lt of 4th Troop-Armand's Corps in 1782 & Adjutant in 1783.

TRUX   GKCo, CBCo, AMd, ML.
  William, of Md. Enlisted as Pvt in GR 21 Jul 1776, prom to Sgt 01 Mar 1777/78, commissioned Ensign 25 Jul 1778, resigned 01 Jul 1779.

WEIDMAN [1], WEIDMANN   P.A., PL, Saffel, HMMR.
  John, of Lancaster City/County, Pa. Served in an Associator Battalion, commissioned Ensign in GR as of 12 Jul 1776, prom to 2nd Lt 14 May 1777, prom to 1st Lt 16 Aug 1777, captured @ Battle of Brandywine 11 Sep 1777, exchanged @ Elizabeth[town], NJ 30 Dec 1780. Born 04 Jun 1756 in Lancaster Co, resident of Lebanon Co, died 06/09 Jun 1830, aged 74, buried in Lutheran Cemetery, Reading.

WEIDMAN [2]   DB79, LW80, P.A.
  John, of Berks/Phila Co, Pa. Commissioned Ensign in GR 10 Aug 1777; appointed GR Adjutant 20 Jun 1779; in GR when disbanded 01 Jan 1781, took supernumerary's ½-pay retirement.

WEISER   P.A., WW.
  Benjamin, of Womelsdorf, Pa. Commissioned Capt in GR as of 08 Jul 1776; court-martialed for misbehavior before the enemy in the attack on Riker's [then Montressor's] Island, NY 14 Oct 1776, found guilty, ordered cashiered with infamy, approved by GW and dismissed 31 Oct 1776. Was then Capt in Pa Militia Co of Northumberland County, stationed in Phila 30 Jan 1777. He was born 1744, and resided on Isle of Que, now Snyder County, Pa. after the war.

WEISER, YEISER   P.A., FBH.
  Frederick, of Pa. Commissioned 2nd Lt in GR as of 12 Jul 1776, resigned 01 May 1777.

WELTNER, WILTNER   AMd, ML, P.A., WW, Adlum, MdHR, S&H.
  William Ludwig/Ludowick, britchesmaker, of Frederick, Md. Was 1st Major in Fredk County Militia in early 1776. Commissioned

Major in GR as of 17 Jul 1776, prevented entire GR from being marched into captivity by Col Hausegger @ Princeton, NJ on 01 Jan 1777, prom to Lt Col 29 Apr 1777. Became CO of GR when Col Arendt was transferred to Ft. Mifflin 18 Oct 1777, on sick leave after Nov 1778, back on duty Oct 1779, was CO when GR was disbanded 01 Jan 1781, took supernumerary's ½-pay retirement. He was German-born, arrived in Phila 16 Sep 1751 on ship **Brothers** from Rotterdam, arrived in Frederick Co before Sep 1757, naturalized in Frederick 17Sep64; death date unknown, but Will probated 17 Jan 1782. He was survived by widow Mary & daughter Mary [Mrs Rev Frederick Henop/Heanop], who were 1788 Md Soldier Land assignees for 200A.

WOELPPER, WILPER,
WOELPER, WOELPERT   P.A., PL, WW, PCC, S&H.
     John David, of Va. Personal acquaintance of Gen Washington, served with his Va troops during entire F&I War. Was Sgt in a Va rgt in 1775, commissioned 1st Lt in 3rd Pa [Col Shee's] Rgt 06 Jan 1776; recommended for captaincy in GR by GW 08 Jul 1776, a fifth company in GR was created for him by Congress and Pa Committee of Safety 17 Jul 1776, comm Capt in GR as of 12 Jul 1776; ordered to join GR in Phila by GW 22 Jul 1776; transferred to Invalid Corps @ request of GW 09/11 Jun 1778, discharged 23 Apr 1783 or 03 Dec 1784. He was German-born, arriving as Johann Davidt Völpert in Phila 09 Oct 1749 on ship **Lydia** from Rotterdam.

YOUNG   DB79, LW80, P.A., Force, FBH.
     Marcus, of Lancaster, Pa. Enlisted in GR as Sgt 20 Jun 1776; recommended for Ensign 08 Nov 1776; commissioned 2nd Lt 08 Jun 1777; prom to 1st Lt 12 Mar 1778; in GR when disbanded 01 Jan 1781, took supernumerary's ½-pay retirement.

OFFICERS SOMETIMES ATTRIBUTED TO THE GERMAN REGIMENT

CALDWELL, COLWELL   FBH.
     Robert, of Pa; 1st Lt German Rgt 15 Jul 1776, wounded and captured at Ft. Washington 16 Nov 1776.

COUSEAU, De   A. Hamilton Papers
     Bernard Pally, Ensign, permitted to resign 07 Aug 1777.

KLEIN   FBH.
     William, Lt Col of a German Volunteer Corps proposed in September 1778. Not associated with German Regiment!

GERMAN REGIMENT SERGEANTS FROM MARYLAND

ALEXANDER   AMd, Brum.
Jacob; enl 28 Jan or 01 Feb 1778, on duty 01 Aug 1780. Sgt's $\frac{1}{2}$-pay pension recd by widow Mary during widowhood 13 Feb 1835.

BALTZEL, BALZEL   HFCo, AMd, ML.
John; enl 1776 as Pvt in Fister's Co, prom to Sgt 01 Dec 1776, comm Ensign in GR 10 Aug 1777.

COLE   GKCo, CBCo, HCP.
John; in Balto Mechanical Co of Militia 04 Nov 1775, enl 16 Jul 1776 as Pvt in Keeports' Co, prom to Sgt in Baltzel's [ex-Keports] Co before 09 Sep 1778, disch 24 Jul 1779 at Ft. Wyoming, Pa.

GAUL   FC78, WP78, 3Vac, AMd.
Richard; enl 16 May 1778 as Pvt for 3 yrs as Frederick Co sub in 3rd Vac [ex-Graybill] Co, prom to Sgt, on duty 01 Aug 1780 as Sgt.

HAIN, HEAN, HAYNE   HFCo,2Vac,AMd, ML, HWN, FBH.
Henry; enl 18/25/26 Jul 1776 as Pvt in Fister's Co, prom to Cpl 01 Mar 1777, prom to Sgt of 2nd Vac [ex-Fister's] Co 12 Jun 1778, comm Ensign in GR 23 Jul 1778.

HELLER   GAB, PGCo, HCP.
Frederick, of Balto Co; enl 1776 as Sgt in Graybill's Co, on duty 25 Jul 1777.

HERRING, HERON   CBCo, AMd.
John; enl 12 Aug 1775, reenl 30 Jul 1776 in GR, prom to Sgt in Baltzel's Co before 09 Sep 1778, disch 24 Jul 1779 at Ft. Wyoming, Pa.

HOSE   WHCo, 4Vac, 79PR, AMd.
Jacob; enl 11 Aug 1776 as Sgt in Heiser's Co, disch as Sgt from Weltner's [ex-Heiser] Co 26 Jul 1779 at Ft. Wyoming, Pa.

JAQUET, JAQUES   WHCo,4Vac,79PR, AMd, Brum,HWN.
John Daniel; enl 21 Jul 1776 as Sgt in Heiser's Co, disch as Sgt from Weltner's [ex-Heiser] Co 26 Jul 1779 at Ft. Wyoming, Pa. Pension applied for by widow, who recd Sgt's $\frac{1}{2}$-pay for life in 1815.

JOHNSON, JOHNSTON   FC78,WP78,3Vac,AMd,Brum,HWN.
William; enl 16 May 1778 as Pvt for 3 yrs as Fredk Co sub, on duty as Pvt 05 Sep 1778 in 3rd Vac [ex-Graybill] Co, prom to Sgt before 01 Aug 1780. Born 1758, was 1788 Md Soldier Land assignee, recd Pvt's $\frac{1}{2}$-pay pension for life in 1827.

JONES, TONE   AMd.
Charles; prom to Sgt after GR service.

KEARNS, KERNS   GKCo, HCP.
Christian, of Balto Co; enl 19 Aug 1776 as 4th Sgt in Keeports' Co, on duty 19 Sep 1776 at Phila.

KEENER   GKCo, HCP.
John, of Balto Co; enl 19 Aug 1776 as 3rd Sgt in Keeports'

Co, on duty 19 Sep 1776 at Phila.

KEYSER   AMd.
  Jacob; prom to Sgt after GR service?, was in 5th Co-2nd Md
  Rgt, disch 13 Feb 1782.

LEATHER, LADDER   HFCo, 2Vac, MB79, Brum.
  John; enl 03 Aug 1776 as Pvt in Fister's Co, prom to Sgt,
  disch as Sgt from Bayer's [ex-Fister] Co 09 Aug 1779 at
  Tioga, Pa. Recd Sgt's ½-pay for life pension in Frederick
  Co beg Dec 1816.

LEWIS   WHCo, 4Vac, 5-77, 79PR, AMd, Brum, HWN.
  William; enl 16 Jul 1776 as Cpl in Heiser's Co, prom to Sgt
  in 4th Vac [ex-Heiser] Co after May 1777, disch from
  Weltner's [ex-Heiser] Co 16 Jul 1779 at Ft. Wyoming, Pa.
  Recd Sgt's ½-pay for life pension in Washington Co beg Jan
  1820, pension applied for by widow.

LITZINGER, LITZENER   GAB, PGCo, HCP.
  William; Pvt in Balto Artillery Co 16 Oct 1775, enl Jul 1776
  as Sgt in Graybill's Co.

LOWE, LOW   HFCo, 2Vac, AMd, BSC.
  Jacob; enl 06 Aug 1776 as Cpl in Fister's Co, prom to Sgt
  in 2nd Vac [ex-Fister] Co, on duty 01 Aug 1780. 1788 Md
  Soldier Land assignee.

MACHENHEIMER, MACKENHEIMER   GAB, PGCo, ML, HCP.
  John; of Balto, enl 28 Jul 1776 as Sgt in Graybill's Co, comm
  Ensign in GR 17 Aug 1777.

MILLER   WHCo, 5-77, HWN.
  John/Jacob; enl 1776 as Sgt in Heiser's Co, on duty 22 May
  1777. Pension applied for by widow.

MORGAN, McCORGAN   WHCo, 5-77, ML.
  David; enl 05 Nov 1776 as Sgt in Heiser's Co, comm Ensign
  in GR 13 Aug 1777.

ROMMELSON, RUMMELSEM
RUMMELSON, KEMMELSTONE   GAB, PGCo, AMd, HCP.
  William, of Balto Co; enl 12 Jul 1776 as Sgt in Graybill's
  Co, disch 16 Jul 1779 at Ft. Wyoming, Pa.

SHULTZ   AMd.
  Valentine; served 3yrs in Capt Baltzel's Co, disch 13 Aug
  1779 at Tioga, Pa. Known only from discharge certificate
  supporting depreciation pay claim.

SHOPPER   HFCo.
  Philip; enl 1776 as Sgt in Fister's Co.

SHROOP   HFCo.
  Philip; enl 1776 as Sgt in Fister's Co.

SMITH   GKCo, ML, HCP.
  Jacob, of Balto Co; enl 15 Jul 1776 as 1st Sgt in Keeports'
  Co, prom to Sgt-Major 01 Oct 1776, appointed Adjutant of
  GR 15 Dec 1777.

SOLLERS, SOLLARS   GAB, PGCo, 3-78, 3Vac, HCP.
  Frederick/Frank, of Balto Co; enl 29 Jul 1776 as Cpl in
  Graybill's Co, prom to Sgt before Mar 1778, disch 28 Jul
  1779 at Ft. Wyoming, Pa.

SPECK   GKCo, CBCo, HCP.

Henry; enl 15/30 Jul 1776 as 2nd Sgt in Keeports' Co, on duty as Sgt in Baltzel's [ex-Keeports] Co 09 Sep 1778, later Ensign in Capt Graybill's Co of Balto Town Militia 25 Sep 1780. Died in Balto 29 Jan 1800, in his 45th year.

STANLEY, STANDLY, SLENDER   HFCo, 2Vac, MB79, AMd.
Christopher/Christofiel; enl 19 Jul 1776 as Pvt in Fister's Co, prom to Cpl, prom to Sgt, disch as Sgt from Bayer's [ex-Fister's] Co 20 Jul 1779 at Ft. Wyoming, Pa.

STAUFFER   GAB,PGCo,3Vac,3-78,AMd,HCP.
George, of Balto Co; enl 30 Jul 1776 as Cpl in Graybill's Co, prom to Sgt of 3rd Vac [ex-Graybill] Co before Mar 1778, disch 29 Jul 1779 at Ft. Wyoming, Pa.

TRUX, TRUCK, TRUCKS   GKCo,CBCo,AMd,Brum,HWN,HCP.
John, of Balto Co; enl 21 Jul 1776 as Pvt in Keeports' Co, prom to Cpl before 09 Sep 1778, prom to Sgt in Baltzel's [ex-Keeports] Co, disch 24 Jul 1779 at Ft. Wyoming, Pa. Recd 50A Md Soldier Land in Allegany Co on 09 Mar 1826 and 215A Federal Bounty Land, recd Sgt's ½-pay for life pension beg 1825; widow Elizabeth of Frederick Co recd pension beg 06 Mar 1832.

TRUX   GKCo, CBCo, AMd, ML, HCP.
William, of Balto Co; enl 21 Jul 1776 as Pvt in Keeports' Co, prom to Sgt 01 Mar 1777, in Baltzel's [ex-Keeports] Co 09 Sep 1778, comm Ensign in GR 25 Jul 1778.

WENTZ, WINTZ   HFCo., CMOB.
George; enl 1776 for 2 [!] yrs as Sgt in Fister's Co, requested courtmartial for being detained in service beyond his enlistment, court found him unjustly detained 06 Aug 1778 and ordered his discharge.

GERMAN REGIMENT CORPORALS FROM MARYLAND

BITTING   GKCo, HCP
  Philip, of Balto Co; enl 21 Jul 1776 as 4th Cpl in Keeports'
Co,   on duty 19 Sep 1776 at Phila.
BOEHM, BEAM   GKCo, CBCo, AMd, HCP.
  Philip, of Balto Co; enl 30 Jul 1776 as Pvt in Keeports' Co,
    prom to Cpl in Baltzel's [ex-Keeports] Co before 09 Sep 1778,
    disch 24 Jul 1779 at Ft. Wyoming, Pa.
BOYER, BYER   PGCo, HCP.
  Mathias; in Balto Mechanical Co of Militia 14 Nov 1775, enl
    1776 as Cpl in Graybill's Co.
BRUCHER, BREECHER   WHCo, 5-77, 79PR, AMd.
  John; enl 17 Jul 1776 as Pvt in Heiser's Co, prom to Cpl before
    22 May 1777, disch as Cpl from Weltner's [ex-Heiser] Co 17
    Jul 1779 at Ft. Wyoming, Pa.
BURK   GKCo, CBCo, AMd, Brum, HCP.
  Jacob/John/James, of Balto Co; enl 28 Jul or 01 Aug 1776 as
    Pvt in Keeports'Co, prom to Cpl after 09 Sep 1778, disch
    24 Jul 1779 at Ft. Wyoming, Pa. Recd $40/yr pension from
    04 Mar 1789, died 03 Dec 1817.
COLE   GKCo, AMd, HCP.
  George; in Balto Mechanical Co of Militia 04 Nov 1775, enl
    15 Jul 1776 as 1st Cpl in Keeports' Co, comm Ensign in GR
    17 Aug 1777.
ETTER   GAB, PGCo, 3Vac, 3-78, AMd.
  Jacob; enl 15 Jul 1776 as Pvt in Graybill's Co, prom to Cpl
    in 3rd Vac [ex-Graybill] Co before Mar 1778, disch 15 Jul
    1779 at Ft. Wyoming, Pa.
FILLER, TILLER   WHCo, 5-77.
  Andrew; enl 1776 as Cpl in Heiser's Co, disch by Surgeon May
    1777.
FREY, FRY   WHCo, 5-77, 4Vac, 79PR, AMd.
  Bernard/Barnard; enl 26 Jul 1776 as Cpl in Heiser's Co, disch
    as Cpl from Weltner's [ex-Heiser] Co 26 Jul 1779 at Ft.
    Wyoming, Pa.
HAIN, HEAN, HAYNE   HFCo, 2Vac, AMd, ML, HWN, FBH.
  Henry; enl 18/25/26 Jul 1776 as Pvt in Fister's Co, prom to
    Cpl 01 Mar 1777, prom to Sgt 12 Jun 1778.
HOCHSHILD, HOSHALL
HONSHITT, HOGSHIELD, HOSHIED   HFCo, 2Vac, MB79, AMd, HWN, HCP.
  Justinius/Jesey/Jesse/John; enl 27 Jul 1776 as Pvt in Fister's
    Co, prom to Cpl by Summer 1778, disch as Cpl from Bayer's
    [ex-Fister] Co 24 Jul 1779 at Ft. Wyoming, Pa. Born 04 Apr
    1756/58 in Holland, married Mary Ellen Hurst (1760-1843)
    on 22 Dec 1779, died 15 Jul 1830 in Balto Co, pension applied
    for by widow.
HOOK   GAB, PGCo, 3Vac, 3-78, AMd, Brum,HCP.
  Joseph; in Balto Co Militia Rgt #36, enl 31 Jul 1776 as Pvt
    in Graybill's Co, prom to Cpl in 3rd Vac [ex-Graybill] Co
    before Mar 1778, disch 30 Jul 1779 at Ft. Wyoming, Pa.

Born 1756, recd pension of $96/yr from 15 Apr 1818, married
Anne Channell in Balto Co in 1821, dropped from pension rolls
by Act of May 1820, living at age 76 in 1832 in Frederick
Co, pens appld for by widow.

HOOVER   HFCo.
George; enl 1776 as Cpl in Fister's Co, on duty 01 Dec 1776.

KELLY, KELLEY   CBCo, AMd.
Patrick; enl 24/30 Jul 1776, Cpl in Baltzel's [ex-Keeports] Co,
disch 24 Jul 1779 at Ft. Wyoming, Pa.

KRAFFT,
KROFFT, CROFT   GAB, PGCo, 3Vac, 3-78,AMd,Brum, HCP.
William, of Balto Co; enl 27 Jul 1776 as Pvt in Graybill's
Co, prom to Cpl after Mar 1778, disch 26 Jul 1779 at Ft.
Wyoming, Pa. Born 1753, died 17 Apr 1829. Widow Catherine
nee Nicodemus recd Cpl's ½-pay pens for life 04 Mar 1835.

LEWIS   WHCo, 4Vac, 5-77, 79PR, AMd, Brum, HWN.
William; enl 16 Jul 1776 as Cpl in Heiser's Co, prom to Sgt
after May 1777.

LINKENFETTER   GKCo, HCP.
Ulrich, of Balto Co; enl 21 Jul 1776 as 3rd Cpl in Keeports'
Co, on duty 19 Sep 1776 at Phila.

LOWE, LOW   HFCo, 2Vac, AMd.
Jacob; enl 06 Aug 1776 as Cpl in Fister's Co, prom to Sgt.

MICHAEL   WHCo, 5-77, 79PR.
John; enl 16 Jul 1776 as Pvt in Heiser's Co, prom to Cpl after
22 May 1777, disch as Cpl from Weltner's [ex-Heiser] Co 16
Jul 1779 at Ft. Wyoming, Pa.

MOPPES   GKCo, HCP.
Frederick, of Balto Co; enl 19 Jul 1776 as 2nd Cpl in Keeports'
Co, on duty 19 Sep 1776 at Phila.

POLEHOUSE, POLLHOUSE   HFCo, 2Vac, WP78, MB79, AMd, JCC.
Thomas; enl 1776 as Pvt in Fister's Co, his bill for $12.67
for bleeding 95 Pvts in GR approved by Congress 26 Apr 1777,
reenl 18 Jun 1778 for 9 mos, prom to Cpl in Bayer's
[ex-Fister] Co 01 Aug 1779, in GR when disbanded 01 Jan
1781, transf to 3rd Co-3rd Md Rgt. See also Thomas Polhouse
in Md unplaceables list.

REEVENACHT   WHCo.
Philip; enl 1776 as Cpl in Heiser's Co, on duty 23 Oct 1776.

ROBINSON, ROBERSON   2Vac, MB79, AMd.
Andrew; enl 25 Jul 1776 as Pvt, Pvt in 2nd Vac [ex-Fister]
Co, prom to Cpl, disch as Cpl from Weltner's [ex-Fister]
Co 20 Jul 1779 at Ft. Wyoming, Pa.

SHATZ, SHOTZ, SHOTTS   HFCo, 2Vac, MB79, AMd, Brum, HWN.
John; enl 29 Jul 1776 as Pvt in Fister's Co, prom to Cpl, disch
as Cpl from Bayer's [ex-Fister] Co at Ft. Wyoming,
Pa. Born 1756, recd Pvt's [?] ½-pay pens for life beg 07
Feb 1818 in Frederick Co, pens appld for by widow.

SHOEMAKER   2Vac, WP78, MB79, AMd, BSC.
Samuel Frederick; enl 08 May 1778 for war as Pvt, Pvt in 2nd
Vac Co, prom to Cpl in Bayer's [ex-2nd Vac] Co 01 Aug 1779,
on duty 01 Aug 1780. 1788 Md Soldier Land assignee.

SMITH   FC78, WP78, 4Vac, 79PR, AMd, Brum.
   James; enl 20 May 1778 as Pvt for war as Frederick Co sub,
   prom to Cpl in Weltner's Co 01 Aug 1779, on duty 01 Aug 1780.
   1788 Md Soldier Land assignee, pensioned @ $40/yr in
   Frederick Co.

SOLLERS, SOLLARS   GAB, PGCo, 3Vac, 3-78, HCP.
   Frederick/Frank, of Balto Co; enl 29 Jul 1776 as Cpl in
   Graybill's Co, prom to Sgt before Mar 1778.

SPECK   PGCo, HCP.
   William, of Balto Co; enl 1776 as Cpl in Graybill's Co.

STANLEY, STANDLY, SLENDER   HFCo, 2Vac, MB79, AMd.
   Christopher/Christofiel; enl 19 Jul 1776 as Pvt in Fister's
   Co, prom to Cpl in 2nd Vac [ex-Fister] Co, prom to Sgt.

STAUFFER   GAB, PGCo, 3Vac, 3-78, AMd, HCP.
   George, of Balto Co; enl 30 Jul 1776 as Cpl in Graybill's Co,
   prom to Sgt before Mar 1778.

STONEBREAKER   WHCo, 4Vac, 79PR, AMd, P.A.
   Adam, from Hagerstown; enl 22 Aug 1776 as Pvt in Heiser's Co,
   prom to Cpl after 22 May 1777, disch as Cpl from Weltner's
   [ex-Heiser] Co 26 Jul 1779 at Ft. Wyoming, Pa. Died 01 Nov
   1827 in Huntingdon Co., Pa., aged 77.

TRUX, TRUCKS   GKCo, CBCo, AMd, HCP.
   John, of Balto Co; enl 21 Jul 1776 as Pvt in Keeports' Co,
   prom to Cpl in Baltzel's [ex-Keeports] Co before 09 Sep 1778,
   prom to Sgt.

TUDDEROW   HFCo.
   Jacob; enl 1776 as Cpl in Fister's Co.

WILHITE, WILHEID   HFCo, Brum, HWN.
   Frederick; enl 1776 as Cpl in Fister's Co. Born 1753, appld
   for pens Jan 1820.

ZEIGLER   AMd.
   John; served 3 yrs, disch 21 Jul 1779 from Capt Bayer's Co
   at Ft. Wyoming, Pa. Known only from discharge certificate
   supporting depreciation pay application.

MARYLAND MUSICIANS OF THE GERMAN REGIMENT

BROWN   Fifer   GKCo, CBCo, AMd, HCP.
John; from Balto Co, enl 21/28 Jul 1776 as a Pvt in Capt
Keeport's Co, became Fifer before 09 Sep 1778 when on duty
at White Plains, NY.

ENGLAND   Drummer   GKCo, CBCo, AMd, HCP.
Benjamin; from Balto Co, was Pvt in Capt Howell's Co 30 Dec
1775, enl 15 Jul 1776 in GR, in Capt Keeport's Co, disch
16 Jul 1779 at Ft. Wyoming, Pa.

FERRINS, FARENCE, FERRENCE Fifer   FC78, MB79, AMd, HWN.
Henry; enl 16/20 May 1778 for war as Frederick County
substitute, drummer in Capt Bayer's Co in Oct 1779, on duty
01 Aug 1780. Born 1765, applied for pension.

FINLEY   Drummer   GAB, PGCo, AMd, HCP.
Peter; from Balto Co, enl 1776, in Capt Graybill's Co, on duty
02 Dec 1776.

GITTEN, GETTIN, GITTING Drummer   WHCo, 5-77, 4Vac, 79PR,AMd.
George; enl 28 Jul 1776 in Capt Heiser's Co, Drummer 23 Oct
1776, Pvt 22 May 1777, disch 26 Jul 1779 at Ft. Wyoming,
Pa.

GITTEN   Fifer   WHCo, AMd.
Jacob; enl 1776, in Capt Heiser's Co.

HEFFNER   Drummer   AMd.
John; enl 1776, in Capt Fister's Co.

HUTCHCRAFT, HATCHCRAFT Drummer   FC78, WP78, 79PR, AMd, BSC.
Thomas; enl 16/19 May 1778 for war as Frederick County
substitute, in GR when disbanded 01 Jan 1781, transf to 4th
Co-3rd Md Rgt, 1782: in 5th Co-2nd Md Rgt. 1788 Md Soldier
Land assignee.

HYATT, HYALT   Fifer   GAB, AMd, HCP.
George; from Balto Co, enl Jul 1776 from Balto Town Militia
Batl, in Capt Graybill's Co, on duty 17 Jul 1776. Applied
for depreciation pay by 1783, but "not found on any muster
rolls for 1779."

McKINSEY, McKENSY   Fifer   FC78, WP78, AMd, HWN.
Joshua; enl 28 Apr 1778 for 3 yrs as Frederick County
substitute, in 4th Vacant Co, in GR when disbanded 01 Jan
1781, transf to 1st Co-3rd Md Rgt, 1782: Cpl in 5th Co-2nd
Md Rgt, reduced to Pvt 10 Nov 1782. Born 1762, 1788 Md
Soldier Land assignee, pension applied for by widow.

McKINSEY, McKENSEY   Drummer   FC78, WP78, AMd, Brum, HWN.
Moses; enl 28 Apr 1778 for 3 yrs as Frederick County substitute,
in 4th Vacant Co, in GR when disbanded 01 Jan 1781, transf
to 1st Co-3rd Md Rgt, 1782: Cpl in 5th Co-2nd Md Rgt, red
to Pvt 10 Nov 1782. 1788 Md Soldier Land assignee. Born
1760, recd Drummer's ½-pay pension for life beg 1815 in
Allegany Co, widow Sarah recd Pvt's ½-pay pension beg 09
Mar 1827.

MATTRELL, MATTRIT   Drummer   WP78, 3Vac.
Adam; enl for war, in 3rd Vacant [ex-Graybill's] Co between

Oct 1777 & Mar 1778.
ROACH, ROCK   Drummer   AMd.
    John; enl 02 Mar 1778, in GR when disbanded 01 Jan 1781, transf
    to 4th Co 3rd Md Rgt, 1782: in 5th Co-2nd Md Rgt as Cpl,
    reduced to Pvt 01 May 1782.
SMITH   Drummer & Fifer WP78, 3Vac, AMd, Brum, HWN, HCP.
    Michael; from Balto Co, enl 28 Apr 1778 for war, in 3rd Vacant
    Co, in GR when disbanded 01 Jan 1781, transf to 3rd Co-3rd Md
    Rgt. 1788 Md Soldier Land assignee. Recd pension Jan 1820,
    pension appld for by widow. See also Michael Smith in
    undetermined Company.

GERMAN REGIMENT PRIVATES OF THE MARYLAND COMPANY ORIGINALLY RAISED
IN FREDERICK COUNTY AND KNOWN AS CAPTAIN FISTER'S COMPANY (JULY
1776 - JANUARY 1777), SECOND VACANT COMPANY (JANUARY 1777 - MARCH
1777), CAPTAIN LORAH'S COMPANY (MARCH 1777 - FEBRUARY 1778),
CAPTAIN HUBLEY'S COMPANY (FEBRUARY 1778 - JUNE 1779), AND CAPTAIN
BAYER'S COMPANY (JUNE 1779 - JANUARY 1781):

AARON, ARRON, ARRINGS   2Vac, WP78, AMd.
  Levi; enl 22 Apr 1776 in Md Flying Camp, reenl in GR, on duty
  01 Aug 1780.
ABELL   HFCo, 2Vac, MB79, AMd.
  John; enl 19 Jul 1776, disch 20 Jul 1779 at Ft. Wyoming, Pa.
ALEXANDER   2Vac, WP78, AMd, Brum.
  Jacob; enl 28 Jan or 01 Feb 1778 for 3 yrs, on duty 01 Aug 1780,
  prom to Sgt.
BAIRFORD   AMd.
  Edward; enl 19 Jun 1780 for 3 yrs, joined Company at
  Northumberland, Pa.
BASHT   AMd.
  William; served 3 yrs, disch 05 Aug 1779 at Ft. Wyoming, Pa.
  Known only from discharge certificate suppporting depreciation
  pay claim.
BECKERSON   HFCo.
  John; enl 1776.
BEIKER   HFCo.
  Michael; enl 1776.
BIRD   HFCo.
  John; enl 1776.
CHARLES   HFCo.
  Adam; enl 1776.
CLINTON   HFCo.
  George; enl 1776.
COLOUR   HFCo.
  Philip; enl 1776.
COPPLE   HFCo.
  Peter; enl 1776.
CORLEY, COLE   2Vac.
  Benjamin, enl 22 Aug 1776, on duty Summer 1778.
CRAMER, CRAMMER, CROUMER,
KRAMER, KREMER, CRAUMER   HFCo, 2Vac, MB79, AMd, HYCO.
  Jacob; enl 19 Jul 1776 in Frederick Co, Md, wounded at
  Battle of Monmouth 28 Jun 1778, returned to duty, disch 20 Jul
  1779. Recd pens of $96/yr in 1818 and died 19 May 1833 in York
  boro, Pa, aged 78; wife Elizabeth aged 70 in 1821.
CRONISE   HFCo, 2Vac, MB79, AMd.
  Henry; enl 01 Aug 1776, disch 24 Jul 1779 at Ft. Wyoming, Pa.
CURLEY, CURLY   MB79, AMd, WW.
  Owen; enl, des, reenl, des, courtmartialled 26 Oct 1781 at Camp
  near Yorktown, Va for des & enlisting with the enemy, sen to
  be hanged, pardoned by GW on 04 Nov 1781.
DALTON, DOLTON   FC78, 2Vac, WP78, AMd.

89

John/Jacob; enl 22 Apr 1778 for 3 yrs as Fredk Co sub, on
  duty/disch 01 Aug 1780.
DELAWTER   HFCo.
  Henry; enl 1776.
DILL   2Vac.
  Robert; enl 31 Jul 1776, on duty Summer 1778.
DORAH, DORON   AMd.
  Dinnis/Dineas; enl 26 Jun 1780 for 3 yrs, joined Company at
  Northumberland, Pa.
DYER, DAYLER   FC78, WP78, AMd.
  James; enl 02 May 1778 for 3 yrs as Fredk Co sub, on duty
  05 Sep 1778. 1788 Md Soldier Land assignee. See also James
  Dyer of undetermined Company who was transf to Invalid Corps.
EGGMAN   HFCo.
  Jacob; enl 1776.
EMERICK, AMRICK, HEMERICK   HFCo, MB79, AMd.
  Peter; enl 25 Jul 1776, disch 24 Jul 1779 at Ft. Wyoming, Pa.
ENGEL, ENGLE   HFCo, MB79, AMd.
  Bartel; enl 31 Jul 1776, died 06/29 Aug 1779 while on the
  Sullivan Expedition.
EVERLY   HFCo, AMd.
  Leonard; enl 1776, disch 02 Dec 1778.
FANTZ   HFCo.
  Jacob; enl 1776.
FARBER   HFCo.
  Jacob; enl 1776.
FETTIE   HFCo.
  Abraham; enl 1776.
FISHER   FC78, 2Vac, WP78, AMd, HWN, MdHR.
  Henry; enl 21 Apr 1778 for 3 yrs as Fredk Co sub [original
  enlistment, $60 bounty receipt, and oath with x-mark extant at
  MdHR], in GR when disbanded 01 Jan 1781, transf to 5th Co-3rd
  Md Rgt, 1782: in 5th Co-2nd Md Rgt. 1788 Md Soldier Land
  assignee, appld for pension.
FISHER   2Vac, MB79, AMd, Brum, HWN.
  Philip; enl 04 Aug 1776, disch 26 Jul 1779 at Ft. Wyoming, Pa.
  Born 1748;recd pension 04 Mar 1789 @ $40/yr, 24 Apr 1816 @
  $64/yr, 08 Apr 1818 @ $96/yr; res in Fredk Co, aged 86.
FOLIOTT, FOLLET   MB79, AMd.
  John; enl 10 Oct 1779, in GR when disbanded 01 Jan 1781, transf
  to 5th Co-3rd Md Rgt, 1782: in 5th Co-2nd Md Rgt, des 30 Jun
  1782.
FROSHOUR   HFCo.
  Adam; enl 1776.
FRYE   HFCo.
  Nicholas, enl 1776. See also Nicholas Frey in Capt
  Graybill's Co.
FULLIM, FOLLEN
FULLAM, FULHAM   FC78, 2Vac, WP78, MB79, AMd.
  Charles/John; enl 23 Apr 1778 for war as Fredk Co sub, in GR
  when disbanded 01 Jan 1781, transf to 5th Co-3rd Md Rgt, prom
  to Cpl before 28 Aug 1781. 1788 Md Soldier Land assignee.

90

GENTNER, GANTNER, KINTER   HFCo, 2Vac, MB79, AMd.
Adam; enl 19 Jul 1776, disch 20 Jul 1779 at Ft. Wyoming, Pa.
GRAFF   HFCo.
Peter; enl 1776.
HAIN, HEAN   HFCo, 2Vac.
Henry; enl 26 Jul 1776, prom to Sgt by Summer 1778.
HAMILTON   HFCo.
Anthony, enl 1776.
HAMMER   HFCo.
Jacob; enl 1776.
HARTMAN, HATMAN, HARDMAN   FC78, 2Vac, WP78, AMd, WW, P.A.
Michael; enl 20 Apr or 15 May 1778 for 3 yrs as Frederick Co
sub, in GR when disbanded 01 Jan 1781, des, courtmartialled
26 Oct 1781 at Camp near Yorktown, Va & sen to rec 100 lashes,
sen approved by GW 03 Nov 1781, 1782: in 5th Co-2nd Md Rgt.
1788 Md Soldier Land assignee, res in Armstrong Co., Pa. in
1835. See also Michael Hartman in Graybill's Co.
HAUSMAN, HOUSEMAN   HFCo, 2Vac, MB79, AMd, Adlum.
Conrad, of York, Pa.; enl 25 Jul 1776, captured at Princeton, NJ
31 Dec 1776, was Col. Hausegger's servant in captivity, retd
to GR in Jan 1777, disch 26 Jul 1779 at Ft. Wyoming, Pa.
HAUSMAN   AMd.
Michael; served 3 yrs, disch 25 Jul 1779 at Ft. Wyoming, Pa.
Known only from discharge certificate supporting depreciation
pay claim.
HAWK   HFCo.
Henry; enl 1776.
HENKEL, HINKEL, HINKLE   FCM, 2Vac, WP78.
Philip; enl 18 Jun 1778 for 9 mos as sub from Frederick Co
Militia, on duty 05 Sep 1778.
HENNINGHOUSE, HANINGHOUSE   HFCo, AMd.
Frederick; enl 1776, disch 26 Jul 1779 at Ft. Wyoming, Pa.
HERRING, FERRINS   HFCo, WP78, MB79, AMd.
Henry, enl 25 Jul 1776, disch 24 Jul 1779 at Ft. Wyoming, Pa.
HILDERBRAND   HFCo.
Henry; enl 1776.
HILL, HULL   2Vac, WP78, MB79, AMd.
Casemar/Camer/Casimer; enl 27 Feb 1778 for 3 yrs, disch 26 Jul
1779 at Ft. Wyoming, Pa.
HOCHSHILD, HOSHIED
HONSHITT, HOSHAL, HOGSHIELD   HFCo, 2Vac, MB79, AMd, HWN.
Justinus/Jesse/Jesey/John; enl 27 Jul 1776, prom to Cpl by
Summer 1778.
HUBER, HEWER, HOOVER   HFCo, 2Vac, MB79, AMd.
Peter; enl 31 Jul 1776, disch 24 Jul or 12 Oct 1779 at Ft.
Wyoming, Pa.
HUGHMORE, HUMORE
HUGHES, MOORE   FC78, 2Vac, WP78, AMd, HWN.
James/John; enl as Hugh Moore 12 May 1778 for war as Frederick
Co sub, in GR when disbanded 01 Jan 1781, transf to 3rd Co-3rd
Md Rgt. Born 1756, applied for pension.
IMFELD   HFCo.

John; enl 1776.
INSINGMINGER   HFCo.
  Philip; enl 1776.
JOHNSON, JONSON   FC78, 2Vac, WP78, MB79, AMd, WW.
  James; enl 20 May 1778 for war as Frederick Co sub, des about
  Sep 1779, courtmartialled 26 Oct 1781 at Camp near Yorktown,
  Va. for desertion & enlisting with the enemy, sentenced to be
  hanged, pardoned by GW 04 Nov 1781.
KEPPLINGER   FCM, 2Vac, WP78, AMd.
  Christopher/Christofiel/Christian; enl 18 Jun 1778 for 9 mos as
  sub from Frederick Co Militia, disch 22 Mar 1779 at Easton,
  Pa.
KEPPHARD, KEEPHART   WP78, MB79, AMd.
  George, enl 13 Feb 1778 for 3 yrs, des before 05 Sép 1778.
KETTLE   MB79, AMd, HWN, BSC.
  Abraham; enl 03 Apr 1779, in GR when disbanded 01 Jan 1781,
  transf to 5th Co-3rd Md Rgt, 1782: in 5th Co-2nd Md Rgt. 1788
  Md Soldier Land assignee. Born 1762, applied for pension.
KING   HFCo.
  Mathias; enl 1776.
KLEIN   HFCo.
  Gottlieb; enl 1776.
KLEIN, KLINE, CLINE   HFCo, 2Vac, MB79, AMd, MdHR.
  John; enl 11 Aug 1776, disch 12 Oct 1779 at Tioga, Pa. Pvt's
  ½-pay for life pension recd by widow Mary M. in Frederick Co
  in 1833.
KUNTZ   HFCo.
  Jacob; enl 1776.
KUNTZ, CUNTZ,
KOONS, CONES   HFCo, 2Vac, MB79, AMd.
  Peter; enl 25 Jul 1776, reenl 01 Jun 1778, in GR when disbanded
  01 Jan 1781,transf to 5th Co-3rd Md Rgt, 1782: in in 5th
  Co-2nd Md Rgt, des 11 Feb 1782.
KURTZ   HFCo.
  Jacob; enl 1776.
LAGO, LEAGO   AMd.
  Charles; enl 01 Apr 1780 for 3 yrs, joined Company at
  Northumberland,Pa., in GR when disbanded 01 Jan 1781, transf
  to 2nd Co-3rd Md Rgt, 1782: in 5th Co-2nd Md Rgt. 1788 Md
  Soldier Land assignee.
LEATHER, LADDER   HFCo, 2Vac, MB79.
  John; enl 03 Aug 1776, prom to Sgt.
LUDWICK   HFCo, 2Vac, MB79, AMd.
  Leonard; enl 03 Aug 1776, disch 24 Jul 1779 at Ft. Wyoming, Pa.
MALADY, MALLADAY, MATODY   FC78, 2Vac, MB79, AMd.
  John; enl 02 May 1778 for war as Frederick Co sub, in GR when
  disbanded 01 Jan 1781, transf to 4th Co-3rd Md Rgt, 1782: in
  5th Co-2nd Md Rgt: "not heard of since Jun 1782 muster."
MAROLF, MAROLE   2Vac, MB79, AMd.
  Rudolph; enl 21 Jul 1776, disch 20 Jul 1779 at Ft. Wyoming, Pa.
MAHONEY, MEHONEY   WP78, 2Vac, MB79, AMd.
  Thomas; enl 02 Apr or 13 May 1778 for 3 yrs, on duty Oct 1779.

92

1788 Md Soldier Land assignee.
MILLER   FCM, WP78, 2Vac.
  Abraham; enl 18 Jul 1778 for 9 mos as sub from Frederick Co
  Militia.
MILLER   HFCo.
  Anthony; enl 1776.
MILLER   HFCo, 2Vac, MB79, AMd.
  Jacob, Sr.; enl 19 Jul 1776, disch 20 Jul 1779 at Ft. Wyoming,
  Pa.
MILLER   2Vac, MB79, AMd.
  Jacob, Jr.; enl 25 Jul 1776, disch 20 Jul 1779 at Ft. Wyoming,
  Pa.
MILLER   HFCo, AMd, MdDAR.
  John; enl 1776, des before Dec 1776. Applied for deprec pay by
  1783. Born ca 1750 in Germany, died March 1795 in Md.
MITTAG, MEDDACK   HFCo, Brum, HWN.
  Frederick; enl 1776. Born 1728, applied for pension Jan 1820.
MOSER   HFCo, 2Vac, MB79, AMd.
  Michael; enl 26/30 Jul 1776, disch 24 Jul 1779 at Ft. Wyoming,
  Pa.
NEVITT, NEVET   AMd.
  John; enl 13 Apr 1780 for 3 yrs, joined Company at
  Northumberland, Pa., disch 13 Nov 1780, 1782: in 5th Co-2nd Md
  Rgt.
POLEHOUSE,
POLLHOUSE, COLHONS   HFCo, WP78, 2Vac, MB79, AMd, JCC.
  Thomas; enl 1776, his bill for bleeding 95 Pvts of GR approved
  by Congress 26 Apr 1777, prom to Cpl 01 Aug 1779. 1788 Md
  Soldier Land assignee. See also Thomas Pollhouse in
  undetermined Company list.
RIDENOUR, REDNOUR,
RIDENHOUR, RIELY   FCM, WP78, 2Vac, AMd.
  Bernard; enl 03/18 Jun 1778 for 9 mos as sub from Frederick Co
  Militia, disch 06 Nov 1780.
RIDENOUR   HFCo.
  John; enl 1776.
RIGGNAGEL,
RICKNOGEL, RICKNAGLE   2Vac, MB79, AMd.
  Jacob; enl 01 Aug 1776, disch 26 Jul 1779 at Ft. Wyoming, Pa.
RINGER   HFCo.
  John; enl 1776.
RITMIRE,
RIGHTMYER, RHYTMIRE   2Vac, MB79, AMd.
  Michael; enl 01 Feb 1780 for 3 yrs, joined Company at
  Northumberland,Pa., in GR when disbanded 01 Jan 1781, transf
  to 5th Co-3rd Md Rgt, 1782: in 5th Co-2nd Md Rgt. 1788 Md
  Soldier Land assignee.
ROBINSON, ROBERSON   2Vac, MB79, AMd.
  Andrew; enl 25 Jul 1776, prom to Cpl.
ROBINSON, ROBERSON   HFCo, 2Vac, MB79, AMd.
  Edward; enl 25 Jul 1776, disch 20 Jul 1779 at Ft. Wyoming, Pa.
ROGERS   AMd.

John; enl 10 Apr 1780 for 3 yrs, joined Company at
Northumberland, Pa.
SHATZ, SHOTS, SHOTZ   HFCo, 2Vac, MB79, AMd, Brum, HWN.
John; enl 29 Jul 1776, prom to Cpl.
SHEAFER   HFCo.
Christian; enl 1776.
SHEAFER   HFCo.
Jacob; enl 1776.
SHOEMAKER   WP78, 2Vac, MB79, AMd.
Samuel Frederick; enl 08 May 1778 for war, prom to Cpl 01 Aug
1779.
SHOEMAKER   MB79.
Michael; enl 1776, disch 24 Jul 1779 at Ft. Wyoming, Pa.
SHOTTER   HFCo.
Valentine, enl 1776.
SHRANZ   HFCo.
George; enl 1776.
SILVER   AMd.
George; enl 31 Mar 1779 for 3 yrs, joined Company at
Northumberland, Pa.,in GR when disbanded 01 Jan 1781, transf
to 5th Co-3rd Md Rgt, 1782: in 5th Co-2nd Md Rgt. 1788 Md
Soldier Land assignee.
STANLEY, STANDLY, SLENDER   HFCo, 2vac, MB79, AMd.
Christopher/Christofiel; enl 19 Jul 1776, prom to Cpl.
SMADRON, SMADERN   WP78, 2Vac.
Jacob; enl 21 Apr 1776, on duty 05 Sep 1778.
SMELTZER   HFCo.
Adam; enl 1776.
SMITH   FC78, WP78, 2Vac, AMd, ML.
Alexander; enl 20 May 1778 for war as Frederick Co sub, named
Surgeon's Mate 01 Aug 1778, declared supernumerary 01 Jan
1781.
SMITH   HFCo.
Henry; enl Aug 1776, disch 25 Aug 1779 at Tioga, Pa.
SNIDER   HFCo, 2Vac, MB79, AMd.
John; enl 01 Aug 1776, disch 24 Jul 1779 at Ft. Wyoming, Pa.
SNIDER   HFCo.
William; enl 1776.
STEINER, STONER   HFCo, MB79, AMd.
Michael; enl 19 Jul 1776, disch 12 Oct 1779 at Tioga, Pa.
STRIDER, STUDER,
STOTER, STOUDER   HFCo, MB79, AMd, Brum, HWN.
Philip; enl 11 Aug 1776, disch 24 Jul 1779 at Ft. Wyoming, Pa.
Born 1752, recd Pvt's ½-pay for life pension beg Dec 1815.
STUDDLEMIER, STOTTLEMEYER   HFCo, HWN.
George; enl 1776. Born 1759; applied for pension, rejected due
to desertion.
TABLER   HFCo.
Jacob; enl 1776.
TAYLOR   2Vac, MB79, AMd.
William; enl 20 Aug 1776, disch 12 Oct 1779 between Tioga & Ft.
Wyoming, Pa.

TIMBLER, TIMHEN, TEMBLIN   FC78, WP78, 2Vac, AMd.
   John; enl 28 Apr 1778 for 3 yrs as Frederick Co sub, on duty
   01 Aug 1780.
WACHTEL, WASHTEL   HFCo, WP78, 2Vac, MB79, AMd.
   John; enl 30 Jul 1776, disch 12/24 Oct 1779 at Tioga or Ft.
   Wyoming, Pa.
WADE   FC78, WP78, 2Vac, MB79, AMd.
   John; enl 05 May 1778 for war as Frederick Co sub, in GR when
   disbanded 01 Jan 1781, transf to 4th Co-3rd Md Rgt, 1782: in
   5th Co-2nd Md Rgt. 1788 Md Soldier Land assignee.
WATKINS   HFCo.
   Martin; enl 1776.
WEAVER   HFCo.
   Jacob; enl 1776.
WESSINGER,
VISINGER, WITSINGER   HFCo, 2Vac, MB79, AMd, HWN.
   Ludwig; enl 04 Aug 1776, disch 20 Jul 1779 at Ft. Wyoming, Pa.
   Applied for pension.
ZIEGLER   HFCo.
   Henry; enl 1776.
ZIMMERMAN   HFCo, 2Vac, MB79, AMd.
   John; enl 25 Jul 1776, disch 12 Oct 1779 at Ft. Wyoming, Pa.

GERMAN REGIMENT PRIVATES OF THE MARYLAND COMPANY ORIGINALLY RAISED
IN FREDERICK (NOW WASHINGTON) COUNTY AND KNOWN AS CAPTAIN HEISER'S
COMPANY (JULY 1776 - MAY 1778), FOURTH VACANT COMPANY (MAY 177-?),
AND LT COL WELTNER'S COMPANY (? - JANUARY 1781):

ARMSTRONG   WHCo, 5-77, 4Vac, 79PR, AMd.
   John; enl 1776 for 2 yrs [?], reenl 27 Jul 1778 for 1 yr, disch
   26 Jul 1779 at Ft. Wyoming, Pa.
ASHLEY   FC78, 4Vac, WP78, 79PR, AMd.
   James W. L.; enl 25 Apr 1778 for war as Frederick County
   substitute, in GR when disbanded 01 Jan 1781, transf to 3rd
   Co-3rd Md Rgt, 1782: Cpl in 5th Co-2nd Md Rgt. 1788 Md
   Soldier Land assignee.
BAIRD, BEARD   WHCo, 5-77.
   Nicholas; enl 1776, on duty May 1777.
BANTZ, BONTZ   FCM, 4Vac, WP78.
   George; enl 18 Jun 1778 for 9 mos as substitute from Frederick
   County Militia, disch 22 Mar 1779 at Easton, Pa.
BELZHOOVER   WHCo, 5-77, 4Vac, 79PR, AMd.
   Jacob; enl 26 Jul 1776, disch 26 Jul 1779 at Ft. Wyoming, Pa.
BENDER, PAINTER,
BENTER, PAINTHER   WHCo, 5-77, 4Vac, 79PR, HWN.
   Henry; enl 27 Jul 1776, disch 12 Oct 1779 at Ft. Wyoming, Pa.
   Born 1748, pension applied for by widow.
BENTER,
BENNER, PAINTER   WHCo, 5-77, 4Vac, 79PR, AMd, Brum, HWN.
   Melcher/Melchior/Michael; enl 17 Jul 1776, disch 17 Jul 1779 at
   Ft. Wyoming, Pa. Born 1739, pension of Pvt's ½-pay for life
   awarded to widow Mary in Washington, DC 01 Apr 1839 as of 01
   Jan 1839.
BISHOP   WHCo, 4Vac, 79PR, AMd, HWN.
   Jacob; enl 26 Jul 1776, disch 26 Jul 1779 at Ft. Wyoming, Pa.
   Born 1756, pension applied for by widow.
BOWARD   WHCo, 5-77, AMd.
   Michael; enl 1776, disch 16 Jul 1779 at Ft. Wyoming, Pa.
BRUCHER, BREECHER   WHCo, 5-77, 79PR, AMd.
   John; enl 17 Jul 1776, prom to Cpl before 22 May 1777.
BUCH   WHCo, 5-77.
   George; enl 1776, on duty May 1777. See also George Buch in
   Keyports' Co.
BURNEY   WHCo, 5-77.
   Thomas; enl 1776, des before 23 Oct 1776, on duty May 1777.
CAMBLER, CAMLER
CAMLEE, GAMBLER   WHCo, 5-77, 4Vac, 79PR, AMd.
   Michael; enl 26 Jul 1776, on duty Oct 1779, paid 01 Jan 1781.
CAVIN, GAVIN, GAVAN   4Vac, 79PR, AMd.
   Francis; enl 04 Aug 1778, disch 26 Jul 1779 at Ft. Wyoming, Pa.
CLIFTON   WHCo, 5-77, 4Vac, 79PR, HWN.
   Thomas; enl 03 Aug 1776, disch 26 Jul 1779 at Ft. Wyoming, Pa.
   Applied for pension.
CRAFFT, CROFT,

KROFT, KRAFT   WHCo, 5-77, 4Vac, 79PR, HWN.
   John; enl 27 Jul 1776, disch 24 Jul 1779 at Ft. Wyoming, Pa.
   Pension applied for by widow.
CROPP, GROOP, GRUPP   WHCo, 5-77, 4Vac, 79PR, AMd.
   John; enl 11 Aug 1776, disch 26 Jul 1779 at Ft. Wyoming, Pa.
DUNCAN   WHCo, 4Vac, 79PR, AMd.
   James; enl 16 Jul 1776, disch 16 Jul 1779 at Ft. Wyoming, Pa.
DUNKLE   WHCo, 5-77.
   Mathias; enl 1776, on duty May 1777.
ETNIER, ITNIER   WHCo, 4Vac, 79PR, AMd.
   John; enl 16 Jul 1776, disch 26 Jul 1779 at Ft. Wyoming, Pa.
FILLER, FILTER   WHCo, 5-77, 4Vac, 79PR, AMd, HWN.
   Frederick; enl Jul 1776 for 2 yrs [?], reenl 09 Jul 1778 for 1
   yr, disch 26 Jul 1779 at Ft. Wyoming, Pa.
FISHER   WHCo, 5-77.
   Balser; enl 1776, died 15 Mar 1777.
FISHER   WHCo, 5-77, 4Vac, 79PR, AMd, Brum.
   Philip; enl 04 Aug 1776 for 2 yrs [?], reenl 09 Aug 1778 for 1
   yr, disch 24/26 Jul 1779 at Ft. Wyoming, Pa. Received
   pension. See also Philip Fisher in Capt Fister's Co.
FLECK, FLIET, FLICK   WHCo, 5-77, 4Vac, 79PR, AMd.
   John; enl 02 Aug 1776, disch 26 Jul 1779 at Ft. Wyoming, Pa.
FLEEGERT   5-77.
   Archibald; died in Philadelphia.
FLEMMING, FLEMON   4Vac, 79PR, AMd.
   Patrick; enl 09 Aug 1776, disch 09 Aug 1779 at Tioga, Pa. Was
   issued Md depreciation pay certificates twice under different
   name spellings.
FOGLE   WHCo, 5-77.
   John; enl 1776, on duty May 1777.
FOGLER   WHCo, 5-77, Brum.
   Simon; enl 1776, on duty May 1777. Received pension @ $20/yr
   from 04 Sep 1793.
FOWEE   WHCo.
   Jacob; enl 1776, des before 23 Oct 1776.
FRIEND   WHCo, 5-77.
   Tobias; enl 1776, des before 23 Oct 1776, on duty May 1777.
FURNIER, FOURNIER, FORNEY WHCo, 5-77, 4Vac, 79PR, AMd.
   James; enl Jul 1776 for 2 yrs [?], reenl 26 Jul 1778 for 1 yr,
   disch 26 Jul 1779 Ft. Wyoming, Pa.
GITTING   WHCo, 5-77.
   Peter; enl 28 Jul 1776, died 18 Mar 1777.
GRASS   WHCo, 5-77.
   Jacob; enl 1776, on duty May 1777.
GREATHOUSE   WHCo, 5-77.
   Jacob; enl 1776, des before 23 Oct 1776, on duty May 1777.
GREECHBAUM   WHCo, 5-77.
   Philip; enl 1776, on duty May 1777.
HARMONY   WHCo, 5-77.
   George; enl 1776, On duty May 1777.
HARTNESS   WHCo, 5-77.
   Robert; enl 1776, des before 23 Oct 1776, on duty May 1777.

HECKET, HACKET, HOCKETT   WHCo, 5-77, 4Vac, 79PR, AMd.
   Jonathan; enl 18 Jul 1776, des 25 Aug 1779 at Tioga, Pa.
HEEFNER, HEFNER   WHCo, 5-77, 4Vac, 79PR, AMd, P.A.,HWN.
   Jacob; enl 18 Aug 1776, disch 12 Oct 1779 at Ft. Wyoming, Pa.
   Born 1757, resided in Richland County, Ohio in 1834, aged 77.
   Pension applied for by widow.
HOOVER, HAVER   WHCo, 5-77, 4Vac, 79PR, AMd.
   Jacob; enl Jul 1776 for 2 yrs [?], reenl 16 Jul 1778 for 1 yr,
   wagoner, disch 12 Oct 1779 at Ft. Wyoming, Pa.
HOTTFIELD, HATFIELD   WHCo, 5-77, 4Vac, 79PR, AMd.
   John; enl 13 Aug 1776, disch 26 Jul 1779 at Ft. Wyoming, Pa.
HOYLE, HOGLE,
HILES, STOYLE   WHCo, 5-77, 4Vac, 79PR, AMd, P.A.
   Conrad; enl 20 Jul 1776, disch 20 Jul 1779 at Ft. Wyoming, Pa.
   Died 17 May 1821 in Fayette County, Pa, aged 61.
KIBLER, KEBLER, KIBBER   WHCo, 5-77, 4Vac, 79PR, AMd, HWN.
   John; enl 27 Jul 1776, disch 26 Jul 1779 at Ft. Wyoming, Pa.
   Born 1760; pension applied for by widow.
KEYSER, GIESER, KEYER   WHCo, 5-77, 4Vac, 79PR, AMd.
   Mathias; enl 10 Aug 1776, des Jul 1779, disch 26 Jul 1779 at Ft.
   Wyoming, Pa.
KLEIN, KLINE, KLEINE   WHCo, 5-77, 4Vac, 79PR, AMd.
   Jacob; enl 01 Aug 1776, disch 26 Jul 1779 at Ft. Wyoming,
   Pa, or disch 26 Aug 1780.
LIESER, LEISER   WHCo, 5-77.
   Adam; enl 1776, des before 23 Oct 1776, on duty May 1777.
LOCHER, LOCKER   WHCo, 5-77, 4Vac, 79PR, AMd.
   Frederick; enl 05 Aug 1776, disch 09 Aug 1779 at Tioga, Pa.
MASSER, MOSER,
MOSEN, MOSES   FC78, 4Vac, WP78, 79PR, HWN, BSC.
   Jacob, enl 12 May 1778 for 3 yrs as Frederick County substitute,
   on duty Oct 1779. 1788 Md Soldier Land assignee. Pension
   applied for by widow.
METZ, METTZ   WHCo, 5-77.
   John; enl 1776, des before 23 Oct 1776, on duty May 1777.
MICHAEL   WHCo, 5-77, 4Vac, 79PR, AMd.
   Henry; enl 22 Aug 1776, disch 26 Jul 1779 at Ft. Wyoming, Pa.
MICHAEL   WHCo, 5-77, 79PR.
   John; enl 16 Jul 1776, prom to Cpl after 22 May 1777.
MILLER   WHCo, 5-77.
   George; enl 1776, on duty May 1777.
MYERS   WHCo, 5-77.
   Francis; enl 1776, on duty May 1777.
O'QUINN, O'QUYN, O'QYNN   FC78, 4Vac, WP78, AMd, P.A.
   Richard; enl 01 May 1778 for war as Frederick County substitute,
   transf to Invalid Corps before 01 Aug 1780, disch 31 Dec 1781.
   Was 1788 Md Soldier Land assignee. See also Richard O'Quinn
   in undetermined Md Co.
PIFFER, FIFER   5-77, HWN.
   Jacob; on duty May 1777. Born 1754; pension applied for by
   widow.
PIFFER   WHCo, 5-77.

Martin; enl 1776, des before 23 Oct 1776, on duty May 1777.
POINTER   79PR, AMd.
William; des, disch 13 Nov 1780.
QUEER, QUIR   WHCo, 5-77, 4Vac, 79PR.
Henry; enl 18 Jul 1776, disch 29 Jul 1779 at Ft. Wyoming, Pa.
REAVER, REEVER,
RAVER, RAYBERT   WHCo, 5-77, 4Vac, 79PR, AMd.
  Christian/Stuffle; enl 27 Jul 1776, disch 26 Jul 1779 at Ft.
  Wyoming, Pa.
RIGGLEMAN, REGLIMAN   WHCo, 5-77, 4Vac, 79PR, AMd.
  George; enl 18 Aug 1776, disch 12 Oct 1779 at Ft. Wyoming, Pa.
ROBERTSON, ROBINSON   WHCo, 5-77.
  John; enl 1776, on duty May 1777.
ROTH, ROTHE   WHCo, 5-77.
  John; enl 1776, on duty May 1777.
ROWLANDS   FCM, 4Vac, WP78, AMd.
  Thomas; enl 06 Jun 1778 for 9 mos as a substitute from the
  Frederick County Militia, on duty 05 Sep 1778.
SAYLOR, SAILOR, TAYLOR   WHCo, 4Vac, 79PR, AMd.
  Alexander; enl 28 Jul 1776, disch 09 Aug 1779 at Tioga, Pa.
SHEESE   WHCo, 5-77.
  Peter; enl 1776, des before 23 Oct 1776, on duty May 1777.
SHOEMAKER   WHCo, 5-77.
  John; enl 1776, des before 23 Oct 1776, on duty May 1777.
SMITH   WHCo, 5-77.
  Eberhart, enl 1776, on duty May 1777.
SMITH   FC78, 4Vac, WP78, 79PR, AMd, Brum.
  James; enl 20 May 1778 for war as Frederick County substitute,
  prom to Cpl 01 Aug 1779.
SMITH   WHCo, 5-77, 4Vac, 79PR.
  John; enl 27 Jul 1776, disch 10 Aug 1779 at Tioga, Pa.
SMITHLY   WHCo, AMd.
  John; enl 02 Aug 1776, disch 12 Oct 1779 at Ft. Wyoming, Pa.
SMITHLY   WHCo, 4Vac, 79PR, AMd.
  Philip, enl 02 Aug 1776, disch 12 Oct 1779 at Ft. Wyoming, Pa.
STATLER, STOTLER, STALTER WHCo, 5-77, 4Vac, 79PR, AMd, HWN.
  Henry; enl 04 Aug 1776, disch 12 Oct 1779 at Ft. Wyoming, Pa.
  Pension applied for by widow.
STONEBREAKER   WHCo, 5-77, 79PR, AMd, P.A.
  Adam, of Hagerstown; enl 22 Aug 1776, prom to Cpl after 22
  May 1777.
STRAYLEY   WHCo.
  Wendel; enl before 23 Oct 1776, died 15 Jan 1777.
STROAM, STRAAM   WHCo, 5-77, 4Vac, 79PR, AMd.
  Henry; enl 17 Jul 1776, disch 17 Jul 1779 at Ft. Wyoming, Pa.
SWEITZER, SWITZER, SCHWIDZER WHCo, 5-77, 4Vac, 79PR, AMd.
  Frederick; enl 1776 for 2 yrs [?], missing at Bonumtown, NJ
  10 May 1777, returned, reenl 16 Jul 1778 for 1 yr, disch 16
  Jul 1779 at Ft. Wyoming, Pa.
TOMM, TOM   WHCo, 5-77, 4Vac, AMd, P.A.,Brum,HWN.
  Henry; enl 1776 for 2 yrs [?], in Hospital at Courthouse,
  Reading, Pa 17 Nov 1777, reenl 27 Jul 1778, transf to Invalid

Corps. Received pension of $20/yr from 04 Mar 1794 & $48/yr from 24 Apr 1816.

WAGNER WHCo, 5-77, 4Vac, 79PR, AMd.
Christopher/Stuffle; enl 10 Aug 1776, disch 12 Oct 1779 at Ft. Wyoming, Pa.

WAGNER, WAGGONER WHCo, 5-77, 4Vac, P.A.
Henry; enl 1776, badly wounded in the leg at Battle of Germantown 04 Oct 1777, reenl 05 Aug 1778. Applied for pension.

WEAVER WHCo, 5-77, 4Vac, 79PR, HWN.
Michael; enl 19 Jul 1776, disch 26 Jul 1779 at Ft. Wyoming, Pa. Born 1751; applied for pension.

WILHELM WHCo, 5-77, 4Vac, 79PR, AMd, P.A., HWN.
George; enl 17 Jul 1776, disch 17 Jul 1779 at Ft. Wyoming, Pa. Born 1753; applied for pension; died in Fayette County, Pa, aged 66.

WISE WHCo, 5-77.
George; enl 1776, on duty May 1777.

YEAKLY, YAKELY, YOCKLEY, JACKELL WHCo, 5-77, 4Vac, 79PR, AMd.
Michael; enl 22 Jul 1776, disch 17 Jul 1779 at Ft. Wyoming, Pa. Applied for depreciation pay by Mar 1785.

YOUNG WHCo, 5-77.
Godfried, enl 1776, on duty May 1777.

GERMAN REGIMENT PRIVATES OF THE MARYLAND COMPANY ORIGINALLY RAISED IN BALTIMORE COUNTY AND KNOWN AS CAPTAIN GRAYBILL'S COMPANY (JULY 1776 -MARCH 1778), THIRD VACANT COMPANY (MARCH 1778 - at least JULY 1778), AND CAPTAIN MYER'S COMPANY (after JULY 1778 - JANUARY 1781):

ALTIMUS, ALTERMAS   GAB, PGCo.
William; enl 1776, allotted 20 shillings/mo of pay to wife, on duty 26 Jan 1777.
ANDREAS, ANDREWS   GAB, PGCo, AMd, HCP.
Wendell/Vendel; enl Jul 1776 from Balto Town Militia Batl., on duty 27 Nov 1776. Appld for depreciation pay by 1783, but "not found on any muster roll for 1779."
APPLE, APPEL   GAB, PGCo.
Christian; enl 1776, on duty 06 Jan 1777.
ARNOLD   FCM, WP78, 3Vac, AMd, HWN.
George; enl 02/18 Jun 1778 for 9 mos as substitute from Frederick County Militia, disch 22 Mar 1779. Born 1751, pension applied for by widow.
BATES, BEATTYS   FCM, WP78, 3Vac, AMd.
Philip; enl 03/18 Jun 1778 for 9 mos as substitute from Frederick County Militia, disch 22 Mar 1779 at Easton, Pa.
BAKER, BACKER   GAB, PGCo, 3-78, AMd, HCP.
Peter; enl 15 Jul 1776 from Balto Town Militia Batl, allotted 25 shillings/mo of pay to wife Christina, disch 15 Jul 1779 from Capt Myers' Co.
BOYER, BYER   GAB, HCP.
Mathias; enl Jul 1776 from Balto Town Militia Batl, allotted 12 shillings/mo of pay to mother, on duty 19 Oct 1776.
BURKE   GAB, PGCo.
Jacob; enl 1776, disch soon after.
CAHILL   FC78, WP78, 3Vac, AMd.
Timothy/James; enl 27 Apr 1778 for war as Frederick County substitute, in GR when disbanded 01 Jan 1781, transf to Md Rgt, 1782: in 5th Co-2nd Md Rgt: "not heard of since Jun 1782 muster." 1788 Md Soldier Land assignee.
CAPPELLE, CAPLE, CAPEL   GAB, PGCo, 3-78, HCP
James; enl 15 Jul 1776 from Balto Town Militia Batl, on duty 03 Apr 1778.
CASTNER, CASNER   FC78, WP78, 3Vac, P.A., AMd, CMOB.
Christian; enl 20 May 1778 for war as Frederick County substitute, courtmartialled 09 Jul 1779 at Ft. Wyoming, Pa for speaking disrespectfully of an officer & sentenced to run regimental gauntlet twice, disch 01 Jan 1781. A Catharina and Catty Castner were with Army at Tioga, Pa. in Aug80, see courtmartial of Pvt John Ammersly of Keeports' Co.
CHARLES see CHARREL   PGCo.
CHARRELL, CHERRELL   GAB, PGCo.
Charles; enl 1776, on duty 02 Dec 1776. Applied for depreciation pay by 1785, but "not found on any muster rolls for 1779."

CITZINGER see ETTZINGER   HCP
COLE   FC78, WP78, 3Vac, AMd.
  Benjamin; enlisted 20 May 1778 for war as Frederick County
    substitute, in GR when disbanded 01 Jan 1781, transf to Md
    Rgt, 1782: Cpl in 5th Co-2nd Md Rgt. 1788 Md Soldier Land
    assignee.
CRETHORN, CRETHO,
CREDO, CROTHORN   3-78, 3Vac, AMd.
  George; enl 02 Aug 1776 or Apr 1777, in GR when disbanded
    01 Jan 1781, transf to 3rd Co-3rd Md Rgt.
CROWDER, CROWER, KROMER   GAB, PGCo, 3-78, 3Vac, AMd, HCP.
  Rudolph; enl 15 Jul 1776 from Balto Town Militia Batl, disch
    15 Jul 1779 at Ft. Wyoming, Pa.
CROWLEY, GROWLEY   GAB, PGCo, 3-78, 3Vac, AMd.
  Michael; enl 15 Aug 1776, disch 14 Aug 1779 at Tioga, Pa.
CUNIUS, CUNNIUS   GAB, PGCo.
  William; enl 1776, on duty 27 Nov 1776.
DANROTH   PGCo, 3Vac, AMd.
  Gottlieb/Godlip; enl 02 Aug 1776, disch 30 Jul 1779 prob at Ft.
    Wyoming, Pa.
DANROTH   GAB, PGCo.
  Lorentz; enl 1776, on duty 02 Dec 1776.
DECKER   GAB, PGCo.
  Henry; enl 1776, allotted 20 shillings/mo of pay to wife, on
    duty 27 Nov 1776.
DEITCH, DYCHE,
DYCH, DRETCH   GAB, PGCo, 3Vac, AMd.
  John Bartholomew; enl 14 Jul 1776, disch 20 Jul 1779 at Ft.
    Wyoming, Pa.
DOWNEY, TAWNEY, TOWNEY   GAB, PGCo.
  Frederick; enl 1776, on duty 01 Dec 1776 at Phila.
ETTSPERGER,
ELZBERGER, ETTZPERGER
ETCHBERGER EBEBERGER   GAB, PGCO, 3-78, 3Vac, AMd, Brum.
  Wolfgang; enl 17 Jul 1776, disch 16 Jul 1779 at Ft. Wyoming, Pa.
    Received pension begining Jan 1820.
ESTIN, ESLING,
ELSING, ESTING   3-78, 3Vac, AMd.
  Paul; enl 30 Jul 1776, disch 30 Jul 1779 at Ft. Wyoming, Pa.
ETTER, ETTEER   GAB, PGCo, 3-78, 3Vac, AMd.
  Jacob; enl 15 Jul 1776, promoted to Cpl before Mar 1778, disch
    15 Jul 1779 at Ft. Wyoming, Pa.
ETTZINGER   PGCo, HCP.
  Wolfgang; enl Jul 1776 from Balto Town Militia Batl.
EISEL, EISSELL,
EYSSEL, EYSEL   GAB, PGCo, 3-78, AMd, Brum, HWN.
  Johannes/John; enl 1776, disch 11 Aug 1779 at Ft. Wyoming, Pa.
    Born 1756. Received pension beg Jan 1820, recd ½-pay for
    life 09 Mar 1832 at Balto.
FENNELL, FANNELL   FC78, WP78, 3Vac, AMd.
  John; enl 20/21 May 1778 for war as Frederick County
    substitute, in GR when disbanded 01 Jan 1781, transf to 5th

Co-3rd Md Rgt, 1782: in 5th Co-2nd Md Rgt: sick at Annapolis.
1788 Md Soldier Land assignee.

FINK, FINCH   3-78, 3Vac, AMd.
  David; enl 07 Aug 1776, disch 07 Aug 1779 at Tioga, Pa.

FRANTZ   GAB, PGCo, 3-78, 3Vac, AMd, HCP.
  Abraham, enlJul 1776 from Balto Town Militia Batl, disch 19
  Jul 1779 at Ft. Wyoming, Pa.

FREY   GAB, PGCo.
  Nicholas; enl 1776, disch soon after. See also Nicholas Frye
  in Capt Fister's Co.

FREYMILLER,
FRYMILLER, FEYMILLER   GAB, PGCo, 3-78, 3Vac, AMd, HCP.
  Jacob; enl 15 Jul 1776 from Balto Town Militia Batl, disch
  15 Jul 1779 at Ft. Wyoming, Pa.

GAUL   FC78, WP78, 3Vac, AMd.
  Richard; enl 16 May 1778 for 3 yrs as Frederick County
  substitute, on duty 01 Aug 1780, prom to Sgt.

GOOD   3Vac.
  George; enl 19 Jun 1778.

GORR, GORE, GOAR   GAB, PGCo, AMd.
  Andrew; enl 1776, on duty 02 Dec 1776. Applied for depreciation
  pay by 1785, but "not found on any muster rolls for 1779.

HALFPENNY   FC78, WP78, 3Vac, AMd.
  Thomas; enl 22 Apr 1778 for 3 yrs as Frederick County
  substitute, on duty 05 Sep 1778.

HALLER   GAB, PGCo, 3-78, 3Vac, AMd, HCP.
  Frederick William/Welhelm; enl 18 Jul 1776 from Balto Town
  Militia Batl, disch 18 Jul 1779 at Ft. Wyoming, Pa.

HARDSTONE,
HARDENSTEIN, HARTENSTEIN   GAB, PGCo, HCP.
  Jacob/John; enl Jul 1776 from Balto Town Militia Batl, on duty
  05 Oct 1776.

HARDY   GAB.
  William; enl 1776, on duty 02 Dec 1776

HARGERODER, HERGERODER   GAB, PGCo.
  Henry; enl 1776, on duty 27 Nov 1776. [See also Henry
  Hargrader/Hergood of Burchardt's (Pa) Co.]

HARLEY, HEARLY   GAB, PGCo, 3-78, 3Vac, AMd.
  Johannes/John; enl 18/19 Jul 1776, disch 18/30 Jul 1779 at Ft.
  Wyoming, Pa.

HARTMAN   GAB, PGCo, HCP.
  Henry; enl Jul 1776 from Balto Town Militia Batl, on duty
  02 Dec 1776.

HARTMAN, HATMAN, HARDMAN   AMd, HCP.
  Michael; served 3 yrs, disch 17 Jul 1779 at Ft. Wyoming, Pa.
  Submitted discharge, but could not be found on 1779 muster
  rolls in 1785 toverify service for depreciation pay. 1788 Md
  Soldier Land Assignee. Born 1760.

HENDRICKS, HENDRICKSON   FCM, WP78, 3Vac, AMd.
  Albert; enl 03/18 Jun 1778 for 9 mos as substitute from
  Frederick County Militia, on duty 05 Sep 1778.

HOFFMAN   GAB, PGCo, HCP.

Jacob; enl 1776, on duty 02 Dec 1776. Resided on Bridge St in Balto, found dead in cellar in Jan 1810.

HOOK   GAB, PGCo, 3-78, 3Vac, AMd, Brum, HWN, HCP.
Joseph; in Balto Co [Militia] Rgt #36, enl in GR 31 Jul 1776, prom to Cpl before Mar 1778.

HULING   GAB, PGCo, 3-78.
Michael; enl 1776, died 02 Feb 1778 at White Plains, NY.

JOHNSTON   FC78, WP78, 3Vac, AMd.
William; enl 16 May 1778 for 3 yrs as Frederick County substitute, on duty as Pvt 05 Sep 1778, prom to Sgt.

KANTZ, KAUTZ,
KUNTZ, SHANTZ   GAB, PGCo, 3-78, 3Vac, AMd, HCP.
Philip; enl 20/25 Jul 1776 from Balto Town Militia Batl, disch 15 Jul 1779 at Ft. Wyoming, Pa.

KAUFFMAN, CAUFMAN, COFFMAN   FC78, WP78, 3Vac, AMd.
Jacob; enl 10 May 1778 for 3 yrs as Frederick County substitute, in GR when disbanded 01 Jan 1781, transf to 5th Co-3rd Md Rgt, 1782: in 5th Co-2nd Md Rgt, deserted 01 Jul 1782.

KEMMELSTONE, See Sgt RUMMELSON   HCP.

KEMP   AMd.
Wilhelm; served 3 yrs, disch 23 Jul 1779 at Ft. Wyoming, Pa. Submitted discharge, but could not be found on 1779 muster rolls in 1785 to verify service for depreciation pay.

KERNS, KEARNS   GAB, PGCo.
Jacob; enl 1776, on duty 01Dec76.

KERSHER, KERSHNER,
KEARSHNER, THERSHNER   GAB, PGCo, 3-78, 3Vac, AMd, Brum, HCP.
Michael; enl 16 Jul 1776 from Balto Town Militia Batl, disch 16 Jul 1779 at Ft.Wyoming, Pa. Born 1752 or 58 in Germany, died 25 Apr 1823. Widow Mary Ann nee Motter recd Pvt's ½-pay for life pension in Allegany Co in 1826.

KEYSER   GAB, PGCo, 3-78, AMd.
Nicholas; enl 1776, on duty 03 Apr 1778. Applied for depreciation pay by 1785, but "not found on any muster rolls for 1779."

KIEFFER   GAB.
Honickle; enl 1776, disch soon after.

KINTZ, KEINTZ, KENTZ   GAB, PGCo, AMd.
Jacob; enl 1776, disch 30 Aug 1780.

KIMMEL, KEMMEL   GAB, PGCo.
Thomas; enl 1776, on duty 22 Jan 1777.

KNEARY, KNERY   GAB, PGCo, HCP.
Lorentz/Lawrence/Lorance; enl 15 Jul 1776 from Balto Town Militia Batl, on duty 22 Dec 1776.

KRAFT, KROFFT, CROFT   GAB, PGCo, 3-78, 3Vac, AMd, Brum, HCP.
William; enl 27 Jul 1776, prom to Cpl after Mar 1778, disch 26 Jul 1779 at Ft. Wyoming, Pa. Born 1753, died 17 Apr 1829. Widow Catherine nee Nicodemus recd Cpl's ½-pay pens for her life 04 Mar 1835.

LANZ, LANTZ   GAB, PGCo, 3Vac, AMd, HCP.
Martin; enl 15 Jul 1776 from Balto Town Militia Batl, disch 15 Jul 1779 at Ft. Wyoming, Pa.

LARAMOT, LARRIMORE   3Vac, AMd.
  Thomas; enl 25 Aug 1776, in GR when disbanded 01 Jan 1781,
  transf to 1st Co-3rd Md Rgt, 1782: in 5th Co-2nd Md Rgt. 1788
  Md Soldier Land assignee.
LIGHTHAUSER,
LEITHAUSER, SIGHHEISER   GAB, PGCo, 3-78, 3Vac, AMd.
  George; enl 26 Aug 1776, disch 22 Jul 1779 at Ft. Wyoming, Pa.
LORENTZ,
LORANTZ, LORANCE   GAB, PGCo, 3-78, 3Vac, AMd, Brum, HWN, HCP.
  Ferdinand/Frederick; enl 15 Jul 1776 from Balto Town Militia
  Batl, disch 15/22Jul 1779 at Ft. Wyoming, Pa. Born 1750,
  ½-pay pension for life to widow Elizabeth in Baltimore 01 Jan
  1839.
LORENTZ,
LORANTZ, LAURENTZ GAB, PGCo, 3-78, 3Vac, AMd, Brum, HCP.
  Wendel/Vendle/Vandel; enl 20 Jul 1776 from Balto Town Militia
  Batl, disch20 Jul 1779 at Ft. Wyoming, Pa. He recd 215A
  Federal Bounty Land. Widow Anne nee Steel recd ½-pay pension
  in Balto 24 Mar 1836.
MALLINS, MALINA, MOLNIX   FC78, WP78, 3Vac.
  William; enl 28 Apr 1778 for war as Frederick County substitute,
  on duty 05 Sep 1778.
MEILEY, MILEY   GAB, PGCo, 3-78, 3Vac, AMd.
  Jacob; enl 11 Aug 1776, disch 11 Aug 1779 at Tioga, Pa.
MIELBERGER,
MILLBERGER, MILLBURGER   GAB, PGCo, AMd, HCP.
  Henry; enl 15 Jul 1776 from Balto Town Militia Batl, on duty
  01 Dec 1776. Applied for depreciation pay by 1785, but "not
  found on any muster rolls for 1779."
MILLER   GAB, PGCo, 3-78, 3Vac.
  Anthony; enl 20 Jul 1776, on furlough Mar 1778.
MILLER   PGCo, HCP.
  Jacob; enl 1776. Born 1753, died 18 Oct 1829, wife named
  Susanna.
MILLER   GAB, PGCo.
  Philip; enl 15 Jul 1776, on duty 04 Oct 1776.
MOORE   GAB, PGCo, AMd, HCP.
  John; enl Jul 1776 from Balto Town Militia Batl, deserted
  05 Oct 1776. Applied for depreciation pay by 1785, but "not
  found on any muster rolls for 1779."
MUMMA, MUMA   GAB, PGCo, 3-78, 3Vac, AMd, HCP.
  David; enl Jul 1776 from Balto Town Militia Batl, disch 20 Jul
  1779 at Ft. Wyoming, Pa. Born 1751, died 30 Oct 1816 in Balto
  Co.
MURPHY   FC78, WP78, 3Vac.
  James; enl 27 Apr 1778 for war as Frederick County substitute,
  on duty 05 Sep 1778.
MYERS, MYER   GAB, PGCo, HCP.
  George; enl 1776, on duty 27 Nov 1776. Born 1755, died 1783,
  wife named Elizabeth.
MYERS   GAB, PGCo, 3-78, 3Vac, AMd, HCP.
  Jacob; enl 20 Jul 1776 from Balto Town Militia Batl, disch

20 Jul 1779 at Ft. Wyoming, Pa. Later served with State Troops and 2nd Md Rgt. 1788 Md Soldier Land assignee.

POPE   FC78, WP78, 3Vac.
William; enl 20 May 1778 for war as Frederick County substitute, on duty 05 Sep 1778.

PROCTER, PROCTOR   WP78, 3Vac, AMd, PMHB.
Thomas; enl 16 Apr or 04 May 1778 for 3 yrs, wounded in Aug 1780 while with Sullivan Expedition, in Sunbury [Pa] General Hospital from at least 04 Sep to at least 18 Oct 1780.

PROCTER, PROETER, BRAETER   GAB, PGCo, AMd.
Joseph/Joshua; enl1776, on duty 02 Dec 1776. Applied for depreciation pay by 1785, but "not found on any muster rolls for 1779."

REGELE, BEGEL   GAB, PGCo, HCP.
Christopher; enl Jul 1776 from Balto Town Militia Batl, on duty 06 Dec 1776.

REINHART, RINEHART   GAB, PGCo.
Simon; enl 1776, on duty 28 Feb 1777.

RICHARDS   FC78, WP78, 3Vac, AMd.
John; enl 20 May 1778 for war as Frederick County substitute, mustered sick at Windsor, NY 01 Aug 1780.

RICH, RICK   GAB, PGCo, HCP.
John; enl Jul 1776 from Balto Town Militia Batl, disch soon after.

RIDER   FC78, WP78, 3Vac, AMd.
William; enl 12/20 May 1778 for war as Frederick County substitute, on duty 01 Aug 1780.

RITTLEMYER, RITTLEMYS   PGCo, 3Vac, AMd.
George; enl 10 Sep 1776, disch 11 Aug 1779 at Tioga, Pa.

ROHRBACH, ROHRBACK, EARBAUGH GAB, PGCo, HCP.
Adam; enl 15/16 Jul 1776 from Balto Town Militia Batl, on duty 22 Dec 1776.

RUMFELT, RUMFIELD,
ROMFELD, ROMFIELD   GAB, PGCo, 3-78, 3Vac, AMd, HWN.
Henry; enl 17 Jul 1776, disch 28 Jul 1779 at Ft. Wyoming, Pa. Born 1761, pension applied for by widow.

RUPPERT, RUTURT   GAB, PGCo, 3Vac, AMd, HCP.
Jacob; enl 15 Jul 1776 from Balto Town Militia Batl, disch 15 Jul 1779 at Ft. Wyoming, Pa.

SCHLIFE,
SHLIFE, SHLIFL   GAB, PGCo, 3-78, 3Vac, AMd, HWN, HCP.
John; in Balto Mechanical Co of Militia 04 Nov 1775, enl 12/20 Jul 1776 from Balto Town Militia Batl, disch 20 Jul 1779 at Ft. Wyoming, Pa. Born 1757, applied for pension.

SCHRYOCK, SHYROCK,
SHRIOK, SHRIACK   GAB, PGCo, 3-78, 3Vac, AMd, Brum, HWN, HCP.
John; enl 16 Jul 1776 from Balto Town Militia Batl, disch 20 Jul 1779 at Ft. Wyoming, Pa. Born 1752, recd pension Jan 1820, recd Pvt's ½-pay pension for life beg 16 Mar 1835.

SEGMAN, SIGMAN   GAB, PGCo, 3Vac, AMd.
Peter, enl 1776. Applied for depreciation pay by 1785, but "not found on any muster rolls for 1779."

SHAFFER   GAB, PGCo, 3-78, 3Vac, AMd, HCP.
   John; enl 29 Jul 1776 from Balto Militia Batl, disch 19 Jul 1779
   at Ft. Wyoming, Pa.
SHIVELEY, SHIVELY   FC78, WP78, 3Vac, AMd.
   John; enl 01 May 1778 for 3 yrs as Frederick County substitute,
   on duty 01 Aug 1780.
SHROVER   AMd.
   Peter; served 3 yrs, disch 29 Jul 1779 at Ft. Wyoming, Pa.
   Submitted discharge, but could not be found on 1779 muster
   rolls in 1785 to verify service for depreciation pay.
SIGWALD   GAB.
   John; enl 14 Aug 1776, disch soon after.
SMITH   GAB, PGCo, 3-78, 3Vac, AMd, HWN, HCP.
   Henry; enl 25 Jul 1776 at Balto, disch 15 Aug 1779 at Tioga, Pa.
   Born 1750 in Lancaster Pa, res in Anne Arundel Co in 1842,
   recd pension.
SMITH   GAB, PGCo, AMd.
   James; enl 1776, on duty 02 Dec 1776. Applied for depreciation
   pay by 1785, but "not found on any muster roll for 1779."
SMITH   GAB, PGCo, 3-78, AMd.
   John; enl 1776, disch 12 Oct 1779 at Ft. Wyoming, Pa.
SMITH   GAB, PGCo, AMd.
   Joseph; Pvt in Capt Howell's Balto Co 30 Dec 1775, enl 1776, on
   duty 01 Oct 1776, in Capt McClellan's Co of Balto Town
   Militia. Applied for depreciation pay by 1785, but "not found
   on any muster rolls for 1779."
SMITH   FC78, WP78, 3Vac, AMd.
   Mathias; enl 19 May 1778 for war as Frederick County substitute,
   on duty 01 Aug 1780. 1788 Md Soldier Land assignee.
SMITH   FC78, WP78, 3Vac, AMd.
   Robert; enl 04/20 May 1778 for war as Frederick County
   substitute, deserted, on duty 01 Aug 1780, deserted in 1781.
SMITH   GAB, PGCo, HCP.
   Roland/Rowland, Jr; in Balto Mechanical Co of Militia 04 Nov
   1775, enl 15/16 Jul 1776 in GR from Balto Town Militia Batl,
   on duty Jan77, in Capt McClellan's Co of Balto Town Militia 04
   Sep 1780. Died prior to 1781, was married to Catherine
   Reister.
SPRENGLE, SPENGLE   GAB, PGCo.
   Henry; enl 1776, on duty 01Mar77.
STRICTER, STRITTER   3Vac, AMd, HCP.
   Joseph; enl 17 Jul 1776 from Balto Town Militia Batl, disch
   16 Jul 1779 at Ft. Wyoming, Pa.
[=?]
STRITER   GAB, PGCo, 3-78.
   Jacob; enl 1776, on duty 04 Apr 1778.
SUMMERS   GAB, PGCo, HCP.
   John, blacksmith; enl 1776, on duty 27 Nov 1776, served in Col
   Nicholson's Troop of Horse 07 Jun 1781.
TROUTS   GAB.
   Peter; enl 14 Aug 1776; disch soon after.
VAUGHN   FC78, WP78, 3Vac, AMd.

Cornelius; enl 21 May 1778 for war as Frederick County substitute, in GR when disbanded 01Jan81, transf to 5th Co-3rd Md Rgt, 1782: in 5th Co-2nd Md Rgt. '88 Md Soldier Land assignee.

WEGER, WAGER   GAB, PGCo, HCP.
Frederick; enl Jul 1776 from Balto Town Militia Batl, on duty 01 Oct 1776.

WELHELM, see HALLER   HCP.

WELTY   GAB, PGCo, AMd, HWN.
John; enl 1776, reenl 03 Jun 1780?, in GR when disbanded 01 Jan 1781, 28Aug81: in 5th Co-3rd Md Rgt. Born 1744, applied for pension.

WILLIAMS   GAB, PGCo, AMd, Brum, HWN.
Joseph; enl 1776, disch 22 Jul 1779 at Ft. Wyoming, Pa. Recd ½-pay pension for life in Annapolis 25 Feb 1824, recd 50A land in Allegany Co 21 Mar 1833.

WILLSDAUGH, WILLSDOCK   GAB, PGCo.
Henry; enl 1776, on duty 02 Dec 1776.
[= ?]

WILSTOCK   PGCo, AMd.
Henry; enl 1776, enl 01 Nov 1779, in GR when disbanded 01 Jan 1781, transf to 1st Co-3rd Md Rgt, 1782: in 5th Co-2nd Md Rgt: not heard of since Mar 1782 muster when on command in Va.

ZARRELL, see CHARRELL.   PGCo.

GERMAN REGIMENT PRIVATES OF THE MARYLAND COMPANY ORGINALLY RAISED IN BALTIMORE COUNTY AND KNOWN AS CAPTAIN KEEPORTS' COMPANY (JULY 1776 - MAY 1777) AND CAPTAIN BALTZEL'S COMPANY (MAY 1777 - JANUARY 1781):

AMMESLY,
EMERSLY, HAMMERSLY   FC78, WP78, CBCo, AMd, CMOB.
  John W.; enl 27 Apr 1778 for war as Frederick County substitute,
    courtmartialled 01 Sep 1779 at Ft Sullivan, Pa. for stealing
    & selling clothing belonging to Catharina Castner, sentenced
    to rec 100 lashes bare back well laid on and stoppage of half
    his pay until Catharina Castner is paid $45, & Catty Castner
    $15 for missing stockings and sleeve buttons, deserted before
    01 Aug 1780.
BARTES, BARTS   WP78, CBCo.
  Samuel; enl 25 Apr 1778 for war, on duty 09 Sep 1778.
BARTOLOMAY, BATHOLOMEY   FC78, WP78, CBCo, AMd.
  Peter; enl 20 May 1778 for war as Frederick County substitute,
    on duty 09 Sep 1778.
BAST   GKCo, HCP.
  Peter, of Balto Co; enl 06 Aug 1776, on duty 19 Sep 1776 at
    Phila.
BAUER, BOWER   GKCo, CBCo, AMd
  John; enl 23 Jul 1776, disch 24 Jul 1779 at Ft. Wyoming, Pa.
BENNET   FC78, WP78, CBCo, Brum.
  John; enl 18 May 1778 for war as Frederick County substitute, on
    duty 05 Sep 1778.   Recd pension of $40/yr.
BIGLER   GKCo, HCP.
  Jacob, of Balto Co; enl 28 Jul 1776, on duty 19 Sep 1776 at
    Phila.
BOEHLER, BAYLOR, BAILOR   GKCo, CBCo, AMd, HCP.
  Daniel, of Balto Co; enl 05 Aug 1776, disch 24 Jul 1779 at Ft.
    Wyoming, Pa.
BOEHM, BEAM   GKCo, CBCo, AMd, HCP.
  Conrad, of Balto Co; enl 24/26 Jul 1776, disch 24 Jul 1779 at
    Ft. Wyoming, Pa.
BOEHM, BEAM   GKCo, CBCo, AMd, HCP.
  Philip, of Balto Co; enl 30 Jul 1776, prom to Cpl.
BROWN   GKCo.
  John; enl 21 Jul 1776, on duty 19 Sep 1776 at Phila.
BRUBACHER,
BRUEBAKER, BRODBECH   GKCo, AMd, HCP.
  Michael, of Balto Co; in Balto Co of Capt Howell 30 Dec 1775,
    enl 15 Jul 1776, "was paid from 01 Nov 1779 to 01 Aug 1780."
BUCH, BOUGH,
BUCK, BOOGHER   FC78, WP78, CBCo, AMd.
  George; enl 04 May 1778 for 3 yrs as Frederick County
    substitute, in GR when disbanded 01 Jan 1781, transf to 1st
    Co-3rd Md Rgt, 1782: in 1st Co-2nd Md Rgt. 1788 Md Soldier
    Land assignee. See also George Buch in Capt Heiser's Co.
BURK, BURKE   GKCo, CBCo, AMd, Brum.

Jacob/James/John, of Balto Co; enl 28 Jul or 01 Aug 1776, prom to Cpl after 09 Sep 1778.

CAMMELL   AMd.
Thomas; served 3 yrs, disch 17 Jul 1779 at Ft. Wyoming, Pa. Known only from discharge certificate supporting depreciation pay claim.

CAPES   GKCo, HCP.
John, of Balto Co; enl 21 Jul 1776, on duty 19 Sep 1776 at Phila.

CARNS, KERNS, KEARNS   FCM, WP78, CBCo, AMd.
Francis; enl 01 Jun 1778 for 3 yrs as substitute from Frederick County Militia, in GR when disbanded 01 Jan 1781, transf to 3rd Co-3rd Md Rgt, 1782: "drafted into Md Line in '81 for the war"-in 5th Co-2nd Md Rgt. 1788 Md Soldier Land assignee.

CARROL   GKCo, HCP.
Joseph, of Balto Co, enl 21 Jul 1776, on duty 19 Sep 1776 at Phila.

CASESS   CBCo.
John; on duty 09 Sep 1778.

CHAMPNESS, CHAMPINS   FC78, WP78, CBCo, AMd, P.A.
James; enl 06 May 1778 for war as Frederick County substitute, transf to Invalid Corps 01 Aug 1780, disch 31 May 1781 or 31 Dec 1781.

COLE   GKCo, CBCo, AMd, HCP.
John; in Balto Mechanical Co of Militia 04 Nov 1775, enl 15 Jul 1776, prom to Sgt before 09 Sep 1778.

DOCHTERMAN   GKCo, HCP.
Michael, of Balto Co; enl 17 Jul 1776, on duty 19 Sep 1776 at Phila.

ELLIOTT, ELLETT   FC78, WP78, CBCo, AMd.
Benjamin; enl 20 May 1778 for war as Frederick County substitute, on duty 09 Sep 1778, disch 01 Aug 1780.

ENERY, ENSEY   CBCo, AMd.
James; enl 18 Jul 1776, disch 10 Oct 1779 at Ft. Wyoming, Pa.

ENGEL, ANGEL,
ENGELLE, ANCKLE   GKCo, CBCo, AMd, HCP.
Peter, of Balto Co; enl 25/30 Aug 1776, disch 14 Aug 1779 at Tioga, Pa.

FITZPATRICK   FCM, WP78, CBCo, AMd.
Philip; enl 06 Jun 1778 for 9 mos as substitute from Frederick County Militia, disch 29 May 1779 at Easton, Pa.

FOX   HCP.
James, of Balto; enl Aug 1776 by Capt Keeports, but not being a German or the son of a German, he was transf to Capt Gale's Co of Md Artillery.

FRANKEN   GKCo, HCP.
John, of Balto Co; enl 18 Aug 1776, on duty 19 Sep 1776 at Phila.

FRANKLIN   CBCo, AMd, BSC.
John; enl 04 Mar 1778, disch 04 Mar 1780. 1788 Md Soldier Land assignee.

FUHRMAN   GKCo, HCP.

Daniel, of Balto Co; enl 10 Aug 1776, on duty 19 Sep 1776.

GROSH, CRUSH   GKCo, CBCo, AMd, HWN, HCP.
Michael, of Balto Co; enl 15 Jul 1776, reenl 01 Jan 1777 for war?, disch 04 Mar 1781. 1788 Md Soldier Land assignee. Born 1750 in Frederick Co, married Christiana Raymer/Roemer, pensioner, died after 24 Mar 1824.

HAHN   GKCo.
Peter; enl 14 Aug 1776, on duty 19 Sep 1776.

HAIFLY, HAVELY,
HAFLICK, HASELIGH   CBCo, AMd, P.A., HWN.
Jacob; enl 08 Jul 1776, sick with swelled belly in Bettering House at Phila Dec 1776, deserted, in Frederick County, Md. Jail 19 Apr 1778, on duty 01 Aug 1780. Pension applied for by widow.

HARRING   GKCo.
John; enl 12 Aug 1776, on duty 19 Sep 1776 at Phila.

HARTZELL   AMd.
George, served 3 yrs, disch 19 Jul 1779 at Ft. Wyoming, Pa. Known only from discharge certificate supporting depreciation pay claim.

HAZELIP, HAISLIP, HASLIP,
HAYLIP, AZELIP   FC78, WP78, CBCo, AMd, Brum, HWN.
Richard B.; enl 24 Apr 1778 for 3 yrs as Frederick County substitute, in GR when disbanded 01 Jan 1781, transf to 1st Co-3rd Md Rgt, 1782: in 5th Co-2nd Md Rgt. 1788 Md Soldier Land assignee. Recd $\frac{1}{2}$-pay pension of $96/yr from 06 Apr 1818 in Washington Co. Born 1753, died Mar 1821, res in Fredk Co.

HAZELWOOD   FC78, WP78, CBCo, AMd.
Thomas; enl 02 May 1778 for 9 mos as Frederick County substitute, disch 20 Mar 1779 at Easton, Pa.

HOEFFLICH, KOEFFLICH   GKCo.
Jacob, of Balto Co; enl 21 Jul 1776, on duty 19 Sep 1776 at Phila.

JONES, TONE   FC78, WP78, CBCo, AMd.
Charles; enl 20 May 1778 for war as Frederick County substitute, in GR when disbanded 01 Jan 1781, transf to 1st Co-3rd Md Rgt, 1782: in 5th Co-2nd Md Rgt, prom to Sgt. 1788 Md Soldier Land assignee.

JOHNSON   AMd.
Nikolas; served 3 yrs, disch 24 Jul 1779 at Ft. Wyoming, Pa. Known only from disch certificate supporting depreciation pay claim. Pvt's $\frac{1}{2}$-pay pension for life recd by widow Rebecca of Queen Anne's Co in 1834.

KARNS, KEARNS, see CARNS

KEES   AMd.
Charles; served 3 yrs, disch 21 Jul 1779 at Ft. Wyoming, Pa. Known only from disch certificate supporting depreciation pay claim.

KENDRICK, HENDRICK   FCM, WP78, CBCo, AMd.
John; enl 28 May 1778 for 3 yrs as substitute from Frederick County Militia, deserted in Jul 1779.

KNEISE, KRUISE,

KREIS, KRIES   GKCo, CBCo, AMd, HWN, HCP.
   Peter, of Balto Co; enl 16/20 Jul 1776, disch 24 Jul 1779 at Ft.
   Wyoming, Pa. Pension applied for by widow.
LANE   AMd.
   Henry; served 3 yrs, disch 19 Jul 1779 at Ft. Wyoming, Pa.
   Known only from discharge certificate supporting depreciation
   pay claim.
LEVY   GKCo, HCP.
   David, of Balto Co; enl 21 Jul 1776, on duty 19 Sep 1776.
LICHTE   GKCo, HCP.
   Christian, of Balto Co; enl 09 Aug 1776, on duty 19 Sep 1776 at
   Phila.
LIMES   AMd.
   Nickolas; served 3 yrs, disch 21 Jul 1779 at Ft. Wyoming, Pa.
   Known only from discharge certificate supporting depreciation
   pay claim.
LOURE, LAWLY   GKCo, CBCo, AMd, HCP.
   Godfried/Gotfried, of Balto Co; enl 28 Jul or 05 Aug 1776, disch
   01 Oct 1779 at Tioga, Pa.
McCOLOUGH   CBCo, AMd.
   Lewis; enl 02 Aug 1776, disch 24 Jul 1779 at Ft. Wyoming, Pa.
McGRAW, McGROUGH   FC78, WP78, CBC0, AMd, BSC.
   Stephen; enl 24 Apr 1778 for 3 yrs as Frederick County
   substitute, on duty 05 Sep 1778. 1788 Md Soldier Land
   assignee.
McKAY, McCAY,
McKOY, McCAW   FC78, WP78, CBCo, AMd, P.A.
   Hugh; enl 19 May 1778 for war as Frederick County substitute, on
   duty 05 Sep 1778, transf to Invalid Corps on or before 01 Aug
   1780, disch 31 Dec 1781 or 15 Sep 1782.
MARKEL   GKCo, HCP.
   Adam, of Balto Co; enl 21 Jul 1776 on duty 19 Sep 1776 at Phila.
MILLER   GKCo, HCP.
   George; enl 19 Aug 1776, on duty 19 Sep 1776 at Phila, in Capt
   McClellan's Co of Balto Town Militia 04 Sep 1780. Born 1752,
   recd ½-pay for life pension 02 Mar 1827.
MILLER   GKCo, CBCo, HCP.
   John, of Balto Co; enl 24/28 Jul 1776, sick on 09 Sep 1778 at
   Phila, became a Sgt. Married Rosannah Ulrich, pensioned as
   Sgt, died 05 Nov 1823.
MONGOAL, MONGALL   GKCo, CBCo, AMd.
   Frederick, of Balto Co; enl 21/22 Jul 1776, disch 24 Jul 1779 at
   Ft. Wyoming, Pa.
MUMART, MUMMARD   FC78, WP78, CBCo, AMd.
   William; enl 25 Apr 1778 for 3 yrs as Frederick County
   substitute, on duty 01 Aug 1780.
MUSLER, MUSSLER
MULLER, MUSHLER   FC78, WP78, CBCo, AMd, HWN.
   Adam; enl 30 Apr 1778 for 3 yrs as Frederick County substitute,
   wounded in Aug 1780, in Sunbury [Pa] General Hospital from at
   least 04 Sep to at least 18 Oct 1780, in GR when disbanded 01
   Jan 1781, transf to 5th Co-3rd Md Rgt, 1782: in 5th Co-2nd Md

Rgt. 1788 Md Soldier Land assignee, pension appld for by widow.

NEVING, NEARVING, NEVIN   FC78, WP78, CBCo, AMd.
William; enl 19 May 1778 for war as Frederick County substitute, disch 01 Jul 1779 at Ft. Wyoming, Pa.

PORTER   FC78, WP78, CBCo, AMd.
Robert; enl 15 May 1778 for 3 yrs as Frederick County substitute, on duty 01 Aug 1780.

QUINLIN, GRUNLIN   WP78, CBCo, AMd.
Cornelius; enl 26 Feb 1778 for 3 yrs, killed at Battle of Newtown, NY 29 Aug 1779.

REITZ, REILY   GKCo, CBCo, AMd, HCP.
Conrad, of Balto Co; enl 21 Jul 1776, disch 24 Jul 1779 at Ft. Wyoming, Pa.

ROUCH, ROACH   WP78, CBCo.
John; enl 01 Apr 1778 for war, on duty 05 Sep 1778. See also Drummer John Roach/Rock.

SCHAEFFER, SHAFFER   GKCo, CBCo, AMd, HCP.
Adam, of Balto Co; enl 21 Jul or 05 Aug 1776, disch 20 Jul 1779 at Ft. Wyoming, Pa.

SCHESLER   GKCo, HCP.
George, of Balto Co; enl 10 Aug 1776, on duty 19 Sep 1776 at Phila.

SCHORCHT   GKCo, HCP.
John, of Balto Co; enl 08 Aug 1776, on duty 19 Sep 1776 at Phila.

SCHREIER, SHRAYER, SHROYER   GKCo, CBCo, AMd.
Mathias, enl 21 Jul 1776, disch 01 Oct 1779 at Tioga, Pa.

SCHUTZ, SHITZ, SHEETS   GKCo, CBCo, AMd, Brum, HWN, HCP.
Jacob, of Balto Co; enl 11/12 Aug 1776, disch 14 Aug 1779 at Ft. Wyoming, Pa. Pvt's ½-pay pension for life recd by widow Hannah 26 Jan 1828.

SETTLEMYER, SETTLEMIRES   GKCo, CBCo, AMd, HCP.
Christopher/Christian, of Balto Co; enl 17 Jul 1776, disch 20 Jul 1779 at Ft. Wyoming, Pa.

SHIRK   CBCo, AMd.
John; enl 07 Aug 1776, died.

SHRIVER   AMd.
George; served 3 yrs, disch 11 Aug 1779 at Tioga, Pa. Known only from discharge certificate supporting depreciation pay claim.

SMITH   CBCo, AMd, HWN.
Christian; enl 01 Oct 1776, on duty 01 Aug 1780. Born 1752, applied for pension.

SMITH   GKCo, AMd, HCP.
John, of Balto Co; enl 30 Jul 1776, disch 12 Oct 1779 at Ft. Wyoming, Pa.

STANTON,
STATON, STAUNTON   FC78, WP78, CBCo, AMd, WW, Brum, HWN.
John; enl 07 May 1778 for war as Frederick County substitute, in GR when disbanded 01 Jan 1781, deserted, courtmartialled 26 Oct 1781 at Camp near Yorktown and sentenced to receive 100

lashes, sentence approved by GW 03 Nov 1781. 1788 Md Soldier Land assignee. Born 1752, recd ½-pay pension for life 23 Feb 1829.

STEIN   GKCo, HCP.
Jacob, of Balto Co; enl 07 Aug 1776, on duty 19 Sep 1776 at Phila.

STITE, FITE, TITE,
SLITE, STITES, STILES   FC78, WP78, CBCo, AMd, WW.
James; enl 14 May 1778 for war as Frederick County substitute, in GR when disbanded 01 Jan 1781, transf to 3rd Md Rgt, deserted, courtmartialled 26 Oct 1781 at Camp near Yorktown and sentenced to receive 100 lashes, sentence approved by GW 03 Nov 1781, 1782: in 5th Co-2nd Md Rgt with note: not heard of since June muster. 1788 Md Soldier Land assignee.

STREIB   GKCo, HCP.
David, of Balto Co; enl 21 Jul 1776, on duty 19 Sep 1776 at Phila.

TRAUT   GKCo, HCP.
Henry, of Balto Co; enl 11 Aug 1776, on duty 19 Sep 1776 at Phila.

TRUX, TRUCKS   GKCo, CBCo, HCP.
John, of Balto Co; enl 21 Jul 1776, prom to Cpl before 09 Sep 1778.

TRUX   GKCo, WP78, AMd, ML, HCP.
William, of Balto Co; enl 21 Jul 1776, prom to Sgt 01 Mar 1777.

WAGNER   GKCo, CBCo, AMd, P.A., HWN, HCP.
Jacob, of Balto Co; enl 21 Jul or 05 Aug 1776, disch 24 Jul 1779 at Ft. Wyoming, Pa. Born 1754, appld for pension, died 04 Nov 1823 in Clarke Co, Ohio, aged 68.

WELLER   GKCo.
John; enl 03 Aug 1776, on duty 19 Sep 1776.

WINK   GKCo, HWN, HCP.
Jacob, of Balto Co; enl 05 Aug 1776, on duty 19 Sep 1776 at Phila. Born 1755, applied for pension.

WOOLFORD, WOLFRED   FC78, WP78, CBCo, AMd.
Thomas; enl 15 May 1778 for 3 yrs as Frederick County substitute, on duty 01 Aug 1780. 1788 Md Soldier land assignee.

GERMAN REGIMENT MEN FROM MARYLAND WHO CAN NOT BE PLACED IN
SPECIFIC COMPANIES:

ALDRIDGE, ALRICH   AMd, HCP, BSC.
  Nathan/Nathaniel, of Balto Co.; Pvt in Capt N. Smith's 1st
  Co of Matrosses 24 Jan 1776, in GR, 28 Aug 1781: in 5th
  Co-3rd Md Rgt, 1782: in 5th Co-2nd Md Rgt.   1788 Md Soldier
  Land assignee. Born 1754 @ Elk Ridge, height 5'-8½".
BARNETT   FC78, WP78, P.A., BSC.
  Robert; enl 07 May 1778 for war as Frederick County substitute,
  sick & absent on muster roll of 05 Sep 1778, transf to
  Invalid Corps on or before 01 Aug 1780, disch 31 Dec 1781.
  1788 Md Soldier Land assignee, recd $40/yr pension in
  Frederick County beg 30 Oct 1819.
BAUSWELL, BOSWELL   AMd, BSC.
  Samuel; deserted 22 Nov 1780, rejoined in 1781, 28 Aug 1781:
  in 4th Co-3rd Md Rgt, 1782: in 5th Co-2nd Md Rgt.   1788
  Md Soldier Land assignee.
BRAUNER   FC78.
  Joseph; enl 18 May 1778 for 3 yrs as Frederick County
  substitute, not on muster roll of 05 Sep 1778.
CONNOLLY, CONNOLY   WP78, WW.
  Edward; enl in Col Harrison's Va Artillery Rgt, deserted to
  the enemy, reenlisted in GR for 3 yrs, arrested, returned
  to original unit, courtmartialled & sentenced to receive
  200 lashes, sentence approved by GW 10 Jun 1778.
CONNOWAY   FC78, WP78.
  James; enl 15 May 1778 for 3 yrs as Frederick County
  substitute, was found to be a deserter from Col Chambers
  unit.
COSGROVE, COSTGROVE   FC78, WP78.
  Matthias; enl 12 May 1778 for 3 yrs as Frederick County
  substitute, deserted before 05 Sep 1778.
DYER, DYRE   AMd, P.A., HWN, MdHR.
  James/Jonathan; enl 01 May 1777, transf to Invalid Corps 05
  May 1777, disch 31 Dec 1781. Recd Pvt's ½-pay pension of
  2/10 Pounds per mo in Anne Arundel County beg 10 Feb 1784.
  See also a James Dyer in Fister's Co.
FLETCHER   FC78.
  Samuel; enl 20 May 1778 for war as Frederick County substitute,
  not on muster roll of 05 Sep 1778.
FUNK   HWN.
  George; Pvt. Pension applied for, born 1750.
GOULD   AMd.
  Edward; mustered sick & discharged 01Jul79.
HALDUP, HOLDUP   FC78, WP78.
  Thomas, enl 27 Apr 1778 for war as Frederick County substitute,
  was deserter from Carolina.
HAMILTON   FC78, HWN.
  John; enl 24 Apr 1778 for war as Frederick County substitute,
  not on muster roll of 05 Sep 1778. Born 1753, appld for

115

pension.
HATTENSTEIN   FC78.
  Samuel; enl 30 Apr 1778 for 3 yrs as Frederick County
    substitute, not on muster roll of 05 Sep 1778.
HEATON   HWN, HCP.
  John/James, of Balto Co; Pvt, Md Line defective Aug 1780.
    Born 1746, pension applied for by widow.
HOBSON, HOPKINS   FCM, WP78, AMd.
  Richard; enl 09 Jun 1778 for 9 mos as substitute from Frederick
    County militia, died 07 Jul 1778.
HOFFMAN   HWN.
  Henry; Pvt. Born 1757, applied for pension.
KETTLE   AMd, BSC.
  Daniel/David; enl 01 Nov 1779, in GR when disbanded 01 Jan
    1781, transf to Md Rgt, 1782: in 5th Co-2nd Md Rgt. 1788
    Md Soldier Land Assignee.
KEYSER, KISER   AMd, BSC.
  Jacob; Pvt in GR, prom to Sgt while in 5th Co-2nd Md Rgt,
    disch 13 Feb 1782. 1788 Md Soldier Land assignee.
LECROSE   AMd.
  John; on duty 01 Aug 1780.
LONASS, LOMAX, LOMASS   HWN, BSC.
  John; Pvt. 1788 Md Soldier Land assignee, recd Pvt's ½-pay
    pension beg 19 Feb 1819, pens appld for by widow.
MacHALL, MacKALL, MacRELL, MACALL   FC78, WP78, AMd.
  Thomas; enl 13 May 1778 for war as Frederick County substitute,
    on duty 05 Sep 1778.
McKINSEY   AMd, BCP.
  Jesse. 1788 Md Soldier Land assignee.
MADERN   FC78.
  Adam; enl 17 May 1778 for war as Frederick County substitute.
    [?= Drummer Adam Mattrell/Mattrit.]
MARTIN   AMd.
  Henry; paid from 01 Nov 1779. Recd Pvt's ½-pay for life
    pension beg 1827 in Frederick County.
MARTIN   HWN.
  John; Pvt. Pension applied for by widow.
MAUNSEL   AMd.
  William; enl Aug 1780, disch 22 Nov 1780.
MAYER   HWN.
  John; Pvt. Applied for pension.
MUMMA, MUMMAW, MUMMARD   FCM, WP78, AMd.
  Christian; enl 02 Jun 1778 for 9 mos as substitute from
    Frederick County Militia, died 27 Jul 1778.
NORRIS   FC78.
  William; enl 04 May 1778 for war as Frederick County
    substitute.
O'QUINN, O'QUYNN   MdHR.
  Richard; "soldier in the GR, wounded in leg @ White Plains
    in 1776[28Oct], disch 10Aug82." [Original disability report
    and discharge extant @ MdHR.] Recd Pvt's ½-pay pension
    of 2/10 Pounds per mo in Anne Arundel Co in Oct & Dec84.

See also Richard O'Quinn in Heiser's Co.

POLHOUSE, POLLHOUSE   FCM.
   Thomas; enl 02 Jun 1778 for 9 mos as substitute from Frederick
   County Militia. See also Thomas Polehouse in Capt Fister's
   Co.

RONNENBERGER   AMd.
   Charles; enl 06 Jun 1780, on duty 01 Aug 1780.

SELAS   AMd.
   Andrew; enl 22 May 1780, on duty 01 Aug 1780.

SELWOOD, SILWOOD   AMd, WW, BSC.
   William; enl 15 Apr 1780, on duty 01 Aug 1780, deserted,
   arrested, court-martialled 26 Oct 1781 @ Camp near Yorktown,
   Va & sentenced to receive 100 lashes, sentence approved
   by GW 03 Nov 1781, on duty with 5th Co-2nd Md Rgt, prom
   to Cpl 01 Oct 1782, reduced to Pvt 27 Dec 1782. 1788 Md
   Soldier Land assignee.

SHANK   HWN.
   John; Pvt. Pension applied for by widow.

SHEARS   HWN.
   Peter; Pvt. Born 1749, applied for pension.

SHULER   FC78, WP78.
   Andrew; enl 06 May 1778 for war as Frederick County substitute,
   deserted before 05 Sep 1778.

SMATTER, SMADERN,
SMITHARD, SMITHERD   FC78, WP78, AMd, BSC.
   John; enl 24 Apr 1778 for 3 yrs as Frederick County substitute,
   on duty 01 Aug 1780. 1788 Md Soldier Land assignee.

SMITH   BSC.
   Michael. 1788 Md Soldier Land assignee. See also Michael
   Smith in Musicians list.

STAUT, STOUT   FC78.
   John; enl 20 May 1778 for war as Frederick County substitute,
   deserted before 05 Sep 1778.

STONE   WP78.
   Frederick; enl for 3 yrs, transferred to the Laboratory before
   05 Sep 1778.

TOMEY   AMd.
   James; enl 1776, disch 26 Jul 1779 @ Ft Wyoming, Pa.

TOMLIN   BSC.
   John; Pvt in GR. 1788 Md Soldier Land assignee.
[?=]
TOOMEY   HWN
   John; Pvt, Md Line. Born 1748, recd Cpl's ½-pay pension 16
   Feb 1820 in Queen Annes Co.

VEACH   AMd.
   Abraham; deserted, disch 22 Nov 1780.

VIEBLER   AMd.
   John.

WALKER   AMd, HWN, BSC.
   John; enl 10 Apr 1780, in GR when disbanded 01 Jan 1781, transf
   to a Md Rgt, 1782: in 5th Co-2nd Md Rgt. 1788 Md Soldier
   Land assignee, recd Cpl's ½-pay pension in Frederick County

beg 1820, widow Mary recd pens beg 1847. Born 1755.

WALTON, WALDON   FC78, WP78.
   John; enl 25 Apr 1778 for 3 yrs as Frederick County substitute,
   deserted before 05Sep78.

WEIGLE, WEEGUEL   FC78, WP78.
   John/Joseph; enl 25 Apr 1778 for war as Frederick County
   substitute, "left @ Frederick Town."

WHIT, WHITE   FC78, WP78.
   William; enl 05 May 1778 for war as Frederick County
   substitute, "was deserter from Carolina."

WILLIAMS   AMd, BSC.
   Daniel; enl 09 Jun 1780, in GR when disbanded 01 Jan 1781,
   28 Aug 1781: in 5th Co-3rd Md Rgt, 1782: in 5th Co-2nd Md
   Rgt. 1788 Md Soldier Land assignee.

WRIGHT   AMd, BSC.
   Samuel; enlisted 03 Jun 1780, on duty 01 Aug 1780. 1788 Md
   Soldier Land assignee.
[?=]

WRIGHT   AMd.
   Samuel; 1782: in 5th Co-2nd Md Rgt, listed as "sick @
   Fredricksburg," died 20 Jan 1782.

BENKLER, BENICKLER   BWCo, P.A.
John; enl as Pvt Jun/Jul 1775 in Capt John Lowdon's
(Northumberland Co) Co, Col Thompson's Batl, marched to siege
of Boston, transf to GR 15 Aug 1776 as Sgt, in Weiser's Co 03
Oct 1776.
CLACKNER, GLECKNER,
KLACKNER, GLICHNER   BWCo, PBCo, DB79, LW80, P.A.
Christian, enl 10 Jul 1776 in Phila as Sgt, in Weiser's Co
03 Oct 1776, Sgt in Boyer's Co 1777-78, comm Ensign in GR 23
Jul 1778.
DIFFENDERFER   5Vac, DB79, P.A., FBH.
David; enl 25 Aug 1776 as Pvt, prom to Cpl 01 Dec 1776, Sgt in
5th Vac [ex-Burchardt] Co, taken prisoner 10 May 1777 near
Monmouth NJ, rejoined GR 24 Apr 1778, comm Ensign in GR 23 Jul
1778.
FRANCIS   Sergeant-Major   GHCo, LW80#1, P.A.
George; enl 04 Nov 1776 in Lancaster, Sgt-Maj in Hubley's Co,
reenl 15 Dec 1777 for war, in GR when disbanded 01 Jan 1781,
transf to 2nd Pa Rgt, reduced to Sgt on 1783 muster roll.
GABRIEL   JBCo, LW80#5, P.A.
Peter; enl 13 Jul 1776 for war in Phila, Sgt in Bunner's Co, in
GR when disbanded 01 Jan 1781, transf to 2nd Pa Rgt, on 1783
muster roll.
HANSS, HAUSS, HANS, HANTZ   5Vac, LW80#2, P.A.
Michael; enl 02/16 Aug 1776 in Phila, Sgt in Burchardt's Co,
transf to Invalid Corps 12 Oct 1780, disch 31 May 1781.
HERBERT   BWCo.
Stewart; enl 15 Jul 1776 as Sgt, in Weiser's Co 03 Oct 1776 at
Phila Barracks.
JOHNSON
JOHNSTON, JOHNSTONE   GHCo, LW80#8, P.A., CMOB.
John; enl 04 Nov 1776 in Phila, reenl 21 Oct 1776 for war, in
Hubley's Co, courtmartialled 20 Jul 1778 "for insolent
behavior to Lt Hudson," found guilty & sentenced to be
reprimanded by Col Weltner in front of the Rgt, on duty May
1780.
LINDEMAN, LINDERMAN   5Vac, LW80#3, P.A.
Frederick; enl 20/21 Aug 1776 in Phila, Sgt in Burchardt's Co
1777-78, on duty May 1780. Resided in Limerick Twp,
Montgomery County after the war.
LUFT, LUFF   PBCo, LW80#6, P.A.
George; enl 10 Jul 1776 for war in Phila, Sgt in Boyer's Co
1777-78, on duty as Sgt May 1780.
MILLER   BWCo.
Joseph; enl 19 Aug 1776, on duty as Sgt in Weiser's Co 03 Oct
1776 at Phila Barracks.
MOSER, MOSSER   JBCo, LW80#10, P.A.
Henry; enl 10 Jul 1776 in Phila as Pvt, prom to Cpl before
Jul 1779, in Bunner's Co, des at Ft. Wyoming 14 Jul 1779 when

his time was up, court martialled, pardoned 27 Jul 1779, reenl
for war, prom to Sgt, on duty May 1780. Died 21 Feb 1825 in
Phila, aged 68.

MULLS   P.A.
   Francis; enl 1776, transf to Invalid Corps 01 Nov 1780.

PRICE   BWCo, 1Vac.
   George; enl 02 Jun or 14 Jul 1776 as Cpl, in Weiser's Co, prom
   to Sgt.

REICHLEY, REISKLEY   GHCo, LW80#9, P.A.
   Lewis; enl 26 Aug 1776 for war in Phila, Sgt in Hubley's Co
   before Apr 1777, on duty May 1780.

SHRADER, SHRIDER   LW80#12, P.A.
   Israel; enl 13 Nov 1779 in Phila, on duty as Cpl for war May
   1780, prom to Sgt after May 1780.

WENTZ   PBCo, LW80#7, P.A.
   Jacob; enl 23 Jul 1776 in Phila, Cpl in Boyer's Co, prom to Sgt
   before May 1780, on duty for war May 1780.

WINAND, WIAND, WEYAND   5Vac, LW80#4, P.A.
   John, enl 24/25 Aug 1776 in Lancaster County, in Bunner's
   or Burchardt's Co, prom to Sgt before May 1780, on duty for
   war May 1780.

WINKLER, WINCKLER   JBCo, P.A.
   John Henry; enl 01 Aug 1776 in Phila, in Bunner's Co, died in
   service.

WISERT, WEISSERT   JBCo, P.A.
   Jacob; enl 20 Jul 1776, in Bunner's Co.

YOUNG   DB79, LW80, P.A., Force, FBH.
   Marcus, of Lancaster; enl 20 Jun 1776 as Pvt, recommended for
   Ensign 08 Nov 1776, prom to Cpl, prom to Sgt, promoted to 2nd
   Lt.

BROWNSBURGH,
BROWNSBURY, BROWNSBERY   GHCo, LW80#15, P.A.
   Lewis; enl 14/21/24 Jul 1776 for war at Germantown, Cpl in
   Hubley's Co, on duty May 1780.
CAHOUN, CALHOUN, GOHOON   PBCo, P.A., AMd.
   James; enl 06 Aug 1776 in Berks County as Pvt in Boyer's Co,
   prom to Cpl. Application made in his name for Md depreciation
   pay.
DEAL   JBCo, P.A.
   Adam; enl 16 Jul 1776, Cpl in Bunner's Co, transf to Invalid
   Corps 16 Oct 1779, prom to Sgt 01 Dec 1780, disch 31 Dec 1781.
DIEFFENDERFER   FBH.
   David, of Lancaster; enl 25 Aug 1776 as Pvt, prom to Cpl
   01 Dec 1776, prom to Sgt.
FESMIRE,
FERMIRE, FIRMIRE   JBCo, P.A.
   John; enl 04 Sep 1776 as Pvt in Phila in Boyer's Co, prom to
   Cpl. Died 02 Sep 1821 in Phila, aged 69.
FUNK   GHCo, LW80#16, P.A.
   George; enl 20 Jul 1776 at Reading, Cpl in Hubley's Co, reenl
   04/19 Oct 1776 for war, on duty May 1780. Resided in
   Lancaster Co in 1835, aged 83.
KLEIN, KLINE,
CLINE, GLEIM   5Vac, LW80#25, P.A.
   Philip; enl 06/07/18 Aug 1776 as Pvt for war at
   Germantown or Lancaster, Pvt in 5th Vac [ex-Burchardt] Co,
   wounded thru left shoulder at Battle of Germantown 04 Oct
   1777, in Rice's [ex-Burchardt] Co, prom to Cpl after May 1780,
   prom to Sgt after disbanding of GR 01 Jan 1781.
MAYER   PBCo.
   Jacob; enl 1776, Cpl in Boyer's Co.
MOSER, MOSSER   JBCo, LW80#10, P.A.
   Henry; enl 10 Jul 1776 as Pvt in Phila, prom to Cpl before
   Jul 1779, Cpl in Bunner's Co, des after his 3 yrs were up @
   Ft. Wyoming 14 Jul 1779, recaptured, sent to run gauntlet &
   red to Pvt, pardoned 27 Jul 1779, reenl for war, prom to Sgt
   before May 1780.
PRICE   BWCo, 1Vac.
   George; enl 02 Jun or 14 Jul 1776, Cpl in Weiser's Co 03 Oct
   1776, prom to Sgt between 18 Oct 1777 and May 1779.
RAHN   BWCo.
   Conrad; enl 15 Aug 1776, Cpl in Weiser's Co 03 Oct 1776.
RIFFERTS, RIFFIT   PBCo, DB79, LW80#14.
   Christian; enl 25 Jul 1776 as Pvt in Phila, in Boyer's Co, prom
   to Cpl between Mar 1779 and May 1780, on duty for war May
   1780. Resided in Phila in 1835, aged 85.
RUDART   WDA
   William, school-master, of Pottsgrove, Berks Co; enl in
   Woelpper's Co, des as Cpl before 13 Mar 1777, believed

121

teaching in Phila. He was listed as age 22, 5'-1½" tall, dark
complexion, black hair.
SHIBLER   JBCo.
  Richard, enl 1776, Cpl in Bunner's Co 03 Oct 1776.
SHRADER, SHRIDER   LW80#12, P.A.
  Israel; enl 13 Nov 1779 as Pvt for war in Phila, prom to Cpl
  before May 1780, prom to Sgt after May 1780.
SHRIDER, SHREDER   JBCo, LW80#13, P.A.
  Philip; enl 20 Jul 1776 for war in Phila, Cpl in Bunner's Co, on
  duty May 1780.
SIPPEREL, CYPRIL, SIPERIL   5Vac, LW80#11, P.A.
  Frederick; enl 18/19 Aug 1776 in Phila, Cpl in 5th Vac
  [ex-Burchardt] Co, des when his 3 yrs were up at Ft. Wyoming
  14 Jul 1779, recaptured, sent to run gauntlet & red to Pvt,
  pardoned 27 Jul 1779, reenl for war, on duty as Cpl May 1780.
WALDMAN   BWCo.
  Nicholas; enl 10 Jul 1776, Cpl in Weiser's Co 03 Oct 1776 at
  Phila Barracks.
WENTZ   PBCo, LW80#7, P.A.
  Jacob; enl 23 Jul 1776 in Phila, Cpl in Boyer's Co, prom to Sgt
  before May 1780.
WILHELM, WILHALM, WILLIAMS   BWCo, 1Vac, P.A.
  Frederick; enl 03/06/09 Aug 1776 in Lancaster as Pvt in Weiser's
  Co, Cpl in 1st Vac[ex-Weiser] Co. Resided in Phila in 1835,
  aged 80.
WINAND, WIAND, WEYAND   5Vac, LW80#4, P.A.
  John; enl 24/25 Aug 1776 in Lancaster in Bunner's/Burchardt's
  Co, Cpl in 5th Vac Co 1777-78, prom to Sgt before May 1780.
YOUNG   Force, FBH.
  Marcus, of Lancaster; enl 20 Jun 1776 as Pvt/Sgt, recommended
  for Ensign 08 Nov 1776, prom to Cpl, prom to Sgt, comm 2nd Lt
  08 Jun 1777.

PENNSYLVANIA MUSICIANS IN THE GERMAN REGIMENT

ALEXANDER   Fifer   PBCo, LW80#17.
    Joseph; enl 12 Jul 1776 in Phila, in Boyer's Co, des after his 3
    yrs were up 14 Jul 1779 at Ft. Wyoming, recaptured, sentenced
    to be shot 24 Jul 1779, pardoned 26 Jul 1779, on duty for war
    May 1780.
BENTIS   Drummer   WDA.
    Peter, laborer, of Norrington, Phila Co; was drummer in Capt
    Archibald Thompson's Co of Pa Flying Camp, enl in Woelpper's
    Co, des before 13 Mar 1777. He was listed as native born,
    5'-5" tall, fair complexion.
BORDIGNON, BORGIGNON   Fifer   LW80#18, P.A.
    Francis; enl 02/04 Oct 1776 in Phila, on duty for war May 1780.
BROWN   Fifer   LW80#108, P.A.
    John; enl 12 Nov 1779 for war in Phila, on duty May 1780.
BUSH   Fifer   BWCo.
    Adam; enl 12 Jul 1776, in Weiser's Co, disch 16 Sep 1776.
FACUNDUS   Drummer   5Vac.
    George; enl 04 May 1777.
FORTNER   Fifer   LW80#19, P.A.
    Peter; enl 11 May 1779 in Phila, in Burchardt's Co, on duty for
    war May 1780.
HART   Drum Major   PBCo, LW80#20, P.A., AMd.
    John; enl 02 Jul 1776 in Phila, in Boyer's Co, on duty for war
    May 1780. Md depreciation pay applied for in his name.
JENKINS   Drummer   GHCo, LW80#21.
    Israel; enl Oct 1776 in Hubley's Co, on duty for war May 1780.
MARX, MARA   Drummer   BWCo.
    William; enl 25 Jul 1776, in Weiser's Co.
MULZ   Drummer   JBCo.
    F.; in Bunner's Co.

GERMAN REGIMENT PRIVATES OF THE PENNSYLVANIA COMPANY KNOWN ONLY AS
CAPTAIN BUNNER'S COMPANY (JULY 1776 - JANUARY 1781):

BANZAY, BANTZER, BONSA   LW80#51, P.A.
   Detmar/Dikmar; enl 12/16 Oct 1776, in GR when disbanded 01
   Jan 1781, transf to 2nd Pa Rgt, on 1783 muster roll.
[=?]
BONTZY, RONSEY   JBCo, DB79.
   Thomas; enl 16 Oct 1776 for war at Phila, on duty May 1779.
DEETZ, DEATS, TEATS   JBCo, DB79, LW80#47, P.A.
   Frederick; enl 20 Jul 1776 for war in Phila Co, on duty May
   1780.
GERLINGER, GARLINGER   JBCo, DB79.
   Leonard/Lewis; enl 20 Jul 1776 at Phila, on duty May 1779.
HAMMEREICH, HAMMERICK,
HAMMICK, AMMERRICH   JBCo, DB79, LW80#56, P.A.
   Henry; enl in 5th Pa Rgt for 1 yr, reenl in GR 17 Jul 1776 for
   war at Phila, wounded in left shoulder at Germantown 04 Oct
   1777, on duty May 1780. Resided and recd pens in Phila in
   1835, aged 94.
HARTMAN   JBCo, DB79, LW80#57.
   Theodore; enl 15 Jul 1776 for war at Phila, on duty May 1780.
HEIDLER, HYDLER   JBCo, DB79, LW80#52, P.A.
   Martin; enl 20 Aug 1776 for war at Phila, on duty May 1780.
HEIMS, HYMES   JBCo, DB79, P.A.
   William; enl 16 Jul 1776 at Phila, on duty May 1779.
HIRSH, HERSH,
MERSH, HERTS   JBCo, DB79, LW80#49, P.A.
   Frederick; enl 20 Jul 1776 for war at Phila, tried & acquitted
   of desertion 01 Oct 1780.
KEISER, KEYSER   JBCo, DB79, LW80#60, P.A.
   John; enl 27 Jul 1776 for war at Phila, on duty May 1780.
KERR   JBCo.
   Philip; enl 21 May 1778.
LEHMAN   DB79, LW80#61, P.A.
   William; enl 29 Jul 1776 for war at Phila, on duty May 1780.
MARSH   DB79, LW80#55.
   John; enl 15 Aug 1776 for war at Lancaster, on duty May 1780.
MYER, MYERS   JBCo, DB79, LW80#58, P.A.
   Jacob; enl 16 Jul 1776 for war at Phila, tried & acquitted of
   desertion 01 Oct 1780.
OTTENBERGER, PLATTENBERGER   JBCo, DB79, LW80#59, P.A.
   George; enl 28 Jul 1776 for war at Phila, deserted when his 3
   yrs were up 14 Jul 1779 at Ft. Wyoming, recaptured, sentenced
   to be shot 24 Jul 1779, pardoned 27 Jul 1779, on duty May
   1780.
RANKEY   JBCo, DB79, P.A.
   Frederick; enl 16/23 Jul 1776 at Phila, on duty May 1779.
RAUCH, RANK   JBCo, DB79, LW80#53, P.A.
   Conrad; enl 17 Jul 1776 at Phila, reenl 23 Jul 1776 for war. on
   duty May 1780.

REYBALL   JBCo.
  George; enl 12 May 1778.
SHEARER, SHAW   JBCo, DB79, LW80#48, P.A.
  Philip; enl 21 Jul 1776 for war at Phila, on duty May 1780.
SHEPPARD, SHEPHERD   DB79, LW80#54, P.A.
  Jacob; enl 10 Aug 1776 at Phila, tried & acquitted of desertion
    01 Oct 1780.
SNIDER, SNYDER   JBCo, DB79, LW80#50, P.A.
  Henry; enl 25 Jul 1776 for war at Reading, on duty May 1780.
STONER   JBCo.
  Richard; enl 1776.
STOVER   DB79, LW80#62, P.A., AMd.
  Nicholas; enl 20 Jul 1776 for war at Phila, disch from Bunner's
    Co in July 1779 at Ft. Wyoming, on duty May 1780. Md
    depreciation pay applied for in his name.
SYBERT   P.A.
  Henry; enl 27 Jul 1776 at Lancaster, in Bunner's Co. Died
    27 Jul 1830 in Phila, aged 70. See also Henry Sivert in Capt
    Weiser's Co.

GERMAN REGIMENT PRIVATES OF THE PENNSYLVANIA COMPANY KNOWN AS CAPTAIN BURCHARDT'S COMPANY (JULY 1776 - APRIL 1777) AND CAPTAIN BOYER'S COMPANY (? - JANUARY 1781):

BLOOM   PBCo, DB79, P.A.
    David; enl 30 Jul or08 Aug 1776 in Berks County, on duty May 1779.
BOTOMER, BOTTOMER   PBCo, DB79, LW80#75, P.A.
    Jacob; enl 09 Aug 1776 in Berks County, wounded in the left side at 2nd Battle of Trenton 02 Jan 1777, recovered & returned to duty, des after his 3 yrs were up 14 Jul 1779 at Ft. Wyoming, Pa, recaptured, sentenced to be shot 24 Jul 1779, pardoned 27 Jul 1779, reenl for war, in GR when disbanded 01 Jan 1781., transf to 2nd Pa Rgt, on 1783 muster roll. Resided in Westmoreland County in 1813, applied for pension.
BROOKHAUS, BROOKHOUSE   PBCo, DB79, P.A.
    Rudolph; enl 09/20 Aug 1776 for war at Phila, on duty May 1779.
BRUNNER   LW80#23, P.A.
    John; enl 18 Aug 1776 at Phila, in Burchardt's Co, on duty May 1780.
CALHOUN,
CAHOUN, GOHOON   PBCo, P.A.
    James; enl 06/13 Aug 1776 in Berks County, prom to Cpl.
CANTWELL   P.A.
    Richard; in Boyer's Co, des Nov 1780.
CHARREL   P.A., AMd.
    Frederick; in Boyer's Co. Md depreciation pay applied for in his name.
CHRISTMAN   PBCo, DB79, P.A.
    Charles; enl 28/30 Jul 1776 for war at Phila, on duty May 1779.
COOK   DB79, LW80#82, P.A.
    Philip; enl 30 Sep 1776 for war at Phila, des 14 Jul 1779 at Ft. Wyoming, Pa, recaptured, sentenced to be shot 24 Jul 1779, pard 27 Jul 1779, disch 1781.
COPPLE, COPPT   PBCo, DB79, P.A.
    Daniel; enl 18/28 Jul 1776 at Phila, on duty May 1779.
COPPUS,CAPPAS, KAPPAIS   PBCo, DB79, LW80#69.
    Peter; enl 10 Dec 1776 at Phila, reenl 01 Jan 1777 for war, on duty May 1780.
DEPERWING,
DEPERUNG, DEBERRING   PBCo, DB79, P.A.
    Henry; enl 13/28 Jul or 03 Aug 1776 at Phila, on duty May 1779.
DELINGER, DILLINGER   PBCo, DB79, LW80#74.
    Frederick; enl 21 Aug 1776 at Chester, on duty May 1780.
DREXLER   PBCo, DB79, LW80#80.
    David; enl 10 Oct 1776 for war at Phila, on duty May 1780.
FERRICK,
FIRMICK, FERRAUGH   PBCo, DB79, LW80#66.
    Michael; enl 20/28 Jul 1776 for war at Phila, on duty May 1780.
FESMIRE, FERMIRE   PBCo, DB79, LW80#79.
    John; enl 04 Sep 1776 for war at Phila, prom to Cpl.

FLEISH   PBCo, DB79, LW80#81.
   Christian; enl 15 Aug 1776 for war at Phila, on duty May 1780.
GERHARD, GERHART   PBCo, DB79, LW80#70, P.A.
   Charles/Conrad; enl 20 Jan 1777 for war at Phila, on duty May
   1780.
GRUMLEY, GRUMLEG   PBCo, DB79, LW80#77.
   Jacob; enl 20 Aug 1776 for war at Phila, on duty May 1780.
HARPER   PBCo, DB79, LW80#84.
   Jacob; enl 02 Aug 1776 for war at Phila, on duty May 1780.
KERLE, KERLS   PBCo, DB79, LW80#65.
   Frederick; enl 21 Jul 1776 at Phila, deserted after his 3 yrs
   were up 14 Jul 1779 at Ft. Wyoming, Pa, recaptured, sentenced
   to be shot 24 Jul 1779, pard 27 Jul 1779, reenl for war, on
   duty May 1780.
KERLE, KERLS   PBCo, DB79, LW80#83.
   William; enl 10 Aug 1776 for war at Phila, on duty May 1780.
KERSTETER, KERETITER   PBCo, DB79, P.A.
   George; enl 29 Jul 1776 for war at Phila, in Burchardt's Co,
   disch at Northumberland Nov/Dec 1779. Resided in Perry Twp,
   Union County in 1821.
KRAMER, KREMER   P.A., HYCO.
   Jacob; enl 19 Jul 1776 in Boyer's Co, served in Baltzel's [?] &
   Boyer's Co, disch 19 Jul 1779. Recd pension and resided in
   York County in 1818, aged 62.   .
LACH, LASH   PBCo, DB79, LW80#76, P.A.
   Philip; enl 14 Jul 1776 for war at Phila, on duty May 1780.
   Died 08 Feb 1822 in Phila, aged 79.
LEHR, LEAR   PBCo, DB79, LW80#72, P.A.
   Henry; enl 20/21 Jul 1776 for war at Phila, on duty May 1780.
LEIDY   PBCo, DB79, LW80#67, P.A.
   Christian/Christopher; enl 20 Jul 1776 for war at Phila, des
   Nov 1780.
REFFET,
RIFFET, REFFETTS   PBCo, DB79, LW80#73. P.A.
   Christian; enl 25 Jul 1776 for war at Phila, on duty May 1780.
RINEHART   PBCo.
   Mathias.
RIVELY   PBCo, DB79, LW80#63, P.A.
   Frederick; enl 21 Jul 1776 for war at Phila, on duty May 1780.
   Resided in Delaware County in 1835.
SHULER, SHUBER   PBCo, DB79, LW80#64, P.A.
   Henry; enl 21 Jul 1776 for war at Phila, in GR when disbanded
   01 Jan 1781, transf to 2nd Pa Rgt, on 1783 muster roll. Died
   10 Jan 1820 in Mifflin County, aged 69.
SUNLITER, SANLITER   PBCo, DB79, P.A.
   John; enl 16/20 Jul or 17 Aug 1776 at Phila, on duty May 1779.
TSCHUDY, SHUDT, JUDY   PBCo, DB79, LW80#68, P.A., Fam.Hist.
   Martin; enl 04 Sep/Oct 1776 for war at Phila, on duty May 1780.
   Baptised 31 Jul 1735 Frenkendorf, Canton Basel, Switz; arr
   Phila 10 Nov 1767 on ship **Sally** with parents.
TUMBELTY, TURNBELTY   LW80#44, P.A.
   John; enl 27 Feb 1780 for war at Northumberland, in Burchardt's

Co, on duty May 1780.
WEIDMAN, WIEDMAN   PBCo, DB79, LW80#71.
   John; enl 10 Aug 1776 for war in Berks County, on duty May 1780.
WHEELER   PBCo, DB79, LW80#78, P.A.
   Frederick/Thomas; enl 10 Aug 1776 for war at Phila, on duty
   May 1780.
WERNER
   Nicholas.   PBCo.

GERMAN REGIMENT PRIVATES OF THE PENNSYLVANIA COMPANY KNOWN AS CAPTAIN G. HUBLEY'S COMPANY (JULY 1776 - ?), CAPTAIN BAYER'S COMPANY (? - JUNE 1779), AND CAPTAIN B. HUBLEY'S COMPANY (JUNE 1779 - JANUARY 1781):

BAKER   GHCo, DB79, LW80#107, P.A.
    Christian; enl 12 Oct or 05 Nov 1776 for war in Phila, on duty
    May 1780.
BEYERLY, BYERLY
    Christian; enl 05 Sep 1776 in Lancaster.
CRANE   GHCo, DB79, LW80#102, P.A.
    John, of Baltimore, Md; enl 23 Oct 1776 for war, on duty May
    1780.
DOMINICK   GHCo, DB79, LW80#98.
    Henry; enl 04 Sep 1776 in Phila, reenl 23 Oct 1776 for war,
    on duty May 1780.
DONAHOO, DONOCHOR   GHCo, DB79.
    Philip/Robert; enl 21 Oct 1776 for war in Phila, on duty May
    1780.
FLOCK, FLOUGH   GHCo, DB79, LW80#103, P.A.
    Mathias; enl 13 Jul 1776 in Phila/Germantown, reenl 23 Oct
    1776 for war, on duty May 1780.
FORTNER   DB79.
    Peter; enl 11 May 1779 for war in Phila.
GARRET   LW80#109.
    Abraham; enl 15 Nov 1779 for war in Phila, on duty May 1780.
HAAG, HAKE, HAGE   GHCo, DB79, LW80#94.
    Christian, enl 28 Aug 1776 for war [?] in Phila, reenl 23 Oct
    1776 for war, on duty May 1780.
HAND   GHCo.
    Burchardt; enl 10 Jul 1776.
HENSELL, HANSEL,
HANTZEL, WENTZEL   GHCo, DB79, LW80#106, P.A., AMd.
    George; enl 29 Sep or 24 Oct or 02 Nov 1776 for war in Phila,
    transf to Invalid Corps 12 Oct 1780, prom to Cpl, disch 31
    Dec 1781. Application made in his name for Md depreciation
    pay.
ISRALO   GHCo, DB79, P.A.
    Caspar; enl 08 Aug 1776 in Phila, on duty May 1780.
KEPHARD, KEPPARD   GHCo, DB79, LW80#96, P.A.
    John; enl 1776, reenl 23 Oct 1776 for war in Phila, on duty
    May 1780.
KUHN, COON   GHCo, DB79, LW80#97.
    John; enl 07 Aug 1776 in Phila, reenl 23 Oct 1776 for war,
    on duty May 1780.
LEAF   GHCo, DB79.
    Mathias; enl 11 Jul 1776 for war in Phila, on duty May 1780.
LEONHARD, LEONARD   GHCo, DB79, LW80#100.
    John; enl 04 Aug 1776 in Phila, reenl 23 Oct 1776 for war,
    on duty May 1780.
LINN, LYNN   GHCo, DB79, LW80#99, P.A.

George; enl 24 Jul 1776 in Phila, reenl 23 Oct 1776 for war, on duty May 1780.

MENCHER, MENGES,
WINSHER, WINGER   GHCo, DB79, LW80#101.
    Christian; enl 25 Jul 1776 in Germantown, reenl 23 Oct 1776 for war, on duty May 1780.

NEBLE, NUBLE   GHCo, DB79, LW80#105.
    Adam; enl 23 Jul 1776 in Germantown, reenl 23 Oct 1776 for war, on duty May 1780.

RICHCREEK   P.A.
    John, of Dover Twp, York County; enl in Hubley's Co, wounded @ Battle of Germantown 04 Oct 1777, transf to Invalid Corps. Died in Conewago Twp, Adams Co 17 Sep 1822, aged 72.

ROOP   P.A.
    Nicholas; in Hubley's Co.

REYSBECKER,
RYBACKER, RYBAKER   GHCo, DB79, P.A., WW.
    John; enl 07/17 Aug 1776 for war in Phila; courtmartialled for desertion & enlisting in another rgt, sentence postponed for further evidence 09 Jul 1777; shot through the hand & shoulder @ Battle of Germantown 04 Oct 1777; on duty May 1779. Applied for pension.

SNIDER, SNYDER   GHCo, DB79, P.A.
    John; enl 13 Aug 1776 in Phila, reenl 23 Oct 1776 for war, wounded in the breast & right side by piece of fence rail splintered by cannon ball @ Battle of Germantown 04 Oct 1777, on duty May 1779. Resided in Phila Co, applied for pension. See also John Snider in Weiser's Co.

STROUD   GHCo, DB79, P.A.
    Robert/Philip; enl 21 Oct 1776 for war in Phila, on duty May 1779.

SHERRICH, SHIRK,
SHERRICK, THIRK   GHCo, DB79, LW80#85, P.A.
    Jacob; enl 05 Aug 1776 in Lancaster, reenl 23 Oct 1776 for war, on duty May 1780. Died 19 Feb 1826 in Franklin County, aged 67.

TURNER, TERNER   GHCo, DB79, LW80#104, P.A.
    Thomas; enl 01 Sep 1776 in Kensington, reenl 23 Oct 1776 for war, on duty May 1780.

WEISLER,
WISLAR, VISLER   GHCo, DB79, LW80#95.
    Jacob; enl 27 Jul 1776 in Reading, reenl 23 Oct 1776 for war on duty May 1780.

GERMAN REGIMENT PRIVATES OF THE PENNSYLVANIA COMPANY KNOWN AS CAPTAIN WEISER'S COMPANY (JULY 1776 - OCTOBER 1776), FIRST VACANT COMPANY (OCTOBER 1776 - ?), AND CAPTAIN RICE'S COMPANY (? - JANUARY 1781):

BARNHEISEL   BWCo, FCDAR.
  John; enl 22 Jul 1776, on duty 03 Oct 1776 at Phila Barracks.
  Died at Quincy, Franklin Co 02 Jun 1848, aged 106!
BISHOP   BWCo.
  John; enl 28 Jul 1776, on duty 03 Oct 1776 at Phila Barracks.
BRODBACH, BROADBACK   DB79, LW80#89, P.A.
  Michael; enl 25 Feb 1779 for war at Phila, on duty May 1780.
CHRISTMAN, CRISTMAN   BWCo, 1Vac.
  John; enl 05/06 Aug 1776, des 03 Sep 1776, on duty at time of
  1st Vacant Company muster roll.
DERR   BWCo.
  John; enl 25 Aug 1776, on duty 03 Oct 1776 at Phila Barracks.
DUNCAN, DUNKIN   P.A.
  James, blacksmith; enl for 3 yrs in Weiser's Co. Resided in
  Huntingdon County in 1818, aged 67.
FICK   BWCo.
  George; enl 10 Jul 1776, des 20 Aug 1776.
GABLE, YABLE, CAPPLE   1Vac, DB79, LW80#91, P.A.
  Henry; enl 01 Oct 1776, reenl 25/26 Feb 1779 for war in
  Northampton County [prob at Easton], on duty May 1780.
GILMAN, GILLMAN   1Vac, DB79, P.A..
  Philip; enl 08 Jun 1776 in Lancaster Co, reenl in GR 17 Aug 1776
  for 3yrs, wounded through the left breast at Germantown 04 Oct
  1777, on duty May 1779. Applied for pension from Phila Co.
HEIER   BWCo.
  John; enl 25 Jul 1776, on duty 03 Oct 1776 at Phila Barracks.
HENRY   BWCo.
  John; enl 12 Aug 1776, des 03 Sep 1776.
HIGGINS, HIGGENS   1Vac, P.A.
  Patrick; enl 18 Aug 1776 at Lancaster, reenl 01 Nov 1776 for
  war.
KEALER   BWCo.
  Caspar; enl 23 Aug 1776, on duty 03 Oct 1776 at Phila Barracks.
KETTLE   LW80#92, P.A.
  Cornelius; enl 25 Feb 1779, reenl 15 Dec 1779 for war at
  Sunbury, on duty May 1780.
KILLMAN   BWCo.
  Philip; enl 14 Jul 1776, on duty 03 Oct 1776 at Phila Barracks.
LESHER   BWCo.
  Peter; enl 15 Aug 1776, on duty 03 Oct 1776 at Phila Barracks.
LEVY   AMd.
  Jacob; in Rice's Co. Applied for Md depreciation pay.
LORASH   BWCo.
  Jacob; enl 06 Aug 1776, on duty 03 Oct 1776 at Phila Barracks.
McLAIN, McCLEAN, McLANE, McLEAN   1Vac, DB79, LW80#88, P.A.,HYCO
  Jacob; enl 29 Jun 1776 at Phila city or 20 Oct 1777 at Easton,

reenl 25 Feb 1779 for war, in GR when disbanded 01 Jan 1781,
transf to Capt Fishburn's Co - Col Harmar's Rgt, disch at
Phila 1783. Recd pens of $8/mo beg 04 Sep 1818, died 18 Feb
1824 in York County, aged 66.

MAST, MATT   BWCo, DB79, LW80#90, P.A.
   Joseph; enl 19 Jul 1776 in Lancaster County, reenl 24 Jul 1776
   for war, on duty May 1780.

MAURST, MARSH   BWCo, P.A.
   John; enl 15 Aug 1776 at Lancaster, in Bunner's Co[?], disch
   Sep 1780.

MICKLEY, MILEY   BWCo.
   Jacob; enl 01 Sep 1776. Res in Lancaster County in 1835, aged
   78.

MYER, MAYER   BWCO, 1Vac, DB79, LW80#87, P.A.
   Eberhart/Everhart; enl 27 Aug/01 Sep 1776 at Phila, reenl
   25 Feb 1779 for war, on duty May 1780.

NEWFANG   BWCo.
   Baltzer, enl 15 Jul 1776, on duty 03 Oct 1776 at Phila Barracks.

PARTNER, PORTNER   BWCo, 1Vac, DB79, P.A.
   John; enl 03/09 Aug 1776 in Lancaster County, des 03 Sep 1776,
   on duty on 1Vac roll, reenl 25 Feb 1779 for war at Easton.

PRICE   BWCo, 1Vac, LW80#93, P.A.
   Abraham; enl 09 Aug 1776, des 03 Sep 1776, on duty on 1Vac roll,
   reenl 25 Feb 1779 for war at Easton, on duty May 1780.

RAZOR   BWCo.
   John; enl 24 Jul 1776, des 30 Sep 1776.

RIEGEL, REGEL, REIGEL   BWCo, P.A.
   Michael; enl 20 Jul 1776, on duty 03 Oct 1776 at Phila Barracks.
   Resided in Mifflin County in 1835, aged 84.

ROMICK   BWCo.
   Joseph; enl 06 Aug 1776, des 03 Sep 1776.

ROSEMEISEL   BWCo.
   Adam; enl 12 Jul 1776, on duty 03 Oct 1776 at Phila Barracks.

SCHIFFER   BWCo.
   Peter; enl 12 Jul 1776, on duty 03 Oct 1776 at Phila Barracks.

SERVEY   BWCo.
   Benjamin; enl 19 Jul 1776, des 03 Sep 1776.

SEYFFERT,
SIVERT, CYBERT   BWCo, 1Vac, DB79, P.A.
   Henry; enl 10 Jun or 27 Jul 1776 in Lancaster County, on duty
   May 1779. See also Henry Sybert in Capt Bunner's Co.

SMITH   BWCo.
   Jacob; enl 21 Jul 1776, on duty 03 Oct 1776 at Phila Barracks.

SMITH   1Vac, DB79, LW80#86.
   John; enl 01 May 1776 at Phila, reenl in GR 02 Dec 1776 for war,
   on duty May 1780.

SNYDER   BWCo, P.A.
   John; enl 16 Aug 1776, reenl 23 Oct 1776 for war, wounded in the
   head at Battle of Germantown 04 Oct 1777. See also John
   Snyder in Capt Hubley's Co.

SPIRE   BWCo.
   Frederick; enl 15 Jul 1776, on duty 03 Oct 1776 at Phila

Barracks.

STOLL, STULL   BWCo, P.A.
Adam; enl 20/21 Jul 1776, des 20 Sep 1776.

TONEY   BWCo.
Peter; enl 02 Aug 1776, on duty 03 Oct 1776 at Phila Barracks.

TRESTER   BWCo.
Frederick; enl 26 Jul 1776, on duty 03 Oct 1776 at Phila Barracks.

TREWITZ, TREVITS, DREBITZ,
TREYWITZ, TREATZ   BWCo, P.A.
Johann Conrad; enl 15/18 Aug 1776, disch Jan 1781. His pension appl states he lost his disch in home fire, was messmate of Michael Yeisley for 1½ yrs. Born 11 Sep 1751 in Herborn, Ger., son of Anton and Anna Catharina Drebitz; resided in Union County in 1822, noted as a fraktur artist.

TUDRO   BWCo.
John; enl 15 Jul 1776, on duty 03 Oct 1776 at Phila Barracks.

WALLMAN   BWCo.
William; enl 27 Jul 1776, on duty 03 Oct 1776 at Phila Barracks.

WARBY, WARLEY   BWCo.
Philip; enl 22 Jul 1776, on duty 03 Oct 1776 at Phila Barracks.

WEIGEL, WEIGLE   BWCo, P.A.
Christopher; enl 28 Jul 1776, wounded in the ankle, disch at Valley Forge in 1778. Resided in Berks County in 1835, aged 79.

WILHELM,
WILHALM, WILLIAMS   BWCo, 1Vac, P.A.
Frederick; enl 06/09 Aug 1776 at Lancaster, prom to Cpl.

WILLIAMS   BWCo.
Vincent; enl 19 Aug 1776, on duty 03 Oct 1776 at Phila Barracks.

YACKEL, CAKEL   1Vac, DB79.
Philip; enl 01 Aug 1776 at Phila, reenl 25 Feb 1779 for war, on duty May 1779.

YEISLEY   BWCo, P.A.
Michael; enl 09 Aug 1776, des 03 Sep 1776, served 18 mos in Weiser's Co, was messmate of Conrad Trewitz for 1½ yrs. Resided in Union Co in 1822.

GERMAN REGIMENT PRIVATES OF THE PENNSYLVANIA COMPANY KNOWN AS CAPTAIN WOELPPER'S COMPANY (JULY 1776 - JUNE 1778), FIFTH VACANT COMPANY (? - ?), AND CAPTAIN-LIEUTENANT SHRAWDER'S COMPANY (? - JANUARY 1781):

BANICK, BANIG   5Vac.
  Ditrick/Dedrick.
BRININGER, BRININGEN   LW80#37, P.A.
  Frederick; enl 09 Nov 1776 at Phila, reenl 29 Dec 1776 for war, on duty May 1780.
BROWN   WDA.
  George Frederick, baker, of Philadelphia city; enl in Woelpper's Co, des before 13 Mar 1777, believed gone to Baltimore. He is listed as German-born, age 19, 5'-6½" tall, fair complexion, marked by smallpox.
CLAUSS   WDA.
  Michael, laborer, of Maytown, Lancaster Co; enl in Woelpper's Co, des before 13 Mar 1777. He is listed as native-born, age 17, 5'-8" tall, fair comlexion, flaxen hair.
DOYLE   LW80#46, P.A.
  Maurice; enl 03/13 Mar 1780 for war at Phila, on duty May 1780, deserted.
DUTTON   5Vac, P.A.
  Abraham; enl 04 Aug 1776, transf to Invalid Corps before 01 Aug 1780, disch 31 May 1781.
FLICKET   WDA.
  John Man, from near Maytown, Lancaster Co; enl in Woelpper's Co, des before 13 Mar 1777. He is listed as Hessian-born, age 32, 5'-3" tall, long black hair, much given to smoking & drinking, and believed returned to Maytown.
GOEBEL
  John; Woelpper's Co, killed @ Battle of Princeton. Cited in Stryker: **Battles of Trenton and Princeton.**
GRUBER   5Vac, P.A.
  George.
HAGAR, HAGER   LW80#38, P.A.
  Andrew; enl 02 Dec 1776 for war in Berks County, on duty May 1780.
HALFPENNY, HAPPENNY   5Vac, LW80#33.
  James; enl 27 Dec 1776 for war in Phila, on duty May 1780.
HAWKE   5Vac.
  Andrew; enl 27 Apr 1777.
HELTER, HILTER   5Vac, P.A., AMd.
  Philip, biscuit baker of 5th St near Market St, Phila; enl 09 Aug 1776, in Shrawder's Co, killed & scalped at Tioga Point 17 Aug 1779. Application made in his name for Md depreciation pay!
HERRGOOD,
HARGOOD, HARDGOOD   5Vac, LW80#36, P.A., AMd, WW, WDA.
  Henry, brickmaker, Berks Co; enl 29 Dec 1776 for war at Lancaster, deserted before 13 Mar 1777, courtmartialled &

sentenced to death, pardoned by GW 03 Sep 1777, on duty May
1780, disch from Shrawder's Co. While deserted he was listed as
German-born, age 25, 5'-7½" tall, brown complexion, believed
with his wife 3 mi this side [east] of Reading. Md
depreciation pay applied for in his name. See also Henry
Hargeroder/Hergeroder of Capt Graybill's Co.

HESS   5Vac, LW80#35.
   Michael; enl 29 Dec 1776 for war at Phila, on duty May 1780.
HESS   5Vac.
   Tobias; enl 27 Apr 1777.
HIGGINS   LW80#39.
   Patrick; enl 18 Aug 1776 for war at Lancaster.
JOHNSON   LW80#42, P.A.
   Hugh; enl 20 Oct 1779 for war at Sunbury, on duty May 1780, paid
   at Carlisle in April 1781.
KEEN   5Vac, LW80#34, P.A.
   Thomas; enl 01 Feb 1777 for war in Phila, on duty May80.
KELLER   5Vac.
   George.
KENNINGTON   WDA.
   John, laborer; enl in Capt Wm West's Co, 3rd Batl, reenl in
   Woelpper's Co 19 Oct 1776, des before 13 Mar 1777. He was
   listed as an Irishman, 5'-1½" tall.
KLEIN, KLINE,
CLINE, GLEIM   5Vac, LW80#25, P.A.
   Philip; enl 06/18 Aug 1776 for war at Germantown, on duty May
   1780, prom to Cpl after May 1780.
KOCHENDERFER   5Vac, LW80#31, P.A.
   John; enl 26 Aug 1776 for war in Lancaster County, on duty May
   1780.
KUHN, COON   5Vac, LW80#26, P.A.
   Christian; enl 23/24 Aug 1776 for war in Lancaster County, on
   duty May 1780.
MAYER, MOYER   5Vac, LW80#41, P.A.
   Peter; enl 24 May 1777 in Heidelberg Twp, Lancaster County, reenl
   17 Mar 1780 for war, on duty May 1780.
MAYER, MYER, MOYER   5Vac, LW80#30.
   Philip; enl 03 Sep 1776 for war in Phila, on duty May 1780.
MOORE   WDA.
   Christopher, laborer; enl in Woelpper's Co, des before 13 Mar
   1777. He is listed as German-born, recently arrived, 5'-5½"
   tall, fair complexion, black hair.
MOORE   LW80#45, P.A.
   Thomas; enl 07 May 1780 for war at Northumberland, on duty May
   1780.
MILLER   5Vac, LW80#24, P.A.
   Mark/Marc; enl 18/19 Aug 1776 for war in Phila, on duty May 1780.
MULZ   5Vac.
   Francis; enl 05 Aug 1776.
PIFER   LW80#40, P.A.
   Henry; enl 18 Aug 1776 at Phila, reenl 13 Mar 1780 for war, disch
   1781. Resided in Phila in 1835, aged 79.

RUMMEL 5Vac, LW80#22, P.A.
Michael; enl 09 Apr/Aug 1776 for war in Phila, on duty May 1780.

SAILOR WDA.
George, shoemaker, of Maytown, Lancaster Co; enl in Woelpper's Co, des before 13 Mar 1777. He was listed as native born, age 21, 5'-10" tall, fair complexion, black hair.

SMELTZER, SMILTZER LW80#43, P.A.
John; enl 13 Feb 1780 for war at Tulpehocken, on duty May80, paid at Carlisle in Apr 1781.

SMITH 5Vac, P.A.
George; transf to Invalid before 01 Aug 1780, prom to Cpl 28 Jan 1781, disch 31 May 1781.

SOENE, SAINE, LAINE 5Vac, LW80#27, P.A.
John; enl 20/21 Aug 1776 for war in Phila, on duty May 1780.

SPECHT, SPECT 5Vac, P.A.
Adam, shoemaker from Schaeffertown; enl 27 Apr 1777, disch at Northumberland Nov/Dec 1779. Died 04 Oct 1824 @ New Berlin, Union County.

STOLL 5Vac, P.A.
Adam; enl 21 Jul 1776.

STROUB, SHAUB 5Vac.
Henry; enl 09 May 1777.

STROUSS LW80#29, P.A., WDA.
George, cooper, of Phila Co; enl 05 Sep 1776 in Phila in Woelpper's Co, des before 13 Mar 1777, on duty for 3 yrs May 1780. Listed while deserted as German-born, age 26, 5'-6" tall. Died 10 Feb 1820 in Phila, aged 75.

SWETZGAY, SWETHE 5Vac, P.A.
Henry; enl 27 Apr 1777. Died 20 Jul 1825 in Berks County, aged 77.

ULERICK WDA.
John Peter, enl in Woelpper's Co, des before 13 Mar 1777. He was listed as being Waldeck-born, age 23, 5'-4' tall, fair complexion, brown hair.

WENICK WDA.
Thomas, hunter; enl in Woelpper's Co, des before 13 Mar 1777. He was listed as being Waldeck-born, age 23, 5'-6¼" tall, a hunter or Yager, a talkative fellow and a cheat.

WAGGONER LW80#32, P.A.
Caspar; enl 09 Nov 1776 for war in Phila, on duty May 1780.

GERMAN REGIMENT PRIVATES FROM PENNSYLVANIA IN UNDETERMINED COMPANIES:

BELCHER   P.A.
 Benjamin.
BOWERS   P.A.
 George.   Died 24 Nov 1827 in Allegheny County, aged 67.
CLIFTON   P.A.
 Thomas.   Died 20 Sep 1832 in Ross County, Ohio, aged 87.
COCKENDORF   P.A.
 John.
DRANK   P.A.
 Peter.
EIRICH   P.A.
 Michael; enl 15 Apr 1776, reenl in GR, disch 1781.
FLOWERS   P.A., Saffel, Force.
 Philip; enl 01 Nov 1776, killed 04 Oct 1777 @ Battle of
   Germantown. Death certified to by ex-Maj Burchardt in 1786 for
   widow's pension.
FORTNEY
 Wender [Wendel?]; wounded @ Princeton 03 Jan 1777. Cited in
   Stryker: **The Battles of Trenton and Princeton**, 1898, Boston.
GERHART   P.A.
 Abraham; enl 1777 in Phila, disch 1781.
HUHN   P.A.
 John.
JANSON   P.A.
 Jacob.   Resided in Greenwood Twp, Columbia County in 1828.
KARCH   P.A.
 Jacob.
KETTLE   P.A.
 Jonas.
KLEICH   P.A.
 Cornelius; enl 01 Jan 1777, disch 1781.
KNOWLAND   P.A.
 Joseph.
KRONEMAN   P.A.
 Leonard.
MANDEVILLE   P.A.
 Philip; enl 01 Sep 1778, disch 1781.
PHILE   P.A.
 Philip; enl in GR, transf to Invalid Corps Jul 1778 or 01 Dec
   1780, prom to Cpl, disch 31 Dec 1781 or 04 Jan 1783 due to
   age. Resided in Phila County, applied for pension.
RINEHART   P.A.
 George S.; in GR when disbanded 01 Jan 1781, transf to 2nd Pa
   Rgt, on 1783 muster roll. Resided in Cumberland County in
   1835, aged 86.
SAILOR   P.A.
 Jacob.   Died 25 Feb 1833 in Phila, aged 81.

SCHROYER   P.A.
  Mathias. Resided in Butler County in 1835, aged 82.
SHIERS   P.A.
  Peter. Resided in Tuscarawas County, Ohio in 1835, aged 88.
SHRUPP, STRUPP   Pa Vital Records
  Henry. Enlisted in GR as Pvt, commissioned Ensign in GR
    20 Aug 1777.

GERMAN REGIMENT PRIVATES OF UNDETERMINED STATE

HARDY
William, courtmartialled 31 May 1777 for deserting & enlisting two different regiments, sentenced to be reprimanded by his commanding officer. Cited in P.M.: v33p267.

HUGHES
James, died during Sullivan Expedition in 1779. Cited in Wright, A.H.: Sullivan's Expedition of 1779 - The Losses.

SMITH
John, courtmartialled 06 Aug 1778, charged with desertion at Paramus, NJ and attempting to go to the enemy, captured at Hackensack, found guilty, sentenced to receive 100 lashes on bare back well laid on. Cited in CMOB. [There are three John Smiths from Maryland and one from Pennsylvania.]

WYNCH, WINCASH
Herman, courtmartialled 07 Jul 1777 at Morristown, NJ, charged with mutiny, neglect of duty, and refusal to take up arms and accroutements, sentenced to receive 39 lashes on bare back. Cited in WW: v8p361 & P.M.: v34p167.

THE GERMAN REGIMENT

New Information for the Second Edition

Additions to Chapter 1 - Congress Resolves

The creation of the German Regiment was definitely covered in Philadelphia's German-language newspapers. The resolution of 26 June appeared on the front page of the PENNSYLVANISCHER STAATSBOTE for 02 July 1776.

Another example of newspaper coverage is when the Congress resolved, on 04 September: "That the Board of War be directed to call in the several recruiting parties of the German Battalion, and they have them formed and armed, with all possible expedition, and forwarded to New York, taking measures, and giving proper directions to have the battalions recruited to the full complement, as soon as the same can be done."

To this the Pennsylvania Assembly added: "The officers of the above battalions are herewith instructed to bring their men to Philadelphia so the Board of War can take the necessary steps to comply with the resolves of the Congress. /s/Richard Peters, Secretary." This was published in German in the STAATSBOTE on 05 September 1776.

The newspapers also helped when the first desertions occurred in the fledgling regiment. A ten dollar reward was offered in the STAATSBOTE for 27 August "by Captain Weiser for the return of Private Andreas Beyer, about 5 feet 8 or 9 inches tall, who claims to have been in Captain Cresap's company on the Quebec expedition, he was believed to have joined a departing militia company; all captains were requested to deliver him for the reward."

The next round of desertion occurred in the company of Captain Bunner, who also placed an advertisement in the STAATSBODE for 16 September 1776 offering "$28 reward for the return of Private Christian Witmann and $8 for Drummer Thomas Rose, missing from the Philadelphia Barracks on 04 September."

Witmann was described as being 5 feet 10 inches tall, skinny build, brown eyes, short curly hair, and is a gifted talker and liar. He was wearing a new beaver hat, a long dove-colored coat probably half silk, a black velvet camisol, buckskin trousers, cotton stockings, and old shoes with silver buckles. He speaks poor English but good German, he is believed headed toward Carolina.

Rose was described as 5 feet 3 inches tall, heavy-set, brown eyes, and black hair tied in queue; was wearing an old wool hat, a brown- colored coat, a nankeen camisol and trousers, white

cotton stockings, and half-worn shoes with brass buckles. He was
described a having been a drum-major in Lord Sterling's Regiment,
and was a incomparably good drummer.

- - - - -

Additions to Chapter 4 - Brandywine and Germantown

Additional Maryland Casualties at Germantown:
Corporal John Ladder (ex-Fister's Co), wounded, still listed on
March 1778 muster role as wounded, returned to duty. [NA130]

Private Philip Caller/Colour (ex-Fister's Co), wounded. [NA130]

Additional Pennsylvania Casualties at Germantown:

Ensign Gottlieb Nebel (Bunner's Co.), wounded, died 11 October
1777 of his wound. [NA130]

- - - - -

The Strange Case of Sergeant John Kredelbach

Unmentioned before, he enlisted as a private in Captain
Woelpper's Company 12 August 1776 and was appointed a sergeant on
01 November 1776. He was captured on 02 January 1777 (probably at
the second Battle of Trenton) according to a February 1777 pay
roll, then was apparently exchanged, as he returned to duty on 20
May 1777. He served about 2 months, then was listed as sick in
hospital for August, September and October. Then, on the 31
October 1777 payroll there is the ominous remark, "Hanged by the
Regulars." [Cited in National Archives microfilm series M246,
roll 131.]

Efforts to obtain more information on this incident have been
fruitless. One wonders what caused the ultimate sentence to be
imposed on Kredelbach.

- - - - -

Addition to Chapter 5 - Valley Forge, New Jersey and New York

The Prussian mercenary John Charles Philip von Krafft visited the
Valley Forge encampment in February 1778 seeking a commission. He
found out officers with a knowledge of field fortifications were
wanted and they were to apply in writing. Krafft visited the
German Regiment on 10 February and had the regimental
quartermaster help him to make out his application in proper
form. While doing this he heard the commanding officer's name was
Baron von Arendt, who had been in the Prussian service. Further
inquiries determined that this was the Lieutenant von Arendt he
had met in Amsterdam in 1776.

On 13 February Krafft wrote a letter to Colonel von Arendt, who
was not in camp, but had gone, on account of sickness, to a house

out in the country. The next two days Krafft lingered with the Germans, he met the regimental adjutant (Linkensdorf) who had also served with the Prussians, and was entertained by them.

Several days later Krafft decided the American offers were not good enough and worked his way through the lines to Philadelphia, where he joined the occupying Hessians as a lieutenant. [Cited in "Journal of Lt. J. C. P. von Krafft, 1776-84." NY HIST SOC COLLECTIONS for 1882, pp17-21.]

The diary kept by the Rev. Henry M. Muhlenberg (at Providence, in Montgomery County, Pennsylvania) records for Wednesday 10 June 1778: "... Messrs. Schaefer, Burchard and Wills and Colonel Weltner's wife came over from the American camp."[Cited in Tappert & Doberstein, transl.: THE JOURNALS OF HENRY M. MUHLENBERG, Philadelphia, 1942-58, see date.]

This is the first of two known visits of Mrs Anna Maria Weltner to see her husband. Burchard is obviously Major Daniel Burchardt of the Germans. The camp mentioned is of course Valley Forge.

When the German Regiment was moved from the Hudson Valley in November 1778 to Easton, Pennsylvania, they were also ordered to escort the Saratoga prisoners across New Jersey. Details of this march are translated from the diary of a young captive Brunswick ensign:

02 Dec: [At Newburgh, NY.] The escort commander arrived with a new escort of two companies. His name is Weltner, he is a German and comes from the Salzburg area. His rank is a colonel, in civil life he is a master tailor in Fredericktown, Maryland. The escort troops are also almost all Germans. Over miserable roads to Little Britain.
03 Dec: Today to Goshen.
04 Dec: [To] Warwick
05 Dec: [To] Harnistown
06 Dec: Rest day.
07 Dec: Past by Sussex to Andover.
08 Dec: Rest day.
09 Dec: Rest day.
10 Dec: We now arrive in New Jersey at Hackettstown.
11 Dec: Bivouacked in middle of woods at John's Mill.
12 Dec: To Pitt's Town.
13 Dec: Arrived at Delaware River.
14 Dec: Crossed the Delaware, over a mile wide, to Pennsylvania, overnighted in Plumstead.
15 Dec: The new commander of the escort is a German, Colonel Mayer, quartered in North Wales.
[Cited from a typescript copy and translation of "Diary of Brunswick Ensign Ernst J.F. Schueler von Senden" in Library of Morristown (NJ) Natl. Hist. Park.]

- - - - -

143

Addition to Chapter 6 - With the Sullivan Expedition

Another German Regiment casualty in upstate New York has been
identified. Corporal James Calhoun of Boyer's (ex-Burchardt)
Company voluntarily joined Lieutenant Lodge's survey party which
was working near Adjusta Town (now Groveland) about 1½ miles
ahead of the troops, when they were fired on by several Indians,
from ambush. Calhoun was mortally wounded on 13 September 1779
and died the next day. [Cited in Journal of Thomas Grant of the
Survey Party, in Frederick Cook, comp.: JOURNALS OF THE MILITARY
EXPEDITION, Albany, NY: Secty. of State, 1887, p142. Boyer's
Company Payroll in National Archives microfilm series M246, roll
130, lists him as killed 15 Sep 1779.]

- - - - -

Addition to Chapter 7 - On the Frontier

Colonel Weltner had the pleasure of his wife's company in
Northumberland during the winter of 1779-80. The details on this
conjugal visit are given by John Adlum, who was previously
mentioned in connection with Colonel Hausegger's appearance in
New York City. Adlum says he made a post-war trip from Frederick,
Maryland to Northumberland on the advice of Mrs Anna Maria
Weltner and her son-in-law, the Rev. Frederick Henop, pastor of
the Frederick-area Reformed congregations. It appears that Pastor
Henop took leave of his parishioners to escort his mother-in-law
to Northumberland. They remained long enough for the pastor to
become acquainted with "all the principal people of the county."
The visit made it possible to give letters of recommendation to
Adlum. [Cited in the unedited "Memoirs of the Life of John Adlum.
The first three Notebooks to December 1784." Typescript on
microfilm @ Hist Soc of York County, Pa, p129.]

- - - - -

Additions to Appendix 3

ADDITIONS TO OFFICERS AND STAFF

ARENDT, Baron d'/de
After returning to Prussia in 1782, he promoted trade with USA.
[Cited in M. D. Learned: Guide to the Manuscript Materials
Relating to American History in the German State Archives,
Washington, DC: Carnegie, 1912, p27ff.]

BENTALOU, Paul NA130.
French mercenary officer. Arrived in Philadelphia from Bordeaux
in November 1776, tried to get cavalry commission, offered second
lieutenancy in GR by Washington, joined Capt Bunner's Co in
winter quarters at Quibbletown, NJ, met General Pulaski during
the night-retreat from Brandywine to Chester and requested to
join his cavalry, resigned from GR as a 2nd Lt in Dec 1777. He
then joined Pulaski's Corps when it was formed in Spring of 1778.

[Cited in Paul Bentalou: PULASKI VINDICATED, Baltimore: Toy, 1826, 41pp. @ Md. Hist. Soc.]

DIFFENDERFER, David
Interviewed at age 91 for write-up in I. Daniel Rupp: HISTORY OF LANCASTER (Pa.) COUNTY, Lancaster: Gilbert Hills, 1844, pp207-211.

HAUSSEGGER, Nicholas
He received land grant of 551 acres in Parcel No. 14 of the Bald Eagle Valley Survey of 1769 for service in the Pontiac War. [Cited in John H. Carter: "Land Grants in Northumberland County, in EARLY EVENTS IN THE SUSQUEHANNA VALLEY, Sunbury: Hist Soc, 1981, p115.] Richards errs in attributing this to Revolutionary service.
Additional information in James F. Davis & Thomas V. Uhrich: A MAN OF NO COUNTRY: THE CASE OF NICHOLAS HAUSSEGGER 1729-86, Lebanon, Pa.: Hist Soc., 1989, 55pp.

JENNINGS, Michael NA130.
Paid as GR Surgeon thru Apr 1778.

LANTZ, Martin NA130.
Enlisted 15 Jul 1776 as Pvt in Graybill's Co for 3 yrs, apptd Quartermaster-Sergeant 13 Nov 1777, paid as QM-Sgt thru May 1778, disch 15 Jul 1779 at Ft.Wyoming, Pa.

LEVY, David NA130.
Enlisted 21 Jul 1776 in Weiser's Co for 3 yrs, GR clerk before May 1777, apptd GR Quartermaster-Sergeant 02 Jun 1778, paid as QM-Sgt to Jun 1779, disch 24 Jul 1779.

LUDWICK, LUDEVIG, Charles NA130.
Appointed Surgeon 15 Nov 1776, GR Surgeon on May 1777 payroll.

MICHAEL, Eberhard NA130.
Resident of Lancaster boro; comm Paymaster 30 Oct 1776, paid as GR Paymaster at least thru Apr 1778.

MIELY, Jacob NA130.
Commissioned Quartermaster of GR 30 Oct 1776, paid thru May 1777.

NEBEL, Gottlieb   NA130.
Sergeant in Bunner's Co May 1777, comm Ensign in Bunner's Co, died
11 Oct 1777 of wound received at Germantown 04 Oct 1777.

POLEHOUSE, Thomas NA130.
Surgeon's Mate in GR 19 Jul 1777.

SMITH, Jacob NA130.
Adjutant pro temp in Mar 1778.

WEIDMAN [1], John (the POW) NA130.
In Woelpper's Co, prom to Ensign 16 Aug 1777, prom to 1st Lt 18
Aug 1778.

WEIDMAN [2], John (the Adjutant) NA130.
Promoted to 1st Lt 14 May 1777.

WURTENBERG, WURTENBERGER, Ludwick NA130.
Appointed Surgeon 18 May 1778, resigned 12 Aug 1778.

ADDITIONAL INFORMATION ON MARYLAND SERGEANTS

ALEXANDER, Jacob NA130. Enlisted at Frederick, Md. 28 Feb 1778
    for 3 yrs, in Bayer's Co, prom to Sgt, in GR when disbanded 01
    Jan 1781, disch.
HAIN, HEAN, HAYNE, Henry NA130. Promoted to Sgt 12 Jun 1778.
INSINGMINGER, EISENMENGER, Philip NA130. Promoted to Sgt in
    Fister's Co 01 Jul 1777, sick Feb 1778, never returned to
    duty.
JOHNSON, JOHNSTON, William NA130. Promoted to Sgt 01 Aug 1779.
LOWE, LOW, Jacob NA130. Reenlisted 27 Feb 1778 for 3 yrs, in GR
    when disbanded 01 Jan 1781, discharged.
MaGAURAN, Francis NA130. Paid as a Sgt in Weltner's
    (ex-Heyser's) Co from 01 Mar 1780, in GR when disbanded 01 Jan
    1781.
MILLER, John/Jacob NA130. Missing at (illegible) Sep 1777, dead
    on Sep 1777 payroll.
SHRUPP, SHRUBB, Henry HFCo, NA130. Enlisted 1776 as Sgt in
    Fister's Co, comm Ens 20 Aug 1777.
SOLLERS, SOLLARS, Frederick/Frank NA130. Enlisted 29 Jul 1776 as
    Cpl/ apptd Sgt in Graybill's Co 28 Jul 1776.
WILHITE, WILHEID, Frederick NA130. Sergeant in Fister's Co Jul
    1777, disch 20/23 Apr 1778.

ADDITIONAL INFORMATION ON MARYLAND CORPORALS

ETTER, Jacob NA130. Promoted to Cpl in 3rd Vac (ex-Graybill's)
    Co 01 Jul 1777.
FROSHOUR, FROSHOWER, Adam NA130. Enlisted in Fister's Co as Pvt
    in 1776, prom to Cpl 01 Jul 1777, sick Mar & Apr 1778, never
    returned to duty.
HARDY, William NA130. Corporal in Graybill's Co, transf to Col
    Spatifort/Stediford Jun 1777.
HOCHSHILD, Jesey NA130. Promoted to Cpl in Fister's Co 01 Sep
    1776.
HOOK, Joseph NA130. Promoted to Cpl in 3rd Vac Co 01 Jul 1777.
HOOVER, George NA130. On duty Jun 1777.
INSINGMINGER, EISENMENGER, Philip NA130. Enlisted in Fister's Co
    as Pvt, prom to Cpl 01 Mar 1777, prom to Sgt 01 Jul 1777.
KRAFFT, CROFT, William NA130. Promoted to Cpl 20 Jun 1778.
LADDER, LEATHER, John NA130. Enlisted as Pvt in Fister's Co 03
    Aug 1776, prom to Cpl before Jun 1777, wounded at Germantown

04 Oct 1777, prom to Sgt.
LANTZ, Martin NA130. Appointed Cpl in Graybill's Co 17 Jul 1776,
    apptd Quarter-master-Sgt 13 Nov 1777.
SPECK, William NA130. Discharged Jun 1777.
STONEBREAKER, Adam NA130. Promoted to Cpl Sep 1777.

ADDITIONAL INFORMATION ON MARYLAND MUSICIANS

DEER, DERR, John Drummer NA130. Deserted from Weiser's Co 05 Jan 1777
FERRINS, FARENCE, Henry Drummer NA130. Returned to Baltimore for reassignment 01 Mar 1781
GITTEN, Jacob Fifer NA130. Appointed Fifer in Heiser's Co, on duty Apr 1778.
HEFFNER, John Drummer NA130. Sick, disch 01 May 1777.
HUTCHCRAFT, Thomas Drummer NA130. Returned to Baltimore for reassignment 01 Mar 1781.
HYATT, George Fifer NA130. Deserted 01 May 1777.
MILLER, Peter Fifer NA130. Paid in Weiser's Co for Dec 1776 thru Feb 1777.
PRICE, Henry Drummer NA130. Appointed in Weiser's Co 20 Mar 1777, last paid Dec 1777.
RIELY, Edward Drummer NA130. In Heiser's Co, on duty Jul 1777, with row-galleys (Penna. Navy) Nov 1778.
SCHLEY, SHLEY, Paul Drummer NA130. In Fister's Co, died 23 Feb 1778.
SPENGLE, Henry Drummer NA130. Appointed 01 Jul 1777, died Nov 1777.
TURVAY, PURVAY, Thomas Drummer NA130. In Fister's Co, on duty Jun 1777.

ADDITIONAL INFORMATION ON FISTER'S, LOHRA'S & BAYER'S MARYLAND COMPANY PRIVATES

From NATIONAL ARCHIVES Microfilm Series M-246, Roll No.130:

ABEY, Leonard.
BARRINGER, David: des 24 Dec 1776.
BEIKER, BACKER, Michael: des 24 Dec 1776.
BERCKSON, John.
BOWEY, Thomas: died 20 Mar 1776.
BUCKNAGLE, Jacob.
CARLE, Adam.
CLEM, John.
COONS, Jacob: died 24 Feb 1777.
DELL, DILL, George.
FISCHER, FISHER, Philip: was wounded in war, died 09 Jan 1839 at Middletown, Frederick Co, Md., aged 82.
HAGINHOUSE, Frederick.
HALLENBRAND, Henry.
HAMMERICH, Peter.
HAWK, HAUK, HAGG, Henry.
HEFFNER, John.
HOCHSHIELD, Christian.
HOOVER, HUBER, George: died 13 Apr 1777.
INSINGMINGER, ISANMANGER, Philip.
KING, Mathias: died 24 Jan 1777.

KUNTZ, Jacob: died 20 Mar 1777.
KURTZ, Jacob: died 29 Jan 1777.
MAIER, Michael.
SCHMELTZER, Adam.
SCHRANTZ, George.
SCHLEY, Paul.
SLANDER, Christian.
STONER, Michael: des 24 Dec 1776, retd.
WEAVER, Jacob: [illegible] 10 Jan 1777.
ZIEGLER, ZEAGLER, Henry: died 26 Feb 1777.

ADDITIONAL INFORMATION ON GRAYBILL'S & MYER'S MARYLAND COMPANY
PRIVATES

From NATIONAL ARCHIVES Microfilm Series M-246, Roll No. 130:

ALTIMUS, William: enl 20 Jul 1776.
ANDREWS, ANDREAS, Wendel: enl 18 Jul 1776.
BAYER, BOYER, Mathias: enl 15 Jul 1776, des 28 Dec 1776.
CAMPBELL, Thomas: taken by order of Board of War.
CHARREL, Charles: enl 07 Aug 1776, missing at Bonoumstown NJ Oct
  1777.
CREDO, CRETHO, George: enl 03 May 1777 for 3 yrs.
CUNIUS, William: enl 07 Aug 1776, disch 07 Mar 1777.
DANROTH, Gottlieb: missing 04 Dec 1776, exchanged & rejoined 28
  Jul 1777.
DECKER, Henry: enl 11 Jul 1776, des 28 Sep 1776.
DOWNEY, TOWNEY, Frederick: enl 27 Aug 1776, des 01 Jan 1777.
DYCHE, John B.: enl 20 Jul 1776, des 11 May 1777, rejoined 07 May
  1778.
ETZINGER, ETTSBERGER, Wolfgang: enl 17 Jul 1776, on duty May
  1778.
EISEL, EYSSELL, John: enl 11 Aug 1776.
FRANTZ, Abraham: enl 20 Jul 1776.
GORR, Andrew: enl 02 Aug 1776, disch no date.
GORR, Richard: enl 15 Jul 1776, des 11 Mar 1777.
HARDENSTEIN, Jacob: enl 01 Aug 1776, des 28 Oct 1776.
HARGERODER, Henry: enl 01 Aug 1776, des 02 Dec 1776.
HARTMAN, Henry: enl 20 Jul 1776, des 01 Jan 1777.
HALLER, HELLER, Frederick: apptd Sgt before Oct 1777.
HOFFMAN, Jacob: enl 06 Aug 1776.
HOOK, Joseph: prom to Cpl 01 Jul 1777.
HULING, Michael: enl 01 Aug 1776.
KERNS, Jacob: enl 15 Jul 1776, died no date.
KNEARY, KENEARY, Lorentz: des Jul 1777.
KEYSER, Nicholas: enl 21 Jul 1776, on duty May 1778.
KINTZ, Jacob: enl 20 Jul 1776, des 01 Dec 1776.
MILLBERGER, Henry: missing at Princeton 04 Jan 1777.
MILLER, Anthony: on duty May 1778.
MILLER, Philip: taken by order of Board of War, aboard the

149

frigate Jun.
MOORE, John: enl 18 Jul 1776, des 11 May 1777.
MUMMA, David: enl 20 Jul 1776, on duty with the butchers May
    1778.
MYERS, George: enl 19 Aug 1776, des Jun 1777.
PROCTER, Joseph: enl 15 Aug 1776, des Jun 1777.
REINHART, Simon: enl 20 Jul 1776.
REGELE, Christopher: enl 17 Jul 1776, des 02 Dec 1776.
RITTLEMYER, George: enl 16 Aug 1776.
ROHRBACH, Adam: disch before 22 May 1777.
SEGMAN, Peter: enl 10 Aug 1776, des 28 Sep 1776.
SMITH, James: enl 04 Aug 1776, des Feb 1778.
SMITH, John: enl 10 Aug 1776.
SMITH, Joseph: enl 25 Aug 1776, des Jul 1777.
SMITH, Roland: des 11 May 1777.
SPRENGLE, Henry: enl 02 Aug 1776, apptd drummer 01 Jul 1777.
STRITER, Joseph: enl 17 Jul 1776, on duty May 1777.
SUMMERS, John: taken by order of Board of War, aboard the frigate
    Jun.
WAGER, WEGER, Frederick: enl 10 Jul 1776, wounded May 1777, dead
    Jun 1777.
WELTY, John: enl 17 Jul 1776, des 01 Jan 1777.
WILLIAMS, Joseph: enl 23 Jul 1776.
WILSTOCK, Henry: enl 25 Aug 1776, des 01 May 1777.

ADDITIONAL NAMES & INFORMATION ON HEISER'S & WELTNER'S MARYLAND
COMPANY PRIVATES

From NATIONAL ARCHIVES Microfim M-246, Roll No.130:

ARMSTRONG, John Jr: sick absent Jun-Jul 1777.
ARMSTRONG, John Sr: with Pioneers Jun, Jul, Nov 1777, with Col
    Biddle Apr 1778.
BAIRD, BEARD, Nicholas: died 12 Sep 1777.
BISHOP, Jacob: wounded Oct 1777, on duty Nov 1777.
BOWARD, BAWARD, Michael: des 03 Jan 1777, retd.
BURNEY, Thomas: never joined Co.
FLEEGERT, Archibald: died May 1777.
FOGLE, John: missing at Chestnut Hill/Germantown 04 Oct 1777.
FOGLER, Simon: wounded Oct 1777, disch 12 Apr 1778.
GITTING, George: on duty Apr 1778.
GREECHBAUM, Philip: sick hospital Jun 1777, dropped from roll Jul
    1777.
GRIBBS, Peter: missing Jul 1777.
GRUBB, John: mentioned Jul 1777 only.
HACKET, Jonathan: wounded Sep 1777, on duty Apr 1778.
HARMONY, George: sick hospital Jul 1777, dropped from roll Sep
    1777.
LOWER, LIESER, LEISER, Adam: waiter in hospital Jun 1777, died 07
    Oct 1777.
MICHAEL, John: with paymaster May 1777, on duty Jun 1777, prom to

        Cpl Sep 1777.
MYERS, Francis: missing at Chestnut Hill/Germantown 04 Oct 1777.
PANTHAR, PENDER, Henry: on duty Apr 1778.
ROBINSON, John: des 18 Jun 1777.
ROCH, Morris: sick hospital Jul 1777, des Oct 1777.
SHEESE, Peter: des Jun 1777.
SIDES, Christian: on duty May 1777, not on roll Jun 1777.
STONEBREAKER, Adam: prom to Cpl Sep 1777.
WISE, George: missing Jun 1777.
YOUNG, Gottfried: sick hospital Oct 1777, disch Mar 1778.

ADDITIONAL NAMES & INFORMATION ON KEYPORT'S & BALTZEL'S MARYLAND
COMPANY PRIVATES

From NATIONAL ARCHIVES Microfilm Series M-246, Roll No. 131:

AMERSLY, John: des after 01 Aug 1780.
BARTON, Thomas, enl 04 Nov 1776, des same day.
BAST, Peter: disch 01 Mar 1777.
BIGLER, Jacob: des 01 Oct 1776.
BROWN, John: missing since 10 May 1777.
BRUBAKER, Michael: des 01 Dec 1776.
COLLINS, Morris: on muster roll for Nov 1777, des 02 Feb 1778.
CARROL, Joseph: disch 01 Nov 1776.
CLINCKER, Peter: enl 27 Oct 1776, with Gen Fermoy May 1777.
DOCHTERMAN, Michael: des 01 Mar 1777.
ELLIOT, Benjamin: des after 01 Aug 1780.
FOWLER, Jonathan: enl 01 Dec 1776, died in hospital 19 Jun 1777.
FRANKEN, FRANKLIN, John: on command 22 May 1777, wagoner.
FROLICK, Christian: 25 July 1776, confined for debts May 1777.
FUHRMAN, Daniel: des 01 Mar 1777.
HAHN, Peter: des 01 Dec 1776.
HAUSER, MAUSER, Ludwick: enl 29 Oct 1776, des 30 Oct 1776.
HILLER, George: enl 19 Aug 1776, disch 07 Apr 1777.
HOEFLICH, HAIFLY, Jacob.
KELLY, Patrick: enl 01 Mar 1777.
LEVY, David: on duty Feb 1778, sick @ Frederick, Md May 1778,
    dropped from rolls Jun 1778.
LICHTE, LICHTY, Christian: des 01 Oct 1776.
LOWREY, Gottfried: armorer at Lebanon Apr 1778.
McCOLLOUGH, Lewis: enl 07 Apr 1777.
MARKEL, MERKEL, Adam: des 01 Nov 1776.
SHINGLEDECKER, Andrew: enl 25 Aug 1776, des same day.
SHOREHT, SCHORCHT, John.
SHIPE, STREIB, David: died 01 Jun 1778.
SHRYER, SCHREIER, Mathias: articifer at work at the Contl.
    Armoury May 1777-Apr 1778.
SHUSTER, SHESLER, George: des 01 Oct 1776.
TRAUTH, Henry: des 01 Oct 1776.
WINCK, Jacob: des 31 Jan 1777.

BENCKLER, John NA131. Appointed Sgt 15 Aug 1776 in Weiser's Co, disch 27 Aug 1777.

BISHOP, John NA131. Enlisted 28 Jul 1776 as Pvt in Weiser's Co, prom to Sgt 01 Aug 1777, disch 01 Feb 1778.

DENHARD, Thomas NA130. Enlisted & apptd Sgt 24 Jul 1776 in Woelpper's Co, died 16 Sep 1776.

DONODEN, DENOUDEN, DONDEN, John NA130. In Burchardt's Co, prom from Cpl before Dec 1777, died 10 Mar 1778.

FRANCIS, George NA130. Appointed Sgt in Hubley's Co 01 Jun 1777, dropped from roll Jan 1778, listed as Sgt-Maj on Hubley's Mar 1778 roll.

GABRIEL, Peter NA130. Appointed Quartermaster-Sgt after Oct 1779.

GLECKNER, GLICKNER, Charles NA131. Appointed Sgt 10 July 1776 in Weiser's Co, disch Aug 1777.

HANSS, HAUSS HANS, HANTZ, Michael NA130. Enlisted 06 Aug 1776, apptd Sgt 01 Dec 1776.

HELLER, Frederick NA130. 2nd Sgt-Maj, listed with Burchardt's Co 22 May 1777.

JOHNSTONE, John NA130. Appointed Sgt in Hubley's Co 25 Jan 1777, on duty when GR disbanded 01 Jan 1781.

KREDELBACH, John NA130. Enlisted as Pvt in Woelpper's Co, apptd Sgt 01 Nov 1776, captured at Trenton 02 Jan 1777, retd to duty 20 May 1777, sick in hospital Aug-Oct 1777, "hanged by the [British] Regulars" Oct 1777.

LUFT, LUFF, George NA130. Appointed Sgt 10 Jul 1776 in Burchardt's Co.

MAAG, Henry NA130. Enlisted for war, appointed Sgt 10 Jul 1776 in Burchardt's Co, comm Ens in GR 15 Aug 1777.

McCURTAIN, Daniel NA130. On duty May 1777.

MULLS, MULZ, Francis NA130. Enlisted and apptd Sgt 05 Aug 1776.

NEBEL, Gottlieb NA130. On duty as Sgt in Bunner's Co May 1777, comm Ens in GR before 11 Oct 1777.

PRICE, George NA131. Promoted to Sgt 01 Feb 1778, disch 20 Jul 1779.

REISHLEY, Lewis NA130. Appointed Sgt in Hubley's Co before 15 Oct 1777, on duty when GR disbanded 01 Jan 1781.

SMITH, Jacob Sergeant-Major NA130 1st Sgt-Maj, listed with Burchardt Co 22 May 1777.

UNGER, UNKER, Christian NA130. Enlisted for 3 yrs, apptd Sgt 15 Jul 1776 in Burchardt'so, missing 27 Dec 1776 at Trenton/Princeton.

VALENTINE, _____ NA130. Sergeant in Burchardt's Co, left the Rgt 01 Apr 1777.

WEIDMAN, WHITEMAN, John NA130. Of Berks/Phila Co; apptd Sgt 01 Nov 1776 in Hubley's Co, comm Ens in GR 10/16 Aug 1777.

WINKLER, WINCKLER, John Henry NA130. On duty as Sgt in Bunner's Co May 1777, died 26 Oct 1779.

WISERT, WEISSERT, Jacob NA130. On duty as Sgt in Bunner's Co May 1777, paid thru Oct 1779.

YOUNG, Marcus   NA130. Commissioned 2nd Lt in GR 08 Jun 1777.

ADDITIONAL INFORMATION ON PENNSYLVANIA CORPORALS

BISHOP, John   NA131. Enl 28 Jul 1776, as Pvt in Weiser's Co, prom
   to Cpl 15 Aug 1776, prom to Sgt 01 Aug 1777.
BRININGER, Frederick   NA130. Appointed Cpl in Woelpper's Co 01
   May 1777, on duty Aug 1777.
BROWNSBERRY, Lewis   NA130. Appointed Cpl in Hubley's Co Oct 1777,
   on duty when GR disbanded 01 Jan 1781.
CALHOUN, CAHOUN, CALHAWN, GOHOUN, James NA130. Killed 14/15 Sep
   1779 near Genesee Town, NY in Indian ambush on Sullivan
   Expedition as volunteer with survey party.
DEAL, DEEL, Andrew   NA130. Enlisted for war in Bunner's Co,
   joined 17 May 1778, on duty Oct 1778.
DIEFFENDERFER, David   NA130. Missing 10 May 1777, listed captured
   Jun 1777, retd from captivity, prom to Sgt.
DONDEN, DENOTIN, Cornelius Jonathan/John NA130. Enlisted for 3
   yrs in Burchardt's Co and apptd Cpl 28 Jul 1776, missing at
   Trenton 27 Dec 1776, listed as rejoined Jun 1777, promoted to
   Sgt before Dec 1777.
FLOWER, Philip   NA130. Appointed Cpl in Hubley's Co 01 Nov 1776,
   killed at Battle of Germantown 04 Oct 1777.
FUNK, FUNCK, George   NA130. Appointed Cpl in Hubley's Co 01 Oct
   1777, on duty when GR disbanded 01 Jan 1781.
HELLER, Frederick   NA130. 2nd Sgt-Maj listed with Burchardt's Co
   22 May 1777.
HORMLY, HARMLOSS, HARMLESS, Henry NA130. Enlisted for war & apptd
   Cpl 10 Jul 1776 in Burchardt's Co, on duty 22 May 1777.
LINDEMAN, Frederick   NA130. Appointed Cpl 01 Nov 1776 in
   Woelpper's Co, prom to Sgt.
MAYER, MOYER, MYERS, Jacob NA130. Enlisted 07 Nov 1776 in Phila
   for war as Pvt in Burchardt's Co, prom to Cpl, Cpl Dec 1777 to
   Oct 1778, des 13 Jul 1779.
MILLER, John   NA130. Appointed Cpl 01 Nov 1776 in Hubley's Co,
   des 01 Feb 1777.
PICKER, PICKERT, PICKIST, Frederick NA130. Enlisted for 3 yrs,
   apptd Cpl 03 Aug 1776 in Burchardt's Co, missing 23 Feb 1777
   at Bonumtown, NJ.
PRICE, George   NA131. Appointed Cpl 14 Jul 1776 in Weiser's Co,
   prom to Sgt before Jan 1778.
RAHN, RONE, ROAN, Conrad NA131. Appointed Cpl 14 Jul/15 Aug 1776
   in Weiser's Co, sick at Easton 22 May 1777, disch before Oct
   1777.
REICHLEY, REISKLEY, Lewis NA130. Appointed Cpl 01 Nov 1776 in
   Hubley's Co, prom to Sgt before 12 Oct 1777.
RIVELY, Frederick   NA130. Enlisted as Pvt in Burchardt's Co, paid
   as Cpl from 01 Nov 1779, on duty Dec 1780.
RUDART, William/Christian NA130. Appointed Cpl 20 Aug 1776, des
   09 Jan 1777, retd 01 Mar 1777, on duty Dec 1777.
SHAFFER, Jacob   NA130. In Bunners Co, on duty May 1777.

SHEBLER, SHIBLER, Reinhart/Richard NA130. Enlisted for 3 yrs, sick at New Holland 10 Jun-Oct 1778.
WILHELM, Frederick NA131. Enlisted 06/09 Aug 1776 as Pvt in Weiser's Co, promoted to Cpl 01 Jan 1778, disch 20 Jul 1779.
WINAND, WIAND, WEYAND, John NA130. Appointed Cpl 01 Sep 1777 in Woelpper's Co.

ADDITIONAL INFORMATION ON PENNSYLVANIA MUSICIANS

ALEXANDER, Joseph Fifer NA130. Deserted 24 Mar 1777, retd, transf to Burchardt's Co 30 Aug 1778.
APPLEGATE, Daniel Drum & Fife Na130. In Bunner's Co, died 15 Jul 1778.
BATES, BENTIS, BANTIS, Peter Drummer NA130. Enlisted & apptd drummer in Woelpper's Co 15 Dec 1776, Left sick in Phila 20 Jan 1777, not returned by Jun 1777, apparent deserter.
CONRAD, John Drum & Fife NA130. In Bunner's Co, des 10 Apr 1777.
DERR, DEER, John Drummer NA131. In Weiser's Co, apptd 25 Aug 1776, des 05 Jan 1777.
FACUNDUS, FOGOUNDTIS, George Ferdinand Drummer NA130. Enlisted 04 May 1777 in Woelpper's Co.
HARRIS, John Fife-Major NA130. On duty 22 May 1777 in Bunner's Co, Drum-major in Jun 1779.
HART, John Drum-Major NA130. Enlisted 02/21 Jul 1776 in Phila for war in Burchardt's Co, apptd Drum-Major 25 Jul 1776, on duty in Bunner's Co until Nov 1780.
JENKINS, Israel Drummer NA130. Appointed 27 Sep 1776, apptd to Hubley's Co 04 Jan/23 May 1777.
LEVI, Jacob Drummer NA131. In Weiser's Co, disch 20 Jul 1779.
MILLER, Peter Fifer NA131. In Weiser's Co, paid thru Feb 1777.
MULZ, Frederick/Francis Drum & Fife NA130. Enlisted 05 Aug 1776, apptd drummer next day in Bunner's Co, transf to Woelpper's Co, apptd fifer 01 Jun 1777, disch as drummer from Bunner's Co 14 Aug 1779.
NEFF, Issac Drummer NA130. Appointed to Hubley's Co 27 Sep 1776, des 15 Jan 1777.
PIERSEY, Jacob Fifer NA130. Appointed 25 Aug 1776 in Woelpper's Co, disch 19 Mar 1777.
PRICE, Henry Fifer NA131. In Weiser's Co, apptd 20 Mar 1777.

ADDITIONAL INFORMATION BUNNER'S PENNSYLVANIA COMPANY PRIVATES

From NATIONAL ARCHIVES Microfilm Series M-246, roll 130:

ARENDBERGER, Peter: des 02 Dec 1776.
BACHMAN, Christian: des Aug 1776.
BANZ, BANZAY, BANTZER, BONSA, Detmar/Dikmar: enl 09 Nov 1776.
BENKLEY, Frederick: des 10 Jan 1777.
BETTINGER, Benjamin: missing at Bonumstown, NJ 10 May 1777.
BLESS, John: died 01 Jan 1777.

BUTTLER, George: des 16 Jan 1777.
CASTER, CARTER, Jacob: on command May 1777.
COBLER, Frederick: enl 09 Nov 1776, des 26 Nov 1776.
CRAMER, Israel: des 15 Nov 1776.
CRAMER, John: des 15 Nov 1776.
DARANITZE, John: missing at Trenton 10 Jan 1777.
DAVIS, Thomas: on command May 1777.
DIES, DEETZ, DEATS, TEATS, Frederick.
FIEDEREN, Gasper: disch 15 May 1777.
FREEMAN, Jacob: missing at Trenton 10 Jan 1777.
HAISS, Frederick: on duty May 1777.
HAUSS, Peter: des 29 Oct 1776.
HEIDLER, HYDLER, Martin: enl 20 Aug/08 Oct 1776.
HEINTZ, HEIMS, HYMES, William.
HELLER, Jacob: des 10 Jan 1777.
KEIPEN, Philip: des 10 Jan 1777.
KING, John: des 18 Jan 1777.
KEISER, KEYSER, KREISTER, John.
KRESSEL, Andrew: enl 04 Nov 1776, on duty May 1777.
LEITZ, Casmier, des 18 Jan 1777.
LONG, John: des 15 Nov 1776.
LORRENT, John: des 15 Nov 1776.
LUDWIG, LUDEVICK, George: enl 19 Mar 1777, on duty May 1777.
MOORE, John: enl 30 Oct 1776, on duty May 1777.
MOSER, Henry: on command May 1777.
MUFF, George: des 16 Jan 1777.
MYER, John, des Aug 1776.
NEIBELT, John: des 29 Oct 1776.
REICHERT, REINHARD, Jacob: died 15 Mar 1777.
ROSE, Thomas: des Aug 1776.
SMITH, John: on furlough May 1777.
STAVER, George: des 21 Jan 1777.
STOUCH, Andrew: des 12 Jan 1777.
VELTY, George: sick in hospital May 1777.

ADDITIONAL INFORMATION BURCHARDT'S PENNSYLVANIA COMPANY PRIVATES

From NATIONAL ARCHIVES Microfilm Series M-246, roll No. 130:

ABLE, Solomon: enl 13 Jul 1776 in Phila for war, joined 21 Sep 1776.
AMEY, AMIE, AMIO, Henry: enl 16 Jul 1776 in Phila for 3 yrs, on duty May 1777.
AUNEFORT, AUNFERT, Andrew: enl 02 Aug 1776 in Phila for 3 yrs, joined 21 Sep 1776.
BEAVER, Nicholas: enl 30 Jul 1776 in Phila for war, on duty Oct 1778.
BLOOM, David: enl 30 Jul 1776 in Phila/Berks County for 3yrs.
CRUMLY, GRUMLEY, Jacob: enl 30 Jul/20 Aug 1776 in Phila for war.
DEHART, Abraham: enl 04 Aug 1776 in Phila for 3 yrs, joined 21 Sep 1776.

DEHMER, Joseph: enl 23 Jul 1776 in Phila for war, joined 21 Sep 1776.

FEIFER, George: enl 04 Aug 1776 in Phila for war, on duty Oct 1778.

FIFLER, FIFLES, John George: enl 23 Aug 1776 in Phila for war, joined 21 Sep 1776.

FILE, PHILE, Philip: enl 17 Aug 1776 in Phila for war.

FRANCK, Peter: enl 21 Jul 1776 in Phila for war, joined 21 Sep 1776.

GREGORY, Jacob: enl 04 Aug 1776 in Phila for 3 yrs, joined 21 Sep 1776.

HAINES, Michael: enl 03 Aug 1776 for 3 yrs, with wagons Oct 1778.

HARDSTRONG, HARTSTONGUE, William: enl 28 Jul 1776 in Phila for war, died 23 Mar 1777.

JONES, John: enl 27 Aug 1776 for 3 yrs, joined 21 Sep 1776.

KASPER, Jacob, delete HARPER on page 127.

KERL, George: enl 25 Jul 1776 in Phila for war, with articifers Oct 1778.

KOSTER, CUSTER, John: enl 05 Sep 1776 in Phila for war, died 17 Jan 1777.

LINDSAY, Thomas: enl 24 Sep 1776 for 3 yrs, des 06 Oct 1776.

MALLIDOR, MUDORE, Adam: enl 07 Nov 1776 in Phila for war, disch 20 Mar 1777.

MARTIN, John: enl 30 Jul 1776 in Phila for war, on duty May 1777.

MURPHY, John: enl 13 Aug 1776 in Phila for 3 yrs, with wagons Oct 1778.

MYERS, MYARS, Jacob: enl 07 Nov 1776 in Phila for war, joined 21 Sep 1776.

RAM, ROAN, Adam: enl 30 Jul 1776 for war, des 07 Jan 1777.

SHAFER, Engelbert: enl 17 Jul 1776 in Phila for war, des 24 Mar 1777.

SHOCK, Philip: enl 03 Aug 1776 in Phila for war, des 26 Mar 1777.

SMITH, George: enl 04 Sep 1776 in Phila for 3 yrs, on duty May 1777.

SUMER, SUMMERS, John: enl 06 Aug 1776 in Phila for war, with wagons Oct 1778.

SUNLIGHTER, SONLITER, John: enl 16 Jul 1776 in Phila for 3 yrs.

ULRICH, ULRICK, Nicolas: enl 07 Sep 1776 in Phila for war, died 03 May 1777.

UNKER, Christian Jr: enl 15 Jul 1776 in Phila for 3 yrs, joined 21 Sep 1776.

WARNER, WERNER, Ludwick: enl 26 Feb 1778, died 08 Jun 1778.

WARNER, WERNER, Nicholas: enl 24 Sep 1776 for war.

WEIDMAN, John: joined 11 Jun 1778.

WEIRMAN, WIERMAN, Francis/Thomas: enl 31 Jul 1776 in Phila for 3 yrs, joined 21 Sep 1776, des 07 Jan 1777.

WENTZ, Jacob: enl 23 Jul 1776 in Phila, prom to Cpl 24 Jul 1776.

WERNER, Nicholas: joined 01 Jun 1778.

WHEELER, Thomas: enl 21 Aug 1776 in Phila for war.

WILLIAMS, Michael: enl 16 Nov 1776 for war, died 06 Mar 1778.

WINDROM, WINDROME, VENDROME, Hugh: enl 22 Aug 1776 in Phila for war.

ADDITIONAL INFORMATION ON HUBLEYS' PENNSYLVANIA COMPANY PRIVATES

From NATIONAL ARCHIVES Microfilm Series M-246, Roll No.130:

BANKS, Joseph: enl 05 Nov 1776, des 25 Mar 1777.
BEYERLY, BYERLY, Christian/Christopher: sick in hospital May 1777.
BOWER, George: enl 13 Jul 1776, des 27 Jul 1777.
BROADBECK, George: enl 27 Jul 1776, died 01 Feb 1777.
BROWNSBERRY, Lewis: enl 24 Jul 1776.
BRIMMER, Henry: enl 21 Aug 1776, des 10 Nov 1776, confined in Main Guard Jul 1777.
CASY, Robert: enl 05 Nov 1776, des 06 Apr 1777.
COYLE, Lewis: enl 07 Mar 1777.
CRANE, John: listed as wounded at Princeton Jan 1777 up to Aug 1777.
DONAHOO, DONOCHOR, DONOCHAN, Robert.
ERLAN, James: enl 12 Aug 1776, des 01 Dec 1776.
FRONIER, George: enl 02 Nov 1776, not listed Jul 1777.
FUNK, George: enl 20 Jul 1776, prom to Cpl 01 Oct 1777.
GERHARD, George: enl 25 Aug 1776, des 27 Nov 1776.
HENSELL, HANSEL, HANTZEL, WETZELL, George: enl 25 Nov 1776, sick at Morristown Jul 1777.
HITTRINGTON, John: enl 15 Oct 1776, des 24 Oct 1776/24 Feb 1777.
ISRAELO, Casper: enl 24 Jul 1776 for 3 yrs, AWOL, rejoined 28 May 1777.
JONES, David: enl 10 Sep 1776, des 11/14 Feb 1777.
JONES, Silas: enl 18 Oct 1776, des 24 Oct 1776.
KELLER, John: enl 31 Aug 1776, des 20 Feb 1777.
KEPHARD, KEPPARD, John, enl 09 Aug 1776.
LEAF, Mathias: enl 08 Aug 1776, on command May 1777.
LLOYD, John: enl 10 Sep 1776, des 11/14 Feb 1777.
MENCHER, Christian: wounded & at Morristown Jul-Aug 1777.
MOORE, John: enl 15 Aug 1776, des 27/29 Nov 1776.
MORGAN, Thomas: enl 05 Nov 1776, missing at Trenton 03 Jan 1777.
NICK, Henry: enl 30 Jul 1776.
ORMOND, William: enl 05 Nov 1776, sick absent May 1777.
REAVELY, Christian: enl 31 Jul 1776, died 05 Feb 1777.
ROAN, Christian: enl 12 Aug 1776, des 14 Feb 1777.
RUDDY, Emanuel: enl 05 Nov 1776, sick absent May 1777.
RYEBECKER, John: enl 27 Jul 1776, missing/des 03/09 Jan 1777, rejoined 28 May 1777.
SHOEMAKER, Thomas: enl 27 Jul 1776, des 29 Mar 1777.
SICKLE, William: enl 21 Jul 1776, on command May 1777.
STONER, John: enl 05 Aug 1776, AWOL May 1777.
STROUD, Philip: enl 05 Nov 1776, on command May 1777.
WISLER, WEISLER, WISLAR, VISLER, Jacob.
ZIMMERMAN, Nicholas: enl 02 Aug 1776, des 09 Sep 1776.

ADDITIONAL INFORMATION ON WEISER'S & RICE'S PENNSYLVANIA COMPANY
PRIVATES

From NATIONAL ARCHIVES Microfilm Series M-246, Roll No.131:

BARNHEISEL, BORNHEUSEL, John: pd for Jul 1777.
BENCKELER, John: paid for Aug 1777.
BISHOP, John: enl 28 Jul 1776, des 05 Jan 1777.
BAILY, BELY, BACKER, John: enl 10 Feb 1777, missing @ Germantown.
BAILY, James: missing at Germantown 04 Oct 1777.
BROADBACK, Michael: joined 03 Sep 1778.
BROWN, William: enl 14 Oct 1776, des 20 Nov 1776.
CEALOR, Joseph, died 16 Jan 1777.
CHRISSMAN, CHRISTMAN, John: enl 05/06 Aug 1776, in Yellow Spgs
    Hosp Apr 1778, des 16 Sep 1778, died/des 06 Feb 1779.
CONELY, Lawrence: enl 30 Nov 1776, des 16/24 Dec 1776.
DAWNEY, TOWNEY, Peter: enl 02 Aug 1776, disch Feb 1778.
EABLE, EAPPLE, Henry: enl 01 Oct 1776, des Oct 1777.
EAYERT, John: disch 31 Jan 1779.
EIKEL, EACKLE, ECHEL, Philip: enl 10 Mar 1777, des Oct 1777.
ERVAN, William: on Dec76-Feb77 payroll, but not paid.
GILLMAN, HILLMAN, Philip: enl 14 July 1776, sick in hospital 22
    May 1777, missing at Germantown, disch 20 Jul 1779.
HENRICK, HENRY, Gottlieb: enl 30 Nov 1776, on command 22 May
    1777, missing at Germantown 04 Oct 1777.
HIGINS, Patrick: enl 1/21 Nov 1776.
HOLDERY, HILDY, Herman: paid for Jul 1777.
HEWER, HINER, HOWER, John: enl 12 Aug 1776, Trenton POW.
KETTLE, Cornelius: des Jul 1780.
LARASH, LORASH, Jacob: enl 06 Oct 1776, POW 03 Jan 1777, sick at
    home May 1777.
LEARBY, Benjamin: on Dec76-Feb77 payroll, but not paid.
LESHER, Peter: paid thru May 1777.
McLAIN, Jacob: enl 01 Sep 1776, des 28 Dec 1776, rejoined 30 May
    1778.
MAUST, MAST, MATT, Joseph: enl 19 Jul 1776, des 05 Jan 1777,
    retd, des Jul 1780.
MAYER, MEYER, MYER, Everhard: enl 22 Aug/01 Sep 1776, des Jul
    1780.
MILLER, Joseph: enl 19 Oct 1776, on recruiting 22 May 1777.
MILLER, Peter: 01 Oct 1776, apptd fifer, des 09 Apr 1777.
MINNERSON, MIENERSON, John: paid for Jul 1777.
MOORE, MOOR, James: enl 14 Nov 1776, des 24 Dec 1776.
NAIL, John: des Oct 1777.
NEUFONG, NEWFANG, Balzer: sick absent 22 May 1777.
PORTNER, John: Princeton POW 03 Jan 1777, des from hospital Aug
    1777, on duty Oct 1777.
PRICE, Abraham: rejoined 08 Jun 1778.
RIEGEL, RIGGLE, Michael.
RIGGER, Elias: enl 02 Mar 1777, pd for Jul 1777.
RISHEL, Martin: paid thru Feb 1777.
RISTER, Frederick: missing at Germantown 04 Oct 1777.

158

ROGER, ROGAN, REGGER, Elias: enl 02 Mar 1777, on furlough May 1777.
ROMICK, Joseph: enl 26 Aug 1776, des 28 Dec 1776, retd, died at Yellow Spgs Hosp 20 May 1778.
ROSMEISEL, ROSEMEISEL, Adam: 22 Jul 1776, disch Oct 1777.
SEYFERT, CYPHERT, Henry: enl 22 Jul 1776, disch 20 Jul 1779.
SHAFFER, SCHIFFER, Peter: des 01 Jul 1777.
SMITH, Andrew: enl 28 Nov 1776, des 16 Dec 1776, retd, missing at Germantown.
SMITH, James: des 24 Dec 1776.
SMITH, Jacob: paid thru May 1777.
SMITH, William: enl 19 Nov 1776, des 24 Dec 1776.
SNIDER, SNYDER, John: des 05 Jan 1777, retd.
SNIDER, William: enl 10 Oct 1776, des 16 Dec 1776.
SPARKS, James: enl 18 Nov 1776, wounded @ Germantown 04 Oct 1777, sick hospital Dec 1777.
SPYER, SPIRE, Frederick: enl 15 Jul 1776, on furlough 22 May 1777.
SWAANER, Peter: enl 28 Nov 1776, des 16 Jan 1777.
TEDEROW, TODRA, TODRO, TUDRO, John: enl 20 Aug 1776, des 03 Dec 1776.
TOMEY, TOMY, Charles: enl 13 Nov 1776, des 16/24 Dec 1776.
TRESTOR, TRISTOR, TREXLER, Frederick: missing at Germantown 04 Oct 1777.
TRYWITZ, Johann Conrad: enl 10 Aug 1776, des 05 Jan 1777.
WALL, WALLMAN, William: enl 27 July 1776, des 24 Dec 1776.
WALTMAN, Nicholas: enl 10 Jul 1776, des 05 Jan 1777.
WEIGEL, WEIGLE, VEIKLE, Christopher/Stophel: des 04 Feb 1778.
WERLOY, WARLEY, WURLY, Philip.
WILHELM, Frederick: enl 03 Aug 1776 for 3 yrs, prom to Cpl 01 Jan 1778.
WILLIAMS, Wenson/Weson: enl 09/19 Aug 1776, sick present Jun 1777, des 15 May 1778.
YAPLE, YEPPLE, YEBEL, EAPPLE, Henry: enl 1/21 Oct 1776, des Oct 1777, retd.
YEISLEY, Michael: enl 09 Aug 1776, disch 07 Mar 1778.
YOUNG, Marks: volunteer paid thru Feb 1777.

ADDITIONAL INFORMATION ON WOELPPER'S & SHRAWDER'S PENNSYLVANIA COMPANY PRIVATES

From NATIONAL ARCHIVES Microfilm Series M-246, Roll No.131:

BANICK, BANIG, Ditrick/Dedrick: enl 01 Jan 1777, on duty Dec 1777.
BOESHORE, John: enl 03 Jun 1777 in Heidelberg Twp-Lancaster Co for 3 yrs, des 09 June 1777.
BOWMAN, Thomas: enl 02 Oct 1776, on duty December 1777.
BROWN, George Frederick: des 02 Jan 1777.
BRUNNER, John: enl 19 Aug 1776, des 20 Dec 1776, retd 01 May 1777, on duty December 1777.

CLAUSS, Michael: des 19 Dec 1776.
COAN, Christian: enl 14 Aug 1776, sick in Hospital December 1777.
DISHLER, David: enl 22 May 1777 in Heidelberg Twp-Lancaster Co
   for 3 yrs, on duty December 1777.
DULL, Christian: enl 25 Aug 1776, on duty December 1777.
FEIL, George: enl 06 Aug 1776, died 05 Mar 1777.
FERDINAND, George: enl 04 May 1777 in Heidelberg Twp-Lancaster Co
   for 3 yrs.
FISHER, Yost: enl 13 Nov 1776, des 08 Mar 1777.
GERHOLD, Nicolaus: enl 26 Nov 1776, missing 02 Jan 1777, POW on
   February 1777 payroll.
GOEBEL, John: enl 13 Nov 1776, missing - killed at Trenton 02 Jan
   1777.
GRUBER, George: enl 02 Feb 1777, on duty December 1777.
HALL, Henry, enl 16 Dec 1776, on command, AWOL October 1777.
HARRINGTON, John: enl 10 Oct 1776, des 05 Nov/11 Dec 1776.
HAWK, HAWKE, Andrew: enl 27 Apr 1777 in Heidelberg Twp-Lancaster
   Co for 3 yrs, on duty December 1777.
HERGOOD, Henry: enl 21/29 Dec 1776, des 09 Jan 1777.
HESS, John Tobias: enl 27 Apr 1777 in Heidelberg Twp-Lancaster Co
   for 3 yrs, on duty December 1777.
KELLER, George: enl 01 Mar 1778 in Heidelberg Twp-Lancaster Co
   for war.
KREDELBACH, John: enl 12 Aug 1776, prom to Sgt 01 Nov 1776.
LECRAN, SECRAN, John: enl 23 Oct 1776, discharged 28 Nov 1776.
MAHLY, MACHLY, Philip: enl 14 Nov 1776, des 10 Mar 1777.
MAYER, MEYER, Peter: enl 24 May 1777 in Heidelberg Twp-Lancaster
   Co for 3 yrs, wounded at Germantown 04 Oct 1777.
MILLER, Maxmillian/Marc/Mark: enl 19 Aug 1776.
MOERE, MOORE, Christopher: enl 09 Nov 1776, POW 26 Dec 1776, des
   03 Jan 1777, retd 01 Mar 1777, Col Arendt's servant in June
   1777.
MULZ, Frederick/Francis: enl 05 Aug 1776, apptd drummer same day.
PEQUA, William: enl 08 Nov 1776, des 08 Mar 1777.
PIFER, Henry: enl 18/19 Aug 1776 at Phila, des 04 Oct 1776, retd
   01 Mar 1777, on command as seaman in November 1777, reenl 13
   Mar 1780 for war, disch 1781. Resided in Phila in 1835, aged
   79.
POLANDER, Adam: enl 29 Nov 1776, left sick at French Creek, sick
   in Pa June 1777.
ROESS, William: enl 28 Jan 1777, des 08/14 Mar 1777.
SAILOR, George: enl 19 Aug 1776, des 19 Dec 1776.
SHAUB, STROUB, Henry: enl 19 May 1777 in Heidelberg Twp-Lancaster
   Co for 3 yrs, on duty December 1777.
SHRANK, Godfried: enl 29 Jul 1776, disch 18 Nov 1776.
SLYHOFF, Godfried: enl 12 Aug 1776, died 08/12 May 1777 in
   Hospital.
SMITH, George: enl 29 Nov 1776.
SOWERMAN, Philip: enl 22 Aug 1776, died 04 Mar 1777.
SPECHT, Adam: enl 27 Apr 1777 in Heidelberg Twp-Lancaster Co for
   3 yrs.
STOLL, Adam, enl 27 Apr 1777 in Heidelberg Twp-Lancaster Co for 3

yrs.

STRAUSS, STROUSS, George: enl 05/08 Sep 1776, des 10/11 Dec 1776, retd 10 Dec 1777, reenl for 3 yrs, on duty May 1780.

SWETHE, SWETZGAY, Henry: enl 27 Apr 1777 in Heidelberg Twp-Lancaster Co for 3 yrs.

TILLY, Baptist: enl 25 Sep 1776, des 15 Mar 1777.

ULRICH, ULERICK, John Peter: enl 09 Nov 1776, believed POW 26 Dec 1776, servant for Col Arendt November 1777, dropped from rolls April 1778.

WEIGEL, John: enl 26 Nov 1776, killed at Trenton 02 Jan 1777.

WEINIG, Herman: enl 09 Nov 1776, des 12 Jan 1777, retd 01 Mar 1777, on duty December 1777.

YUNGIUS, YOUNGYOST, John: enl 18 Nov 1776, missing 02 Jan 1777 at Trenton, believed POW February 1777, believed deserted on May 1777 payroll.

INDEX

VEACH, Abraham, 117
VEIKLE,
 Christopher/Stop
 hel, 159
VELTY, George, 155
VENDROME, Hugh, 156
VIEBLER, John, 117
VISINGER, Ludwig,
 95
VISLER, Jacob, 130,
 157
VOLPERT, Johann
 Davidt, 80
VON SENDEN, Ernst
 J. F. Schueler,
 143
VON KRAFFT, John
 Charles Philip,
 142
VON STEUBEN,
 Friederich
 Wilhelm, 22
 Insp. General,
 44
VON ARENDT,
 Baron/Col./Lieut
 ., 142
VON DONOP, Colonel,
 9
WACHTEL, John, 95
WADE, John, 95
WAGER, Frederick,
 108, 150
WAGGONER,
 Caspar, 136
 Henry, 100
WAGNER,
 Christopher/Stuf
 fle, 100
 Henry, 19, 100
 Jacob, 114
WALDMAN, Nicholas,
 122
WALDON, John, 118
WALKER, John, 117
 Mary, 118
WALL, William, 159
WALLMAN, William,
 133, 159

WALTMAN, Nicholas,
 159
WALTON, John, 118
WARBY, Philip, 133
WARLEY, Philip,
 133, 159
WARNER, Ludwick,
 156
 Nicholas, 156
WASHINGTON, 11, 12,
 15, 18, 20, 22,
 23, 24, 26, 28,
 29, 33, 34, 49, 51
 Colonel, 50
 General, 3, 4,
 6, 7, 10, 14,
 21, 24, 25, 37,
 39, 41, 43, 44,
 45, 46, 48, 55,
 80
 George, 1
 Lord, 11
WASHTEL, John, 95
WATKINS, Martin, 95
WAYNE
 Anthony, 6, 7,
 44, 50
 General, 19
WEAVER, Jacob, 95,
 149
 Michael, 100
WEEDON, 17, 20
WEEGUEL,
 John/Joseph, 118
WEGER, Frederick,
 108, 150
WEIDMAN, J., 3
 John, 5, 18, 30,
 43, 44, 45, 48,
 79, 128, 145,
 152, 156
WEIDMANN, John, 79
WEIGEL,
 Christopher, 133
 Christopher/Stop
 hel, 159
 John, 161
WEIGLE,
 Christopher, 133

 Christopher/Stop
 hel, 159
 John/Joseph, 118
WEINIG, Herman, 161
WEIRMAN,
 Francis/Thomas,
 156
WEISER, Benjamin,
 3, 5, 51, 79
 Captain, 131,
 141
 Frederick, 5, 79
WEISLER, Jacob,
 130, 157
WEISSERT, Jacob,
 120, 152
WELHELM, 108
WELLER, John, 114
WELTNER, 11, 37
 Colonel, 24, 26,
 36, 38, 39, 40,
 41, 43, 44, 46,
 77, 143, 144
 L., 25
 Lt. Col., 35,
 47, 96
 Ludowick, 14,
 34, 44, 47, 67
 Ludwick, 5, 9,
 18
 Major, 6, 10, 15
 Mary, 47, 80
 Mrs. Anna Maria,
 143, 144
 William
 Ludwig/Ludowick
 , 79
WELTY, John, 108,
 150
WENICK, Thomas, 136
WENTZ, George, 25,
 83
 Jacob, 120, 122,
 156
WENTZEL, George,
 129
WERLOY, Philip, 159
WERNER, Ludwick,
 156